The Overseas Student Question

Of related interest:

Freedom to Study:
Requirements of Overseas Students in the UK

The report of a survey by the Grubb Institute (Bruce Reed, Jean Hutton and John Bazalgette), Overseas Students Trust, 1978.

Available from: Overseas Students Trust, 14 Denbigh Street, London SW1. £3.50 inc. p & p.

The Overseas Student Question
Studies for a Policy

Edited by
Peter Williams

HEINEMANN . LONDON
for the Overseas Students Trust

Heinemann Educational Books Ltd
22 Bedford Square, London WC1B 3HH

LONDON   EDINBURGH   MELBOURNE   AUCKLAND
HONG KONG   SINGAPORE   KUALA LUMPUR   NEW DELHI
IBADAN   NAIROBI   JOHANNESBURG
EXETER [NH]   KINGSTON   PORT OF SPAIN

ISBN 0 435 83485 1

Filmset by Northumberland Press Ltd
Gateshead, Tyne and Wear
Printed in Great Britain by Richard Clay (The Chaucer Press) Ltd
Bungay, Suffolk

Contents

List of Tables

The Overseas Students Trust was established in 1961, as an educational charity, by a group of leading transnational companies. Its broad purpose was to improve the provision made in the UK for the increasing number of students from overseas, and thereby help to ensure that they made the best use of their stay here. The companies held the view that the widest interests were served if students, particularly those from developing countries, were encouraged and enabled to pursue their studies in the UK, so long as appropriate provision was made for them.

The Trust has, during the past twenty years, initiated and supported a large number of schemes operated by welfare, academic and student agencies and was mainly responsible for the formation of the UK Council for Overseas Student Affairs (UKCOSA) which it continues to fund. The Trust has also sponsored independent investigation and research into various aspects of the overseas student question. In 1976 it commissioned the Grubb Institute for Behavioural Studies to undertake a survey of the requirements of overseas students in the UK, and published the report of this survey in 1978 under the title *Freedom to Study*. In 1979 it commissioned and published two monographs with statistics entitled *Overseas Students: some Facts & Figures* and *Overseas Students & Government Policy 1962–1979*.

The Trust is administered by a Committee composed, at present, of representatives of the following companies: Barclays Bank International, BAT Industries, Blue Circle Industries, British Petroleum, ICI, Inchcape Group, Shell International Petroleum, Standard Chartered Bank, UAC International. The Trust derives its income from these companies and others with overseas interests.

Preface

During the fifteen years that I have been associated with the Overseas Students Trust, I have often been asked if we can measure the value of the Trust's work. If that means a numerical reckoning of friends made for Britain, or export orders won, then the answer must be 'no'. Nevertheless I believe that there are benefits in many directions, immeasurable indeed in both senses of the word, deriving from the fact that men and women, often at an impressionable age, have come from overseas to pursue part of their education in this country. An important proviso of this assertion is that there are proper arrangements which meet the students' requirements for making the most of their stay here.

Belief in the benefits and, at the same time, recognition of that proviso led to the Trust's formation twenty years ago. Since then, from similar motives, a variety of initiatives have flowed: notably, the sponsorship (with the Trust's sister organisation, the Fund for International Student Co-operation) of the National Union of Students' survey of overseas students, published in 1967 as *International Community?*; the foundation of the UK Council for Overseas Student Affairs in 1968; the 1970 enquiry, under the auspices of the British Council of Churches, into the churches' role and work with overseas students; the commissioning of the Grubb Institute's survey of overseas students' requirements, published by the Trust in 1978 as *Freedom to Study*. In my introduction to that report I expressed the Trust's belief that the issues surrounding the subject of overseas students needed to be widely and sensibly debated on a basis of sound and up-to-date knowledge. This, we hoped, would lead to the evolution of a coherent policy for the future, taking account of the many varied interests engaged.

It was in this hope that we started discussions in 1978 with a wide range of people in education, industry and government, leading in November 1979 to a private meeting, chaired by Lord Seebohm, at which there was endorsement of the Trust's proposals for a series of linked studies to look at the overseas student question simultaneously from a number of different aspects. (This proposal proved timely in view of the government's decision to put overseas students' tuition fees on to a new footing from 1980.) Accordingly, work was commissioned and put in train: research into the economic costs and benefits of overseas students, incorporating a sample survey of students and institutions by a market and social research agency; a study of the foreign policy implications of overseas students; an enquiry into the needs of developing countries for study abroad; a comparative study of the situation and policies on foreign students of the main 'receiving' countries. The authors of these studies worked in close collaboration with the Trust and with each other through all the stages of their research, and indeed the sample survey was deliberately designed to serve the needs of all four studies.

In October 1980 a private colloquium, chaired by Lord Carr of Hadley, explored the issues raised by the studies and at that meeting the policy options were aired which are discussed in the final section of this book.

The Trust sees *The Overseas Student Question* as a companion volume to *Freedom to Study*. Taken together, we hope that these two books can chart a course that will be beneficial to all the interests engaged in this important question, not least the overseas students themselves. Amid the welter of statistical argument and all the discussion of national interests and policies, we should not lose sight of them.

There is not room in a short preface to do justice either to the heartening record of collaborative enthusiasm which has gone into the making of this book, or to the many people whose friendly and effective co-operation have helped to turn an idea into print. Some of those people are named elsewhere, but I must make special mention here of the debt the Trust owes to Lord Carr and Sir Charles Carter for their wise counsel and support over many months; and most of all to Professor Peter Williams, without whom this project would not have taken shape.

14 Denbigh Street
London SW1
January 1981

Anthony Birch
Chairman,
Overseas Students Trust

Foreword

I am very glad to write a foreword to this book and to commend it to as wide a readership as possible. The overseas student question has generated more heat than light in the recent past and therefore nothing but good can come from a long, cool look at its various aspects. I believe that the studies commissioned by the Overseas Students Trust and published here offer us such an opportunity.

It is a subject where policy is complicated by the variety of interests engaged. By way of illustrating this complexity, it is instructive to note that for the past thirty years it has been the overseas departments of state which have taken responsibility for the reception of overseas students, a responsibility they have largely delegated to the British Council, itself wholly funded by those departments and their offshoots. Yet active visible policy most closely affecting overseas students has in the past fifteen years been formulated and executed by domestic departments of state, primarily the Department of Education and Science in respect of tuition fees, and the Home Office as regards immigration and employment. In so far as overseas students are of 'interest' to, or even an 'obligation' of, the United Kingdom, it is largely as elements in her foreign policy, taken at its broadest. Thus policy decisions taken for reasons quite understandable in the light of domestic constraints have proved less easy to comprehend when viewed in the context of Britain's overseas relations.

Another difficulty which besets rational consideration of the overseas student question is the near-impossibility of calculating political or even trading benefits. The argument about the actual cost of an overseas student and the savings to be effected is comparatively straightforward because it is an argument about facts and figures in a single economic dimension. But discussion about the benefit to UK interests or our standing in the world from the presence of overseas students presumes so many shared perceptions even before the task of measurement can be attempted. Furthermore the time scales of 'savings' and 'benefits' are so different. For example, any effect on British investment overseas may be so far off in time that the link between cause and effect can scarcely be recognised, and the case for overseas students is thus the victim, because unfortunately in politics the short-term tends to pre-empt the long-term and the urgent usurps the place of the important.

We can be all the more grateful therefore that the papers brought together in this book rehearse so comprehensively the many political and commercial factors in the overseas student equation. Of particular interest to me as Chairman of the CBI Education and Training Committee is the discussion in Chapter 4 of the connection between foreign students and British overseas business. Professor Blaug in his fascinating study (Chapter 3) finds little hard evidence to satisfy him that there is a causal connection between the two. Yet the enquiry undertaken by the Overseas Students Trust, with the help of the Department of Trade, the British Council and the CBI, is pretty emphatic in its findings to the contrary. A study of the replies to my letter sent to the chairmen of more than forty of Britain's largest exporters and firms with interests abroad makes plain that the majority set much store for their business interests by the foreign national who has had some of his education in Britain. Also, one of the clearest impressions I have of the discussions at the Trust's private colloquium was the importance attached by the leading industrialists present to the maintenance of as large a population of overseas students as possible in the years ahead.

The colloquium provided a unique opportunity to range over the many aspects of the overseas student question, and it was particularly pleasing that the occasion was used not for looking back in recrimination but solely to explore the bases on which a good policy for the future would be built.

I believe that such a policy must keep in mind a number of key elements. First, there must be real acceptance that there was and is a problem, and that means must be found of regulating the inflow of overseas students. Next, conversely, we should be convinced of the benefits to Britain of having overseas students here; but, since there can be no question of seeking a return to the old unregulated system, we probably need a scheme of selective discrimination in order both to discharge our obligations and to foster our particular interests, taking account of such diverse benefits as research, foreign influence, aid, trade, etc.

The process begun at the colloquium of a collective clearing of minds about what one is trying to achieve in terms of international stability, winning the battle for the minds of men, trade, aid, research, a broad outlook in higher education, etc., needs to be continued. The benefits sought cannot be precisely quantified and will in any case be long-term; nevertheless, it is recognised that some quantification is inherent in the process of policy implementation at the point of committing government funds, and it will be necessary at some point to set figures on any proposals if one is to carry conviction.

There is also need to devise mechanisms for selective help to overseas students that will reconcile national priorities with the principles of individual application and the preservation of institutional autonomy in the process of selection and admission.

Such careful preparatory work as these proposals call for should be put in hand now against the time when the right climate once again exists and sufficient resources for implementation become available.

Again, these are not matters to be laid solely at government's door. Industry and the educational world should be involved, both in the thinking and the implementation. In view of the weight of opinion in favour of overseas students' programmes, as evidenced in the replies to my letter quoted in Chapter 4, one may reasonably ask industry what part it feels it can and should play in maintaining the conditions which engender benefits to UK trade through these means.

It is at this point that I should like to put in a plea for some careful thought about how we provide for overseas students once they have arrived in this country. Although the book does not treat this aspect, it takes on a new urgency when overseas students are no longer subsidised objects of charity but have become clients and purchasers of services – at £5000 per annum. Sir Rowland Wright, of Blue Circle Industries, and a former Chairman of ICI, dwelt at the colloquium on the importance of a well co-ordinated approach to the arrangements made by institutions for the reception of their overseas students. In his words 'caring pays, because overseas students will expect value for money'.

Another element in this question to which Sir Rowland Wright said thought should be given – and I agree – is the grey area of policy where immigration rules impinge on the lives of overseas students, often to the detriment of race relations. This is a delicate but vital aspect of the overseas student problem, and it calls for clear objectives and honest thinking.

In all future policy-making on the overseas student question, I

believe it to be vital that we consult with other countries; whether
it be to avert unnecessary hostility, the better to meet the needs of less
developed countries, or to plan a collective approach with other rich
host countries. The British experience must be seen in the wider
context of the international mobility of students which is one of the
foundation stones of a peaceful, stable and interdependent world.

Robert Carr
January 1981

Acknowledgements

The Overseas Students Trust would like to express its grateful ap-
preciation to all those who have contributed to the making of
this book. In addition to the editor and the authors of the studies,
these include: Mr Alan Bartlett, Sir Kenneth Berrill, Dr Kingman
Brewster, Mr Rupert Bristow, Miss Irene Carey, Lord Carr, Sir
Charles Carter, Mr Geoffrey Caston, Mr Keith Court, Professor Ralf
Dahrendorf, Dr Bertie Everard, Mr Tommy Gee, Miss Margaret
Greville, Miss Jean Hutton, Mr Darrell Jackson, Professor Richard
Jolly, Dr Edwin Kerr, Mr Alan Parker, Mr William Plowden, Mrs
Barbara Preston, Mr Bruce Reed, Miss Christine Scotchmer, Lord
Seebohm, Dr Tom Soper, Sir Peter Tennant, Mr Jack Thornton, Mr
Gordon Wilson and Sir Rowland Wright.

The Trust also wishes to acknowledge the helpful collaboration
of the Department of Education and Science, the Foreign and
Commonwealth Office, the Home Office, the Overseas Development
Administration, the Department of Trade and Treasury; the British
Council and the Confederation of British Industry.

Notes on Contributors

Mark Blaug is Professor of the Economics of Education at the University of London Institute of Education. He is the author of *Introduction to the Economics of Education* (1970), *Economic Theory in Retrospect* (1978) and *Methodology of Economics* (1980). He is a consultant to various UN agencies.

Guy Hunter of the Overseas Development Institute has long experience of research and consultancy in Africa and Asia. He is the author of *The New Societies of Tropical Africa* (1962), *Education for a Developing Region* (1963) and other studies in development.

Jean-Pierre Jarousse is a Research Fellow at the Institute of Education, European Cultural Foundation in Paris. He has worked in the Sociological Economics Group linked to the Centre National de la Recherche Scientifique where he published studies on the socio-economic bases of students' options and attitudes.

John Oxenham is Fellow in Education and Development at the Institute of Development Studies at the University of Sussex. His interests are the relationship between schooling and employment and the effectiveness of adult education and training.

Alan Smith is Director of the Brussels office of the Institute of Education, European Cultural Foundation. He was formerly External Relations Officer of the West German Rectors Conference. He is the author of several reports on European Co-operation in Higher Education.

William Wallace is Director of Studies at the Royal Institute of International Affairs. He is the author of *The Foreign Policy Process in Britain* (1975), editor of *Britain in Europe* (1980), and joint editor of *Policy-Making in the European Communities* (1977) and *Economic Divergence in the European Community* (1981).

Peter Williams is Professor of Education, and has been Head of the Department of Education in Developing Countries at the University of London Institute of Education since 1978. He worked as an educational planner for many years in Kenya and Ghana and served in the Secretariat of the International Commission for the Development of Education at Unesco.

Christine Woesler de Panafieu is 'Privatdozentin' (Associate Professor) of Sociology at the University of Oldenburg, Federal Republic of Germany. She has published a number of studies, notably on the Sociology of Science and on Educational Planning. She has also worked as a research consultant for UNESCO and the Institute of Education, European Cultural Foundation.

Maureen Woodhall is Visiting Research Fellow at the University of Lancaster and an Honorary Research Associate of the University of London Institute of Education. She has also worked at the International Institute for Educational Planning in Paris and is a consultant to the OECD.

1. The Emergence of the Problem:
Editorial Introduction

Athens, Constantinople, Toledo and Salamanca, the Cavendish Laboratory Cambridge ... In different centuries each of these places has been a magnet for scholars from many countries, their fame stretching far and wide. And other countries and continents have played similar roles at other times – India, Egypt, Timbuctoo. The tradition of centres of learning has been that of an intellectual forum, international in character, a concept and a reality transcending the bounds of a particular nation or culture. The role of the wandering scholar, travelling far to such places in pursuit of wisdom, finds a place in the traditions of many societies.

The contemporary foreign student in Britain or elsewhere, though typically different perhaps in many important respects from the travelling scholar of former times, is heir to this great tradition and fulfils many of the same roles as his predecessors – as a bearer of new ideas and as a carrier of new science and technology. He is also in a sense a cultural mediator, playing an important bridging role between societies and interpreting one culture to another. As such, the overseas student is one of the many vital strands, individually weak but collectively strong, which constitute the fabric of international society and hold in check the fissiparous forces of nationalism. Professional ties, intermarriage and bonds of personal loyalty and friendship crossing the boundaries of individual countries are all fostered by study abroad.

Contemporary perceptions, at least, are that in former times study abroad was largely an individual phenomenon, the archetype being a scholar, often already accomplished in his own right, seeking out renowned masters in famous centres abroad. Today we are concerned with a movement of a rather different character; a mass movement of the partially educated, often in search as much of qualifications as of knowledge and wisdom. The scale has grown enormously, as Smith and colleagues point out in Chapter 7, so that throughout the world there are now an estimated one million persons studying abroad in higher education alone. Approximately 300,000 of these are in the United States; and 60,000 are in Britain which in recent years has been the third largest receiver after the US and France. Beyond the narrowly defined tertiary level of education, there are tens of thousands of other foreign students in lower level educational establishments, in practical training schemes, in language study and the like. The number of overseas students in Britain doubles, to 120,000, when this wider definition is applied. And even then, as explained in Chapter 2, certain groups are still excluded from the count.

The Growth of Study Abroad

What has accounted for this surge in international study? In part clearly it is the emergence of the physical possibility through development of transport and communications of travelling abroad to pursue one's education. International communication has also created an awareness of the opportunity to study abroad. Courses and awards are now notified in internationally available handbooks, and postal application and acceptance has become commonplace. The fact that entry to courses is now so often by way of paper qualifications has not proved a particular obstacle, for whole education systems became interlocked in the colonial era. On the one hand the diplomas and degrees obtained in the colonies were given a measure of recognition for entry to higher education in the metropoles. And on the other hand the qualifications obtained in the 'mother country' had prestigious value in the job market of the colonies. These relationships have not entirely disappeared in the post-colonial era of independent states. And here, in speaking of qualifications, one comes on to one of the major factors fuelling the rise in foreign study and training – the so-called 'Diploma Disease' as Ronald Dore has named it.[1] This causes people to study mainly for certificates and their market value, education being very much a means to an economic end. This economic valuation of foreign study is particularly noticeable at the individual private level, but it is also recognised at the societal-public level. For with the development of political philosophies which place a major part of responsibility for economic and social development on the shoulders of governments, the public authorities have become increasingly interested in planning the supply of skilled manpower and have themselves begun to sponsor students in foreign study through scholarship and bursary awards. Governments of rapidly developing countries in particular have seen foreign study as an important means of meeting crucial manpower requirements. This has also become an important dimension of international co-operation and aid schemes both on a bilateral and on a multilateral basis. The student sponsored by his own or another government (or sometimes by a private foundation or firm) has become an important new feature of international student flows.

Whilst the private and public interests in access to overseas educational opportunities have thus reinforced one another as generators of demand for overseas education and training, they are not in fact always in harmony. To some extent foreign study has been associated with the 'brain drain' phenomenon whereby newly qualified graduates have failed to return to their countries of origin, preferring instead to avail themselves of the attractive employment opportunities in the countries of study. This is particularly serious where public funds have financed the study programme; but even when privately financed, the overseas study may have caused a scarcely affordable loss of foreign exchange and a nil return on the country's investment in those lower levels of education preceding the overseas course of study.

The very growth of overseas student numbers, for the reasons mentioned above, has however contributed to a worldwide consciousness of the overseas student phenomenon as a 'problem'. For, the increase in international flows has taken place in the face of other trends of a contrary nature, now becoming more perceptible and particularly entering into international awareness at a time of economic recession. The rise of nationalism, replacing the older concept of 'empire' may be quite largely responsible. Empires – British, French, Portuguese, Austro-Hungarian, Turkish and so on – are by their nature multinational. Although many recent empires were built on overtly racialist principles, nationality was played down or even suppressed under most imperial systems.

Ideologically, if not always in practice, the principle of free movement within the bounds of imperial sway was proclaimed, and the colonial peoples had right of access to the metropolis. Reasons of expense and difficulties of communication were among the reasons why comparatively few exercised this right. Rudimentary educational provision in the territories meant that few colonials were in any case qualified to do so.

The advent of cheap mass transport and the rather rapid development of many colonial territories in the 1940s and 1950s would certainly have spelled an end to this right, even if national independence had not intervened. For at the end of the 1950s and in the 1960s rather large scale immigration to Britain and France from their colonies was experienced. Had national independence not arrived on the scene to provide an acceptable rationale for stopping this immigration, it would have been necessary to invent it. National independence spelled the end of the idea of a 'mother country' to which all subjects of the Queen or President had the right of access. In its place arose the ethnic nation state whose nationals did *not* have the right to reside or work in the former metropole; and its students in the erstwhile mother country then became a separate category, whom it was necessary to count and to some extent control even if only to distinguish them from regular immigrants. Correspondingly one can see that in a country such as Britain the notion of a rather clearly distinguishable British national interest often differing from that of our former Empire became more sharply delineated in this post-colonial era.

These past two decades have also been years of accountancy, a golden age of cost-benefit analysis. Costs have been scrutinised, benefits analysed and calculated in all sorts of areas of activity. The economists have had a field day, insisting that accepted obligations and cherished relationships should now be subjected to cold economic calculus. Values and obligations can only be sustained if they contribute directly to our economic self-interest: and that contribution should preferably be calculable. It is amusing to speculate on whether a marriage or a football team could survive the strict application of these principles.

At any rate, as part of this process in Britain the costs of higher education came to be seriously scrutinised for the first time in the 1960s, notably at the time of the Robbins Committee Report on Higher Education in 1963.[2] As part of the same exercise the cost of subsidising overseas students was calculated as a separate item of public expenditure. It was seen now as being in large measure a form of overseas 'aid' (another area where international relationships came to be expressed in strictly calculable terms). All at once 'the subsidy to foreign students' became known about and treated as an option: something which was regarded for the time being as acceptable and outweighed by the benefits, but an item which in different circumstances might be manipulated. The sudden awareness in the first half of the 1960s of the existence and size of 'the subsidy' represented in a sense the end of the 'age of innocence' in respect of overseas students in Britain. Once the cost of educating overseas students stopped being seen as an uncalculated part of the natural order of things, and became instead a matter of cost and choice, the need for 'a national policy' was with us.

That is the starting point of this book, the need for a national policy on overseas students. However much the internationalists among us may regret in some ways the passing of the 'age of innocence' in international relations when passports, entry certificates, work permits and the rest were unnecessary – and may indeed look forward to a new era of world community in the future – we live here and now in a world of nation-states pursuing their national interests and guarding their national privileges. It is scarcely conceivable that a country such as Britain with a static population could contemplate the repetition in the 1980s of the experiences of the 1970s when, as Chapter 2 and Appendix B show, the number of overseas students in our publicly financed tertiary education system tripled and their share of our higher education student body doubled.

The Individual Perspective

Although overseas students in Britain have thus become a matter of state policy, the individual perspectives have not become irrelevant and must still be given due attention. Much of the demand from overseas for study opportunities in Britain is in fact a private demand from individuals and the families which support them. The British tradition is to see the relationship between the individual student and his college tutor or lecturer as fundamental to our education system. There is great sympathy, one might say an in-built preference, for arrangements which provide for an individual to be admitted on merit by an institution to which he individually applies rather than as a nominated representative of a category or group.

There is sympathy for the idea of the poor but bright unsponsored student, for the political refugee, for the person of idiosyncratic and unconventional mind to find a place in our system 'in spite of the bureaucrats'. Any arrangements under a new policy for overseas students have somehow to protect this tradition.

However, the complicated and compromising nature of the challenge becomes fully apparent when we reflect that individualism can be selfish and may obstruct other values and policy preferences which we may hold. We may find that support we offer to poor developing countries is allocated to train doctors and engineers who are unwilling to return home and contribute to the progress of their fellows. The overseas student body, like any bunch of individuals, has its fair share of playboys, of those travelling for pleasure, of parasites.

The experience of the individual overseas student at his university or college is also an intensely personal matter and is not in essence a matter of state policy. True, the quality of that experience will be affected by the extent to which positive discrimination (special advisory services or reserved student accommodation, for example) or negative discrimination (on fees, the right to earn through work, etc.) is exercised, and such discrimination often emanates from state policy. But basically the relationship between student and teacher, student and institution, is not mediated through the state. These important dimensions of the overseas student question will accordingly not find any prominent place in this book. As explained in the Preface, they have been explored in depth in this work's companion study, *Freedom to Study*,[3] also sponsored by the Overseas Students Trust. The main contribution of the present work to our knowledge and understanding of the individual and personal dimension of overseas students in Britain is found in Appendix A which summarises the important findings of a major survey (1500 returned questionnaires) of the circumstances of individual overseas students by Mark Blaug and his colleagues of the University of London Institute of Education.

Why a National Policy is Necessary

Let us revert to the national perspective and consideration of the possible elements of national policy. Three possible reasons may be adduced for wishing to have a national policy on overseas students which would control the numbers, and possibly also the composition of overseas students in Britain. First, there might be concern if the costs of overseas students were not purely financial but also involved a diminution of opportunity for British students. This might be the case even where any subsidy element had been removed by the imposition of full-cost fees. If it were found for example that overseas students were in effect 'buying up' places which would otherwise have been available to and filled by British students – that in other words there was a major displacement effect – intervention might be considered justified. The proportions of overseas students in British higher and further education are shown in Tables 2.2 and 2.3. In broad terms it seems doubtful whether overseas students have seriously deprived British students of places in recent years, largely because of the sluggish British demand for higher education. Certainly some displacement has occurred insofar as UK nationals might like, for example, to occupy all the medical places available in the British higher education system – though in areas of intense home demand like courses for initial qualifications in medicine, the proportion of overseas students seems actually to have been much lower than average (Table 2.3). Another possibility to be borne in mind is that on individual courses the proportion of overseas students might in fact rise so high that British students attending those same courses were somehow disadvantaged by, for example, the inadequate language competence of the foreign students. Evidence of rather considerable concentration on some individual courses is given in Chapter 2 and Appendix A.

A second set of possible grounds for regulating overseas student numbers would be if, on general grounds of social policy, it were considered that overseas students were crowding British 'living space' and creating undue pressure on the housing stock, social services, recreational facilities, etc. This aspect of the problem is not in fact explored further in the present book.

The third reason, which is the major focus of this book, is the consideration that overseas students in Britain are subsidised at quite considerable public cost and the question arises of gearing levels of expenditure on the subsidy to possible expected benefits. The scale of the cost and the nature and possible extent of the benefits are central issues. If we consider the cost side of the equation first, the financial costs to the British state of overseas students have largely arisen from the system of British finance of public higher and further education. This is partly by fee which the student, the student's family, or – more usually in the case of British students – a local education authority pays, and partly by a grant to the institutions. The normal British practice in respect of overseas students, until the policy of full-cost fees was introduced in 1980, was to subsidise overseas students by the difference between their fee levels and the cost of their education. This subsidy level varied considerably over time as inflation took its toll on the overall cost, and as the amount of the fee element rose. Fee rates for the years since 1967 are set out in Table 2.5 which records how the previous system of uniform fees for home and overseas students was abandoned in 1967 and never restored, though the differential has varied considerably. Although a fairly substantial level of overseas fee was levied in 1967, in subsequent years governments did not have the will to raise the fee level in step with inflation: and in real terms (constant prices) the overseas fee steadily fell until the mid-1970s. The amount of the subsidy for higher education, estimated at £9m in 1963 by Robbins, had risen according to Treasury estimates to £102m by 1978/79 plus a further £25m at the latter date in non-advanced further education. These figures appear to have been arrived at by calculating an average annual recurrent cost for students in different levels of tertiary education, multiplying this by the number of overseas students and then deducting their fee payments. Blaug recalculates the figure at about £53m higher in 1978/79 than the Government estimate for that year (p. 68). He argues that the Government's figure for the cost per head was an *under*estimate insofar as it failed to take account of the distribution of overseas students, who were highly concentrated in science and technology and at postgraduate level (both factors making for much higher than average costs) and also left capital costs out of account: these factors together easily outweighed the effect of government *over*estimation through ignoring the research element in costs, and the use of average rather than long-term marginal cost.

Previous Attempts at Regulation

Subsidisation of overseas students in the public education system has of course been the practice for very many years. As explained above, for a long time access for overseas students to our higher education system on the same terms as for home students was regarded as part of Britain's global responsibilities, more particularly towards our colonies and the independent Commonwealth. After 1960 the mood changed for a number of reasons which have been given. As the number of overseas students grew and the value of the subsidy to them mounted, Britain became increasingly unwilling to treat overseas students on the same basis as home students and introduced fee discrimination. However, for a variety of reasons such as historical links, the role of English as a world language, the high quality and short duration of British degree courses, the 'cheap' pound from the mid-1960s to the mid-1970s, etc., demand from overseas for places in the UK system has generally been strong. In some overseas countries particular national circumstances fuelled this demand. For example restricted access to education for Chinese in Malaysia, the oil boom in Middle Eastern countries, Nigeria and Venezuela, the tertiary education policy of the Hong Kong government – all these combined to increase the flow of these countries' nationals to Britain. Consequently overseas student numbers in the publicly financed sector of education, after remaining fairly constant in the 1960s, rose dramatically in the 1970s and by 1978/79, when the number was nearly 87,000, they stood at almost three times their 1970 level (Appendix Table B.1).

The question was how this growth could be regulated by the authorities. As is explained in Chapter 2, moderate (and not so moderate) fee increases were tried by successive Labour governments but without much permanent success. Regulation through exhortation was attempted in the mid-1970s, but the approach lacked sharp teeth for it was often in the interest of education institutions and departments to admit more overseas students and set up new courses as a way of expanding their activities. The actual funding arrangements through the University Grants Committee and the Advanced

Further Education Pool constituted a system of incentives and rewards which worked in exactly the opposite direction from government exhortation.

By 1979 action of some kind was inevitable because of the intensification of the problem and the serious national economic situation. Both major political parties seemed to be agreed that the system was unsatisfactory in three major respects. First, numbers were growing rapidly, involving a substantial and rising government subsidy, and government did not seem able to control this growth even though there were many competing claims on the use of public funds. Second, the subsidy was indiscriminate, benefiting all foreign students regardless of their country of origin or courses and irrespective of any British interest in receiving and subsidising them. Third, because of extraordinary levels of concentration, quite sizeable parts of the tertiary education system were catering for overseas students almost exclusively. The argument seems persuasive that the previous arrangements had to be modified to cope with these problems.

The 'solution' adopted by the Conservative government was the 'full-cost fees' option announced as a policy in 1979 and implemented from September/October 1980. Whilst some would see a number of advantages in this policy as an instrument of control, it is a blunt instrument and it is not clear that it is likely to be any more successful than the previous policies in dealing with the matter of giving expression in a sensitive way to the actual interests involved. In the precise form adopted, the main forms of differentiation implicit in this new policy are in favour of the European Community and refugees (both given home fee status), some priority for research students (a modest sized bursary system for some of them), a presumption in favour of rich individuals and rich countries who would more easily pay the fees, and – because of the differential pricing system (p. 39) – more incentive to take arts and social science courses than science or technology.

British Interests and Obligations

If, as seems likely (see p. 44), there is a sharp fall in numbers of overseas students as a result of these full-cost fees, the question is whether important British interests would suffer or obligations would be neglected. Policy involves choice, as has been said, and a weighing of costs and benefits. A full-cost fee scheme drastically reduces the cost to the British state of overseas students, but it may also involve some loss of benefits if some overseas students are deterred from coming to Britain. One of the purposes of the several authors of this book is to explore in more detail what the benefits

from the reception of overseas students in Britain might be and to
search for new bases for policy which might give adequate weight
to them. The interests and obligations may be considered under
various headings and the remainder of this introduction will be
devoted to exploring these. It will basically discuss *British* interests
and obligations. Many of these are in fact joint interests with other
nations, and Chapters 5, 7 and 8 discuss the implications of this
for direct consultation with other countries in working out new
approaches to overseas students.

What then are the interests and obligations *vis-à-vis* overseas
students that Britain should take into account?

First and most obviously a major interest and obligation of any
British government is to reduce public expenditure to a necessary
minimum. Any system of regulation of overseas student numbers
through quotas or fees takes that as its starting point. The issue
to be discussed is whether there are compensating benefits to Britain,
and/or whether there are British obligations, which justify the
expenditure of public funds on overseas students, either at the recent
level of subsidy or at some other level. In debates on overseas student
policy the following seem to be the main British interests and obligations identified:

(*A*)   *British interests*
　　(1)   Educational
　　　　(i)   Attracting bright scholars;
　　　　(ii)   Value of international element in educational insti-
　　　　　　tutions;
　　　　(iii)   Research output of overseas students;
　　　　(iv)   Reciprocal access for British scholars to overseas
　　　　　　institutions.
　　(2)   Economic
　　　　(i)   Spending on goods and services;
　　　　(ii)   Balance of payments;
　　　　(iii)   Future export orders for goods and services.

　　(3)   Political
　　　　(i)   Direct influence and goodwill towards Britain;
　　　　(ii)   Promotion of democratic values.

(*B*)   *British obligations*
　　(1)   Formal obligations
　　　　(i)   Treaty obligations;
　　　　(ii)   Cultural exchange agreements;
　　　　(iii)   Pledges under international schemes of co-
　　　　　　operation.

  (2) Informal responsibilities
- (i) Assistance to developing countries;
- (ii) Countries educationally dependent on Britain;
- (iii) Students already on course;
- (iv) Refugees.

Many of the various possible benefits listed seem to be real but are not easily quantifiable. There are of course 'hardline' economists who insist that what cannot be measured probably does not exist. But observation of behaviour by individuals and business corporations suggests that many economic decisions have to be made on the basis of convictions and hunches. William Wallace of the Royal Institute of International Affairs, draws the parallel (p. 112) with firms' prestige advertising, where any payoff is long-term and is very difficult to assess in isolation from other factors which have simultaneously affected the volume of sales. One previous attempt at quantifying the economic benefits of overseas students in Britain – by the London Conference on Overseas Students Working Party[4] – put benefits exclusive of fee payments at £105m in 1976; but this carried little conviction and is fiercely criticised by Blaug (p. 69) whose own study provides rough orders of magnitude rather than precise numbers but even so comes to the conclusion that economic benefits have not exceeded the long-run costs of subsidising overseas students at the levels of subsidy involved up to 1979. In other words, he argues, it has not been possible to make a case on purely economic grounds for the level of subsidies of overseas students that obtained in the late 1970s. Nevertheless it is important to try to weigh up as many as possible of the potential benefits and not only those that can be measured in financial terms, and this is what is attempted here.

A. British interests

A.1 Educational

(*i*) *Attracting bright scholars.* Britain does or could gain from attracting outstanding intellects from whatever source to enhance the standard of academic work in her institutions with benefit to their British colleagues. It is not clear that general subsidisation has in fact achieved this but schemes such as the Commonwealth Scholarships or the new postgraduate research award scheme obviously point in this direction.

(*ii*) *Value of international element in educational institutions.* This partly concerns the inculcation in British academic institutions of a consciousness of belonging to a wider international community, and the combating of parochialism among staff and students. In many disciplines, and particularly the social sciences, a full understanding of phenomena is only possible in a comparative context, in which the contribution of case studies drawing on foreign experience can be extremely illuminating. When UK students are studying overseas countries, their languages and cultures, an admixture of students from the countries concerned is particularly valuable. However, it is not clear that the present concentrated distribution of overseas students maximises these benefits to British institutions, staff and students.

(*iii*) *Research output of overseas students.*   A high proportion of postgraduate research students in British universities and colleges, especially in science and technology, is from overseas. Where they are producing individual theses and dissertations their research output can be seen as an unpaid contribution to the generation in Britain of knowledge and scholarly activity. In other cases the student is an unpaid or underpaid assistant in a research team working under supervision, sometimes even on outside research contracts, and there may be some saving to Britain in terms of costs of research work. Blaug (p. 70) estimates the value of this work at about £13m. Government recognition of the dependence of some British university research programmes on the presence of overseas students was shown in 1980 by its willingness to establish a research fund of 1500 awards (about 8% of overseas postgraduates at levels prevailing then).

(*iv*) *Reciprocal access for British scholars to overseas institutions.* Somewhat surprisingly Unesco figures for 1976 show Britain as sixth in the list of countries exporting students (Table B.5). However, a large proportion of Britons overseas was registered as being in Canada, and there is some doubt about the definition of 'overseas student' in that country (see p. 203). There is considerable potential value to British research and industry in having our students gain access to overseas educational institutions, particularly in areas of advanced technology. Knowledge of other languages and cultures, best acquired abroad, may be highly relevant to the export drive. As the world 'shrinks' it may eventually come to be seen as a normal part of a complete education that one should have a period of study in another country. To the extent that access for our scholars and students to overseas institutions depends on an open and welcoming posture towards foreigners by our own education system, we can reckon some benefit from having overseas students here. The Government ruled in 1980 that overseas students under specific schemes on a full reciprocal basis can pay the home level of fees, but seems mainly to have been thinking of reciprocity on a rather narrowly accountable 'knock-for-knock' basis between institutions. Reciprocity and exchange have so far been mainly with developed countries; the 'balance of trade' in students with developing countries is nearly all one way – into the United Kingdom.

A.2 Economic

This whole range of issues is discussed by Blaug in Chapter 3, while Chapter 4 focuses specifically on the commercial benefits to Britain of overseas trade and investment.

(*i*) *Spending on goods and services.* Beyond their tuition fees, which Blaug estimates at £66m for the public sector in 1979/80, the 120,000 public and private sector overseas students spend considerable sums of money in Britain. They may purchase British travel services in coming to the UK, and when here they appear to spend something like £300m per year (£200m p.a. for those in the publicly financed sector). Blaug calculates that about £140m of overseas students' total expenditure represents the net addition to aggregate demand generated by their consumer expenditure. But he points out that whereas this will be counted a benefit by those who value the employment effects of this expenditure highly, others will regard such expenditure as basically inflationary and will not acknowledge any benefit accrued whatever. Therefore he calculates the benefit at anywhere between £1m and £140m, according to political perspective.

(*ii*) *Balance of payments.* In earlier years when foreign exchange shortage was a major constraint to economic growth, the foreign currency earned from overseas students might have been an important consideration. However the current Government position, supported by Blaug, is that these foreign exchange receipts confer no special benefit on the British economy at the present time (see p. 82).

(*iii*) *Future export orders for goods and services.* This has been seen in rather narrow terms of placing of export orders for British goods, particularly in the engineering sector. The argument is that familiarity with British machinery, British firms, British standards and practice during the study and training period will lead later to more orders for British goods. This seems to be widely believed by British companies surveyed by the Overseas Students Trust (Chapter 4) and by British educational institutions; to some extent by the Government itself. However everybody agrees that the benefits are virtually impossible to quantify since so many other factors influence the placing of orders and the lag times are great between a student's stay in Britain and the time when he would be in a position to influence decisively the placing of an order. A more general consideration is the creation of a climate favourable to British business. The companies approached reiterated their conviction that those who have studied and trained in the UK are easier to do business with, and help to create a climate of economic goodwill favourable to British investment and trade. Blaug (Chapter 3) confirms there is a positive statistical correlation between growth of overseas student numbers in one period and the subsequent growth of British export markets, but points out that such a correlation is not the same thing as proved causation and that in any case the correlation holds good with reverse order chronology. On the other hand he finds the correlation between overseas country *shares* of British exports and *shares* of overseas students in Britain to be extremely weak. This might be expected given that the developed countries which are our biggest export markets have the most advanced education and training facilities.

A.3 Political

The place of overseas students as an element in Britain's overall relations with other countries is fully explored in Chapter 5 by William Wallace, who points out that the issue of overseas students has to be seen within the overall context of foreign cultural policy. For reasons he adduces, Britain has been somewhat reluctant to have any co-ordinated foreign policy, with the result that the overseas departments of government have often left, by default as it were, the overseas students issue to be handled by the Department of Education and Science and the Treasury from their essentially cost-saving perspective.

Although reception of foreign students in Britain is only a small element in our overall policies and programmes towards other countries one would presume that the looked-for effects would be twofold.

(*i*) *Direct influence and goodwill towards Britain.* Britain has wide-spread security and economic interests in other countries. She has extensive overseas trading links in terms of both visible and invisible trade: her overseas investments are substantial and British shipping and aviation have large international networks. To the extent that a beneficent attitude by overseas authorities towards Britain and her interests can be fostered by study opportunities in Britain, a considerable 'return' may be obtained from the continuing presence of foreign students in Britain. Many overseas governments do have a substantial identifiable part of their leadership – political, military, commercial – who have in the past been educated in the United Kingdom and the testimony of overseas British diplomatic and commercial representatives has been that such leaders have generally been helpfully oriented towards Britain by their study experiences here. (The possibility of a contrary effect – unhappy study experiences leading to negative attitudes towards Britain – was one reason for the setting up of the Overseas Students Trust twenty years ago and for its early concern with overseas student welfare.) Of course it is more difficult than hitherto to identify the leaders of tomorrow, and it is to be expected that the proportion of overseas leaders that is British trained will fall. Moreover the direct benefit is hard to assess, and may equally be sought through other channels parallel to overseas study programmes. If the experience of Britons working abroad is to be believed, study in Britain is a potent force in forming and maintaining useful overseas relationships for this country and in securing our overseas interests. In this connection the links between educational exchanges, the spread of the English language, and British commercial advantage is often stressed.

(*ii*) *Promotion of democratic values.* Beyond the advantages to be gained from the specific promotion of 'things British', this country's interests may be furthered to the extent that other countries share our general outlook on life. In the 'battle for the minds of men' with totalitarian regimes, the importance of fostering democracy, tolerance, scepticism, cannot be overestimated if our way of life and thought is to survive. To the extent that this is important, British society (and other Western societies) should be open for inspection by the youth and rising professionals and politicians of other countries. Our interest here is less in a love of Britain, Shakespeare and Queen Victoria, and more in an adherence to constitutionality, respect for minorities, tolerance and the rule of law. In fostering these we shall in fact be contributing to our own ultimate safety and well-being.

B. British obligations

The third of the foreign policy objectives spelled out by the Central Policy Review Staff in its report a few years ago on Britain's overseas representation[5] (the first two were external security and promotion of the country's economic and social well-being) was to 'honour certain commitments or obligations which the UK has voluntarily entered into or cannot withdraw from' (see Chapter 5). Bonds between countries, as between individuals, are built up on trust and we cannot simply renege on our international obligations and responsibilities.

B.1 Formal obligations

(*i*) *Treaty obligations.*   The most important of these involves our accession to the European Community and our consequent obligation to treat EC nationals, in many important respects, as favourably as our own citizens. Britain has agreed to honour this obligation, even to the most painful extent of treating students from overseas departments of France such as Réunion more favourably than those from neighbouring Commonwealth Mauritius, or from our own dependencies such as Hong Kong.

(*ii*) *Cultural exchange agreements.*   These account for only a modest proportion of the overseas student flow to Britain, but again constitute an obligation which we must honour.

(*iii*) *Pledges under international schemes of co-operation.*   An example is the Commonwealth Scholarship and Fellowship Plan to which Britain has pledged a certain number of places rather than a sum of money. She was urged by her Commonwealth partners at the Commonwealth Education Conference in Sri Lanka in 1980 to shield Commonwealth Scholars and Fellows from the effect of the fee increases.[6]

B.2 Informal responsibilities

(*i*) *Assistance to developing countries.*   The particular needs of developing countries for study opportunities in Britain form the subject of contributions by Guy Hunter of the Overseas Development Institute and John Oxenham of the Institute of Development Studies, University of Sussex, in Chapter 6. The Central Policy Review Staff listed this as one of the major objectives of our overseas policy, essential also to our vital long-term interests in an increasingly interdependent world. About 80% of overseas students in Britain come from developing countries, and subsidised fees were of major assistance to those countries. It afforded relief to the budget in the case of sponsored students, and to their foreign exchange reserves in respect of both sponsored and private students. The withdrawal of the subsidy has increased the burden on them. Since the number of British technical assistance awards has not risen to offset the effect on private students of the rise of fees, and since Britain's overall foreign aid budget has in any case been cut in absolute terms, the impact of recent changes on developing countries is all the more painful, as the following quotation from the 1980 Commonwealth Education Conference report testifies:

> The recent increase of tuition fees in some countries – even to the point of charging the full economic cost – has become a burning issue between developed and developing countries of the Commonwealth. Some countries have been charging differential fees for some time, but the problem has now become acute as it affects a larger number of students from developing countries and is likely to disrupt the developmental plans of these countries and their programmes for human resources development. Developing countries are traditionally dependent on these same sources within the Commonwealth for assistance. However, developed countries are forced sometimes to adopt policies such as the reduction of public expenditure to put their economies in sound order, and these may affect overseas students.[7]

The overall effect of the rising real costs of study in Britain in recent years has been to shift the country composition of the body of students coming from developing countries away from the poorest countries and towards the middle-income and other oil-rich countries (p. 30). While there are many pertinent questions that can be asked about the extent of developing countries' overall benefit from foreign study – the issues of brain drain, of foreign exchange loss, of cultural dependence, of demoralisation of local institutions naturally arise – the evidence seems to be that developing countries' own perception of their interests is that foreign study and training will be needed and officially supported for some years. This is certainly the thrust of the evidence given to Oxenham and his colleagues in the course of the enquiry reported in Chapter 6. It is borne out by data from worldwide international student flows which suggest that, taking developing countries as a whole, the growth and development of indigenous education systems have not yet brought about any diminution of the flow of students abroad.

(*ii*) *Countries educationally dependent on Britain.*   Certain of the smaller Commonwealth countries have over a long period integrated their education systems with that of Britain. Not having resources of their own to construct workable comprehensive higher education systems, they chose to make use of British facilities for a large proportion of their specialised needs. Many of these countries are small and poor; some in fact are still dependencies of the UK. In some cases Britain actually discouraged them from embarking on expensive provision for themselves, so their dependence on the UK has been in part a result of British prompting. Appendix Table B.3 includes a list of 34 small (mainly Commonwealth) countries with populations of under a million which had over one per thousand of their 20–24 age group studying in the UK in the recent past; the proportion being in many cases in the region of ten times as high as that for France, Germany and Italy (whose students will be here at home rates), a hundred times that for India and a thousand times that for China or the Soviet Union. Because higher education facilities take several years to plan, construct and make operational, these countries face particularly acute transitional difficulties.

(*iii*) *Students already on course.*   The Government has normally honoured the principle that students who are already committed to a course should be relieved of newly imposed fee rises beyond the level of inflation. This is straightforward for students enrolled on one particular course, but problems have arisen for those students who originally came to the UK to pursue a sequence of courses and who were then caught in mid-stream, so to speak. Under previous arrangements they could qualify through the school or non-advanced further education system for entry to higher education in this country, and then pay the home level of fees (and even in some cases obtain an LEA grant), but this has been made no longer possible.

(*iv*) *Refugees.*   This group has special needs and in recognition of them refugee students have been permitted to pay the home level of fees.

From the foregoing listing one can see that there are many different aspects to the overseas student question. Indeed the central message of this book is that policy on overseas students is multi-dimensional and that a wide range of considerations must be weighed in the balance when such policies are formulated. This has implications for the machinery of government and funding mechanisms as is discussed in Chapter 8. Policy-makers are confronted all the time with choices in the allocation of scarce resources among multiple objectives. Another of the perennial problems in public policy formulation is the lack of any neat one-to-one fit between programmes and objectives, means and ends. A single objective may be served by more than one programme: and any programme may serve more than one objective.

Even if overseas study programmes do yield the foregoing more or less tangible benefits to Britain, it must be asked first, which of these interests and objectives should have priority or whether other more desirable benefits could be obtained for the same outlay; and second, whether the same benefits might be obtained at lower cost through programmes other than overseas study courses. As regards the first question, the comparative valuation of different elements in the national welfare comes down ultimately to a question of values rather than of calculation. We shall revert to discussion of priorities for support between different groups of overseas students in Chapter 8. As for public expenditure choices between overseas student programmes and other objectives, because subsidies were part of the Department of Education and Science (DES) budget, the sum to be saved from scrapping them in favour of full-cost fees was being compared with very real domestic political sacrifices such as school meals and school transport. A more appropriate comparison, however, might have been with other objectives of overseas expenditures, like defence. Overseas student support decisions should not be taken exclusively in the DES.

In relation to the second question, both Blaug in Chapter 3 and Wallace in Chapter 5 ask whether better directed programmes might be more cost-effective than an indiscriminate subsidy. Some of these alternative expenditure programmes might be outside the orbit of overseas student policy altogether: others might fall within it. Thus Blaug asks whether in-plant industrial training attachments and trade promotion visits should not be examined as an alternative approach to subsidising engineering courses for overseas students in the quest for more exports. Wallace points out that in our efforts to educate a pro-British leadership in friendly overseas countries, it is getting more difficult than in the previous era of ruling dynasties to identify who the 'stars' of tomorrow will be. And in that case, perhaps the short British Council visit for personnel already 'on the way up' is preferable to pre-career training for a mass of unsifted students? Again, are there more direct ways of promoting the English language abroad than through overseas students coming to Britain?

The problem is, as Wallace suggests, that although overseas study programmes constitute only one small part of British influence on the rest of the world – an influence which is also mediated through the press and radio, books and films, artists and sportsmen, tourists and businessmen, diplomats and migrants – it is very hard to isolate the effect on the situation abroad of any one element in our co-operative programmes and cultural contacts. Referring to different possible ways of assisting educational development overseas he concludes that because of the problem of attributing costs and benefits, prudence requires a 'judicious blend' of several activities.

British Policy in the Global Context

In the foregoing pages the argument has concentrated on the perspective of interests and obligations of this country in receiving overseas students. In justifying any subsidisation of fee levels, or granting of scholarships to overseas nationals for study in our colleges and universities, the cost to the taxpayer must be justified largely in terms of *British* welfare that would be forgone if such expenditure were not incurred.

Nobody would deny that there is a sense in which our interests in the matter of overseas student programmes may be competitive with those of other nations: we may be competing with America, Germany, France and Japan for trade influence, even though in alliance with them we compete for political influence in the Third World against the Eastern Bloc.

It is important to emphasise that we do have a common, shared interest in our overseas student policies both with our 'clients' in the developing countries who are the main sources of demand for places in our higher education system, and with our allies/competitors in the rest of the Western industrialised world. The contribution to the growth and prosperity of the developing countries by helping them to fill vital manpower needs in their economies and just as importantly to lay the foundations, through staff development programmes, for the expansion of their own higher education systems, can be substantial. In the 'post-Brandt'[8] era of growing interdependence between North and South, reciprocal student flows and the sharing of professional knowledge and know-how may be one of the surest ways of sustaining dialogue and co-operation. By contrast the damage that may be done to these relationships by lack of consultation and precipitate action was demonstrated by the angry reactions of many Commonwealth developing countries to Britain's unheralded announcement of full-cost fees.

With our Western allies on the other hand there is also a considerable commonality of interest, as Alan Smith and his colleagues of the Institute of Education of the European Cultural Foundation show in Chapter 7. The British predicament of rising numbers of overseas students is not unique; nor is our burden the heaviest. Our own experience is part of a worldwide phenomenon affecting North America and Western Europe as well as ourselves. Smith and colleagues show that restrictive action by one affected country may well have serious effects on other receiving countries.

One clear message from the papers in this volume therefore seems to be that Britain must approach the overseas student problem in a global perspective, taking account of the interests of both the sending and other receiving countries. Hopefully in so doing Britain will be taking the surest road to the maximisation of her own long-term advantage from overseas student programmes.

Notes

1. R. Dore, *The Diploma Disease*, London, Unwin Educational Books, 1976.
2. *Report of the Committee on Higher Education*, HMSO, Cmnd 2154, October 1963.
3. The Grubb Institute, *Freedom to Study: Requirements of Overseas Students in the UK*, Overseas Students Trust, 1978.
4. London Conference on Overseas Students, *Overseas Students: a subsidy to Britain*, Report of the Working Party on the Costs and Benefits of Overseas Students in the UK, London, 1979.
5. Central Policy Review Staff, *Review of Overseas Representation*, HMSO, 1977.
6. Commonwealth Secretariat, *Eighth Commonwealth Education Conference Report* (Colombo, Sri Lanka, 5–13 August, 1980). London, Commonwealth Secretariat, 1980, paragraph 49.
7. Commonwealth Secretariat, *Eighth Commonwealth Education Conference Report*, paragraph 194.
8. The reference is to the 'Brandt Report' – *North–South: a programme for survival*. Report of the Independent Commission on International Development Issues under the chairmanship of Willy Brandt, Pan Books, 1980.

2. Overseas Students in Britain: the Background

by Peter Williams

This chapter contains two sections. The first summarises the statistical and other data available about overseas students in Britain up to the end of 1980. The second surveys the evolution of government policy towards overseas students in the 1960s, 1970s and the start of the 1980s.

The Overseas Student Body: Trends and Profile

Nature of the data

The major source of information on overseas students in Britain is a compilation of figures published by the British Council under the title 'Statistics of overseas students in Britain'. This appears annually, normally about two years after the academic year to which the data apply. A major handicap for all those working on overseas student issues is that at any point of time the information being used tends to be two or three years out of date.

The British Council figures contain three different commonly used totals for the number of overseas students in Britain:

(1) *Overseas students in higher education* (59,625 in 1978/79).

(2) By adding to this students on non-advanced courses in further education (27,154 in 1978/79) we obtain a second aggregate: *overseas students in publicly financed higher and further education institutions* (86,779 in 1978/79).

(3) When one then adds students attending private establishments outside the publicly financed sector of education (estimated at 32,780 in 1978/79), one arrives at *Total overseas students in Britain* (119,559 in 1978/79).

The British Council definition of an overseas student for purposes of inclusion in its statistics is

a person over the age of 18, whose permanent home is overseas, who has come to Britain for full-time study, research and practical training of at least six months and who is expected to return to his own country at the conclusion of his studies or training. In academic institutions such a person generally pays the increased fees for overseas students introduced by the British Government in 1967.[1]

It is well to note the omissions from this list, for the total British contribution to the education and training of overseas nationals is even greater than the 120,000 computed by the British Council. Four major categories of omissions are:

(1)   Students in publicly financed institutions who, though having a permanent home overseas, have qualified under the regulations to pay the home student rate of fee. Nobody knows the precise number involved but it could be as many as 10,000 overseas individuals (beyond the 87,000 who have been paying the overseas fee). Ever since the separate overseas student fee was introduced in 1967, institutions have tended to report their overseas students by the criterion not of permanent residence but of level of fee paid. When the public subsidy to overseas students is at issue, this omission is the most serious of the ones in the present list.

(2)   Those on short courses of less than six months. Again the numbers are not known, but there are thought to be large numbers of European students who come for short language courses in Britain, and a number of students and trainees come for periods of six months or less under the British aid programme.

(3)   Those in state or private secondary schools, or those under age 19 elsewhere (e.g. in further education colleges). Many of those in the state and private school system (probably mainly the latter) may be hoping to qualify for places in the further and higher education system and moreover, under the regulations that have been in force, to qualify by virtue of residence for home fee status and even local education authority grants. In a survey undertaken for the Overseas Students Trust, Blaug found that 21% of a sample of overseas university and polytechnic students in 1979/80 had taken 'A' levels in Britain (see p. 242). New fee levels and changing rules on eligibility for home

fee status at tertiary level *may* therefore eventually result in lower overseas enrolment at secondary level.

(4) Students in private sector institutions not covered by the British Council returns. The British Council recognises that its coverage of correspondence colleges, secretarial schools, English language establishments, etc. is incomplete, and some believe the numbers in institutions of all kinds in this category may be much larger than Council figures show. *Au pair* students of English are also excluded.

Another major problem with these Council statistics is that they are *stock* figures at a single point of time and do not indicate the year of study of students. Without *flow* figures of arrivals and departures, or grade enrolment (and particularly first-year student numbers) it is difficult to assess how changing fees are affecting trends. Fortunately some information has become available recently from DES on entrants to higher education (see Table 2.7) but if data on new overseas entrants were available in all sectors of the system, much better forecasts would be possible for total numbers in the UK two or three years ahead. It sometimes seems to have been overlooked in the debates on overseas student numbers that current stock figures partly represent intakes several years ago.

Numbers and growth of overseas students, by sector

Table 2.1 shows the numbers of overseas students in Britain and their distribution by sector. One can see that in the most recent years the grand total has contained three main constituents – university students comprising about 30%; other advanced and non-advanced further education around 40%; and the remaining, mainly private, category around 30%. The proportion in publicly-financed institutions who were benefiting from any government subsidy before full-cost fees were introduced was thus about 70% of the total enumerated by the British Council.

Table 2.1 also shows the growth and changing composition of overseas student numbers over a twenty-year period (fuller data on a year by year basis is available in Appendix Table B.1). Overall, numbers roughly trebled in this time: after growing by approximately 50% in the 1960s they doubled during the 1970s. The publicly financed sector of education witnessed a much faster rate of growth than the non-public sector: indeed in the 1970s the public sector tripled in size while the non-public sector is actually recorded as having declined. This helps to explain the rising level of government concern over the cost to public funds of educating large numbers of overseas students.

Table 2.1 Growth and composition of overseas student numbers 1958/59 to 1978/79 by main category, (figures in brackets denote percentages of grand total)

Sector/level of education	1958/59	1968/69	1973/74	1977/78	1978/79	Change 1968/69 to 1978/79 (%)
A. Publicly financed institutions						
Universities						
1. Post-graduate	n.a.	9019 (13)	15144 (16)	18552 (15)	18915 (16)	+ 110
2. Under-graduate	n.a.	6956 (10)	10177 (11)	17336 (14)	18225 (15)	+ 162
3. **Total** universities (1 + 2)	10672 (25)	15975 (23)	25319 (27)	35888 (29)	37140 (31)	+ 132
4. Other advanced further education	n.a.	5554 (8)	9755 (10)	22675 (18)	22485 (19)	+ 305
5. **Total** higher education (3 + 4)	n.a.	21529 (31)	35073 (37)	58563 (47)	59625 (50)	+ 177
6. Non-advanced further education	n.a.	8744 (13)	18091 (19)	27544 (22)	27154 (23)	+ 211
7. **Total** publicly financed institutions (5 + 6)	21113 (50)	30273 (43)	53164 (56)	86107 (70)	86779 (73)	+ 187
B. All other institutions (private sector)						
8. Non-publicly financed education	20987 (50)	39546 (57)	42045 (44)	37652 (30)	32780 (27)	− 17·1
Grand total overseas students in Britain						
9. (7 + 8)	42100 (100)	69819 (100)	95209 (100)	123759 (100)	119559 (100)	+ 71·2

Source: British Council, *Statistics of Overseas Students in Britain,* successive editions.

In the *university* sector one notes that overseas numbers trebled in the 1960s and 1970s. Within universities the undergraduate element remained strong: it rose from 40% in 1973/74 to 49% five years later. This development has confounded the Robbins Committee expectation that, as university institutions developed overseas, students would be much less inclined to come to Britain for study at undergraduate level.[2] The trend may be quite largely because of a tendency for wealthy but possibly vulnerable minorities, especially in Malaysia and certain other Asian countries, to seek undergraduate places in Britain for their children.

In the *non-university* sector of higher and further education (i.e. polytechnics, colleges of education and other further education establishments) the growth was spectacular, doubling every five years during the 1970s. There was a rapid increase of overseas students in advanced courses, mainly in polytechnics. Enrolment at non-advanced level was almost entirely concentrated outside the poly-technics. The figure of 27,200 non-advanced students in 1978/79 con-tained a large element (13,100) of students taking General Certificate of Education (GCE) and Scottish Certificate of Education (SCE).

Overseas students *outside the publicly financed sector* constitute something of a catch-all category with some very disparate elements. As can be seen in Appendix Table B.2, it includes those in private colleges, nursing training and hospital work, language assistants and trainees in government and industry. Overseas student nurses, once the largest group, grew from about 6000 to 20,000 in the 1960s, but in the 1970s they receded to 7400, under 40% of their former number. This decline was largely offset by recorded numbers in private colleges (language, secretarial, GCE studies, etc.) increasing from 9000 to 18,000 between 1972/73 and 1978/79.

Proportions, concentration and subjects of study

Not just the overall number, but also the proportion and distribution of overseas students in the total UK student body, is of interest to policy-makers, particularly in the context of discussions of whether overseas students have in some sense been marginal to the system or alternatively have displaced home students. Table 2.2, covering higher education only, suggests that the proportion of overseas students doubled in six years up to 1977/78, after dropping sharply in the 1960s.

Table 2.2 highlights the stagnation of home enrolments, which grew from 438,000 to only 453,000 (3·4%) over an eight-year period in which overseas numbers grew from 26,000 to 56,000 (115%).

Table 2.2 Proportion of overseas students in UK higher education

Year	Total enrolment (*thousands*)	Of which overseas (*thousands*)	Overseas (%)
1971/72	464	26	5·6
1972/73	473	30	6·3
1973/74	481	34	7·1
1974/75	487	40	8·2
1975/76	505	48	9·5
1976/77	515	55	10·7
1977/78	509	57	11·2
1978/79	508	58	11·4
1979/80	509	56	11·0

Sources: Committee of Vice-Chancellors and Principals, and other sources.

The rise in the proportion of overseas students in Britain must be seen in the context of mushrooming higher education demand abroad which caused students there to 'overflow' into foreign study. At a time of exceptionally sluggish demand in Britain, the proportion of overseas students consequently rose. The figure of 11% in Table 2.2 is of course an average figure. In individual institutions, at some levels of study, in particular subjects and on some individual courses, the proportions are sometimes very high (and in other cases they may be negligible):

(1) In terms of *institutions* one finds that in British universities, for example, an average figure of 11% for overseas students has been compounded of proportions of as much as 34% at the University of Manchester Institute of Science and Technology, 19% overall at the University of London, but only about 4% at Keele or Leicester Universities. Within London University some individual Schools such as Imperial College, the Institute of Education, London School of Economics, and School of Oriental and African Studies have had around a third of their students from overseas, and the School of Hygiene and Tropical Medicine as much as three-quarters. In polytechnics and further education colleges one has also encountered very high concentrations of overseas students, especially in the London area.

(2) There is a similar contrast between *levels of study*. In the universities the number of overseas postgraduate students, at

Table 2.3   UK publicly financed higher and further education: overseas students by subject groups 1977/78

Subject group	Universities						Other higher and further education		Total publicly financed higher and further education		
	Undergraduates			Postgraduates			Advanced	Non-advanced		As percentage of total overseas students	
		Overseas students			Overseas students						
	All students	Number	As percentage of student body	All students	Number	As percentage of student body	Overseas students number	Overseas students number	Overseas students number	All students	Classified students only
Education	3286	241	7·3	8403	1354	16·1	1290	45	2930	3·4	4·3
Medicine, dentistry and health	27517	1120	4·0	3233	1427	44·1	406	95	3048	3·5	4·5
Engineering and technology	34311	7399	21·6	6900	3971	57·6	8468	5019	24857	28·9	36·4
Agriculture, forestry and veterinary science	4698	112	2·4	1084	606	55·9	32	143	893	1·0	1·3
Science	53110	2920	5·5	11756	4103	34·9	2357	602	9982	11·6	14·6
Social, administrative and business studies	56807	3248	5·7	10702	4021	37·6	7534	1967	16770	19·5	24·6
Architecture and other professional and vocational subjects	4202	221	5·3	1714	569	33·2	1461	1022	3273	3·8	4·8
Language, literature and area studies	30420	1000	3·3	3182	1184	37·2	217	151	2552	3·0	3·7
Arts other than languages	24110	1075	4·5	2700	923	34·2	910	1053	3961	4·6	5·5
Other and unclassified	—	—	—	394	394	—	—	17447	17841	20·7	—
Total	238461	17336	7·3	50068	18552	37·1	22675	27544	86107	86107 = 100	68266 = 100

Note: 394 unclassified postgraduate students have been included so as to make this table consistent with those based on British Council figures.

over 18,000 in 1978/79, was only slightly in excess of the number of overseas undergraduates. But the overseas postgraduates constituted 37% of the total student body at that level, whereas the overseas undergraduates were only 7% of all undergraduates (Table 2.3). At postgraduate level overseas students seem to have been concentrated more heavily in taught courses than in research degree courses.

(3) The distribution by *subject* is also uneven. Table 2.3 reveals the pattern for universities and shows the subject distribution for the rest of higher and further education. Data relating the overseas students to the total student body by subject were available only for the universities. At undergraduate level, overseas students are most numerous in engineering and technology where they constituted 21% of all students in 1977/78, but in almost all other subject areas they accounted for only 2–6% of the total student body. At postgraduate level their proportions were much higher, as we have noted, but with unusually high proportions in engineering and technology (57%), agriculture and forestry (56%) and medicine (44%). The largest numbers of overseas students at postgraduate level are in science, in social administrative and business studies and in engineering and technology. These last two subject groups are also much the most important in non-university higher and further education, with science a long way behind in third place. The overall pattern certainly confirms the point made by Oxenham in respect of the Third World that students come to Britain mainly to pursue development-oriented applied studies rather than arts and pure science (see p. 154). When the data are analysed by individual subject (rather than subject groups) figures recently compiled show that overseas proportions rise to very high levels in some cases. To take two large groups in 1978/79, 70% of 885 students on university taught postgraduate economics courses and 54% of 965 students doing research courses in electrical engineering were from overseas. In the case of some less well patronised subjects the proportions of overseas students reached 70–80% of the total student body.

(4) When the effects of institution, level and subject are combined and examined at *course* level, one finds some individual courses with heavy concentrations of overseas students. In the case of non-university institutions an analysis made for the London area in 1978/79 shows a high proportion of courses at all levels with over 25% overseas students. Indeed many of the higher

degree courses appear to have existed almost entirely for overseas students: some had 100% overseas enrolment.

Countries of origin

There are also heavy concentrations among overseas students in terms of nationality. Table 2.4 shows the countries providing most overseas students in the public sector in recent years. Malaysia and Iran jointly accounted for over a quarter of the total in 1978/79, and the top seven countries (Malaysia, Iran, Nigeria, Hong Kong, USA, Greece and Iraq) accounted for half the total. Until 1978/79 none of our eight partners in the European Community had as many as one thousand students in UK public sector institutions, and in that year only Germany (Federal Republic) was listed. At the end of the 1960s the two foremost sending countries accounted for only 13% of the total and the top seven countries for 37%: so the degree of concentration had increased.

The numbers from individual sending countries are shown in Appendix Table B.3. Numbers from developed countries are on the whole small: developing countries account for about three-quarters of overseas students in Britain. Analyses by Alan Phillips of World University Service show that among the group of developing countries trends in the 1970s have very much reflected, as one would expect, the economic fortunes of the sending countries. Although the overall number of overseas students in Britain has risen so sharply, the share – and in many cases the absolute number – of students from poor developing countries has fallen. This tendency does not appear to have been offset by the official aid programme. The numbers have risen fastest from OPEC countries and Malaysia (see Figure 2.1).

Listings of the kind represented by Table 2.4 say something of concentrations in Britain, but do not indicate the importance of study in Britain to individual overseas countries. Some quite small countries are near the top of the list of sending countries. Other very large ones such as China, USSR, Indonesia, Brazil and Japan do not appear at all. One way of indicating the importance of study in Britain to a country is by means of an index relating the number of its students in Britain to its population aged 20–24, and Appendix Table B.3 presents the necessary data.* Gibraltar comes easily top with 55 students per 1000 population aged 20–24. Brunei has 33 and Cyprus 27. Malaysia has 11, but Iran 4 and Nigeria only 1.

---

*The author is indebted to Sir Charles Carter for having compiled this information.

Table 2.4 Countries with more than 1000 students in UK publicly financed institutions, selected years, in rank order

1964/65		1969/70		1974/75		1978/79	
1. Nigeria	4082	1. USA	2360	1. Malaysia	7010	1. Malaysia	13308
2. India	2758	2. Malaysia	1713	2. Iran	5222	2. Iran	9095
3. Iraq	1604	3. India	1668	3. Nigeria	3533	3. Nigeria	5896
4. USA	1531	4. Pakistan	1577	4. USA	3248	4. Hong Kong	5133
5. Pakistan	15–3	5. Nigeria	1473	5. Hong Kong	2931	5. USA	3720
6. Ghana	1355	6. Kenya	1275	6. Greece	2735	6. Greece	3148
7. Malaysia	1200	7. Cyprus	1179	7. Kenya	1946	7. Iraq	2482
8. Iran	1107	8. Sri Lanka	1153	8. Cyprus	1892	8. Sri Lanka	2068
9. Kenya	1087	9. Iran	1074	9. India	1881	9. Jordan	1875
		10. Canada	1057	10. Sri Lanka	1659	10. Singapore	1786
		11. Hong Kong	1053	11. Pakistan	1311	11. Cyprus	1587
				12. Iraq	1278	12. Rhodesia	1534
				13. Turkey	1178	13. Turkey	1463
				14. Canada	1097	14. Kenya	1166
				15. Singapore	1010	15. India	1162
						16. Canada	1061
						17. Germany (F.R.)	1032
						18. Libya	1014

Note: The 1964/65 and 1969/70 figures for Pakistan include students coming from what is now Bangladesh.
Source: British Council *Statistics of Overseas Students in Britain*, various editions.

Figure 2.1   Overseas students in Britain: changes in numbers by country groupings, 1975/6 to 1978/9

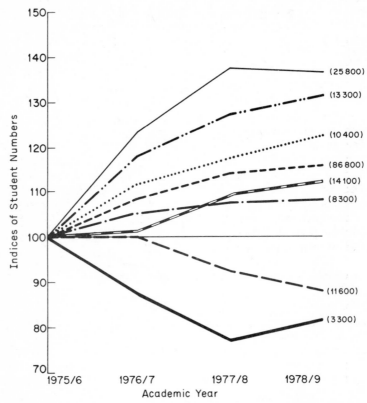

Notes: The numbers for 1975/6 academic year are used as base 100

The total number of students for 1978/9 academic year is shown in brackets

━━━━━━ Poorest Developing Countries

━━ ━━ Poorer Developing Countries

━━·━━ Poor Developing Countries

━━··━━ Malaysia

·········· Wealthier Developing Countries

──────── OPEC and Middle Eastern Countries

▭▭▭▭▭▭ Other Countries (Developed and unclassified)

━━━━━ All Countries

Source: Phillips, Alan, *British Aid for Overseas Students.*

Many small Commonwealth countries have a very high dependence on the UK, both for historical reasons and because their size is such that they cannot hope to construct fully viable comprehensive education systems at tertiary levels. The other groups of countries with a relatively high dependence are several Eastern Mediterranean and Middle East countries, especially those formerly under British control, and a few of the smaller Western European countries outside the European Community.

Personal circumstances of overseas students

The survey by Blaug and colleagues, an abridged version of which appears as Appendix A, has shed considerable light on the personal circumstances of overseas students in higher education in Britain. This survey yields important new information particularly on the financial sponsorship, income and expenditure of overseas students and on their motivations for study here. There are also valuable data on their personal characteristics (including socio-economic status) and on their academic profiles.

Government Policy on Overseas Students 1963–80

Developments up to 1979

The measures announced in 1979 regarding full-cost fees represented the culmination of developments over two decades. Twenty years ago overseas students in Britain were much fewer in number than currently (Table 2.1 and Appendix Table B.1), and their numbers and growth were not a matter of major public concern. They paid fees at the same level as British students. In the 1960s and 1970s a number of developments combined to make overseas students, their numbers, and the terms on which they study in Britain an 'issue'. These developments included the escalation abroad, particularly in developing countries, of demand for higher education and for study opportunities in Britain; the coming of independence, and the shedding of direct British responsibility, for large areas of the world; British economic and financial crises; the mounting real cost of higher education, and a greater degree of consciousness of this; changes in attitude and policy towards immigrants with whom many overseas students tend inevitably to be identified.

The Robbins Committee on Higher Education which reported in 1963 was, as noted in Chapter 1, among the first to draw attention to the element of subsidy to overseas students as a form of foreign aid. The Committee estimated the subsidy at £9m for the 20,000 overseas students in higher education at that time. The Committee

Table 2.5   Tuition fees – Comparison of actual (cash) fees with the same fees expressed at constant 1979 prices

(for the academic years 1968/69 to 1974/75 the increases were left to the discretion of universities and local education authorities)

		Universities									Non-university public sector									
		Home students				Overseas students					Advanced					Non-advanced				
		Postgraduates		Undergraduates			Postgraduates		Undergraduates		Home Students		Overseas Students			Home Students		Overseas Students		
Year	Retail prices indices Nov.	Actual (£)	Nov.79 prices (£)	Actual (£)	Nov.79 prices (£)	Category 1980/81	Actual (£)	Nov.79 prices (£)	Actual (£)	Nov.79 prices (£)	Actual (£)	Nov.79 prices (£)	Actual (£)	Nov.79 prices (£)	Category 1980/81	Actual (£)	Nov.79 prices (£)	Actual (£)	Nov.79 prices (£)	Category 1980/81
Nov.	100	70	265	70	265		250	945	250	945	45	170	250	945		30	115	150	570	
1975/76	144.2	140	230	140	230		320	525	320	525	115	190	320	525		100	165	200	330	
1976/77	165.8	182	260	182	260		416	595	416	595	150	215	416	595		104	150	260	375	
1977/78	187.4	750	950	500	635		850	1080	650	825	500	635	650	825		165	210	360	450	
1978/79	202.5	815	955	545	640		925	1085	705	825	545	640	705	830		165	195	390	460	
1979/80	237.7	890	890	595	595		1230	1230	940	940	595	595	940	940		165	165	520	520	
1980/81	(295.1)	1105	890	740	595		1525	1230	1165	940	740	595	1165	940		205	165	645	520	
						Continuers New arts etc.	2000	1611	2000	1611			3300	2660	Continuers New laboratory-based			1890	1525	Continuers New laboratory-based
						New science etc.	3000	2416	3000	2416			2400	1935	New classroom based			1380	1115	New classroom based
						New medicine etc.	5000	4027	5000	4027										

Source: First Report of the House of Commons Education, Science and Arts Committee, 1980, Appendix C: modified to include fees for new overseas students in 1980/81 and fees for the non-advanced sector. For the non-advanced sector, fee levels cited here are those given in *Overseas Students and Government Policy 1962–79* (Overseas Students Trust 1979) Appendix I

proposed an increased fee for both home and overseas students, with no differential; it recommended a fund, as part of British aid, to help needy overseas students; and forecast 50,000 overseas students in 1980/81 out of a total of 558,000 for all students. Paragraph 175 of its Report reads

> In our judgement this expenditure is well justified. It is a form of foreign aid that has a definite objective and yields a tangible return in benefit to the recipients and in general goodwill. It is however an open question whether the aid is best given by subsidising fees; and it is a further question to what extent Parliaments of the future will permit it to grow without limit.[3]

A differential fee for overseas students was however announced by the Labour Government in December 1966, when Mr Crosland was at the DES. The overseas student fee for 1967/68 was set at £250 in higher and advanced further education compared with £70 for home students. As Table 2.5 shows, in constant money terms the fee of £250 set in 1966 was in fact higher than the overseas undergraduate fee level in 1979/80 before full-cost fees were introduced.

This 1967 fee rise apparently caused a hiccup in the rising trend of overseas applications and entrants to British universities. A paper by Blaug and Layard (forthcoming, 1981) shows that the number of overseas first degree applicants through the Universities Central Council for Admissions (UCCA) fell from a record number of 9643 for 1967 (applications for entry had mostly been lodged before the announcement of higher fees in December 1966) to a low point of 7068 in 1969 and they did not fully recover their 1967 level until 1972. Actual entrants through UCCA fell from a then peak of 2274 in 1967 to 1923 in 1969 before starting to recover (see Table 2.6).

Fees remained at their 1967 levels until 1974, since when fees for both home and overseas students have been raised several times (Table 2.5). In real terms (constant prices), as Table 2.5 shows, fees were in 1974 at only just over half their 1967 level. The freezing of fees over this period occurred in spite of discussion proposals[4] put out by Mrs Shirley Williams in 1969 for a more restrictive policy on overseas students admission and of a firm proposal by an Expenditure Committee Report in 1973 on Postgraduate Education[5] that full-cost fees and a scholarship scheme charged to overseas aid should be instituted.

From 1975 to 1979 the Government raised fees each year, and in 1977/78 it introduced a new type of differential by levels of study. Fee increases were particularly steep in 1977 when they rose by 56% for undergraduates and 104% for postgraduates: but since fees for

Table 2.6   Overseas applicants and entrants to first degrees in universities, numbers and percentages, 1965–72

Years	Applicants	Entrants	Percentage of applicants who entered
1965	6972	1254	18·0
1966ᵃ	8360	1984	23·8
1967	9643	2274	23·7
1968ᵇ	7704	1995	24·6
1969	7068	1923	27·2
1970	7618	2246	29·5
1971	9016	2326	25·8
1972	10393	2815	27·0

Notes: [a] Oxford and Cambridge excluded before 1966;
[b] Heriot Watt and Ulster excluded before 1968.
Source: UCCA Reports, individual years.

home students increased by as much or more (in fact by over 300% for home undergraduates in 1977) the absolute and proportionate fee differentials between home and overseas students were actually lower in 1979 than in 1975.

The 1974–79 Labour Government thus raised fees but it reduced the percentage differentials. Indeed there was during this period the intention, stated more than once, of removing the differentials altogether, when the economic climate permitted. The Government also embarked on an alternative method of limiting overseas student numbers, and of thus reducing the scale of the British public subsidy, by imposing numerical limits. In July 1976 Mr Mulley (at the DES) announced that the Government 'cannot accept the continued rapid growth in the number of overseas students coming to our institutions .... I am therefore proposing to ask universities and local education authorities to aim at overseas student intakes in 1977/78 and subsequent years which will stabilise total numbers at recent levels.'[6] 'Recent levels' were defined as 1975/76 totals of 48,000 overseas students in higher education; and Government later proposed[7] that the reduction would continue still further to 44,000 in 1981/82.

By 1978/79 however this policy did not appear to be 'biting'. University numbers in 1978/79 at 36,500 were about 5000 higher than the 1975/76 level; and the total out-turn for higher education was 58,800 – 12% of the UK student body – or nearly 11,000 higher than the target levels. The extent to which the system was out of control may however have been exaggerated by a tendency to consider total enrolments rather than the underlying trend in admissions. A rapid rise in overseas numbers in publicly financed institutions to 1976/77 reflected fast increasing admissions a few years earlier when fee levels were lower and inflation rates less. Admissions grew more slowly after 1976. Thus whereas overseas undergraduate entrants to British universities had risen between 1972 and 1975 from 4300 to 6900 (60%), in the next three years to 1978 they increased less dramatically from 6900 to 7900 (14%). In higher education overall it transpires that already by October 1979, before the full-cost fees policy was announced, initial entrants to higher education had dropped below the level in Mr Mulley's baseline year of 1975/76. Table 2.7 makes this clear.

Table 2.7   Overseas initial entrants to full-time higher education in Great Britain (thousands)

Academic year of entry	Universities	Public sector	All higher education
1967/68	2·6	3·0	5·6
1968/69	3·1	2·5	5·6
1969/70	3·1	2·6	5·7
1970/71	3·5	2·6	6·1
1971/72	3·7	3·2	6·9
1972/73	4·3	3·4	7·7
1973/74	5·1	4·5	9·6
1974/75	5·9	6·0	11·9
1975/76	6·9	8·3	15·2
1976/77	7·4	9·7	17·1
1977/78	7·7	8·8	16·5
1978/79	7·9	8·2	16·1
1979/80 (*prov*)	7·2	7·2	14·4

Source: Department of Education and Science Statistical Bulletin 12/80 September 1980

New policies for overseas students were thus anticipated in 1979, whatever the outcome of the General Election that year. Mrs Shirley Williams, as Labour Secretary of State for Education and Science, was already publicly floating proposals for applying the then existing public fee subsidy to overseas students more selectively, to help priority groups.[8]

Full-cost fees policy, November 1979

After the May 1979 election, the new Conservative Government, as part of urgent expenditure cuts, decided upon an increase in overseas student fees for 1979/80 of 20%, which was over and above the 9% already announced by the previous administration. Later in the year, on 1 November 1979, the full-cost overseas student fee policy was formally announced in a White Paper entitled 'The Government's Expenditure Plans for 1980/81' (Cmnd 7746). The accompanying Department of Education and Science Press Notice stated, *inter alia*

> Given the overriding need to reduce public expenditure while giving priority to home students, the Government considers it right to remove progressively the current subsidy in the education budget of around £100m a year on provision for overseas students. Accordingly, as from the start of the academic year 1980/81, all overseas students who begin courses of higher and further education in Great Britain will be expected to pay a fee covering the full cost of tuition.

The minimum recommended fees for overseas students in 1980/81 were as shown in Table 2.8. For overseas students no fee differentiation was made between university undergraduates and postgraduates. Continuing overseas students had their fees raised by 24% for 1980/81, the same percentage rise as for home students (incorporated in the home student figures in Table 2.8).

Three aspects of the 1980/81 overseas student fee structure should be particularly noted. First, it represented a very considerable rise in fees for many categories of overseas students. For new university postgraduates the increase was one of from 63 to 307%, for undergraduates from 113 to 432%, depending on subject studied; in polytechnics and further education, for advanced students from 155 to 251%, and for non-advanced students from 165 to 263%, depending on subject studied and level. Second, the principle of differential tuition fees by subject of study, geared to calculations of differences in costs of a place in different groups of disciplines, was applied for the first time.

Third, the policy was to reduce public expenditure through the reduction of public grants to educational institutions. Institutions were to lose that part of their *existing* grant which corresponded to the recent proportion of overseas students in their total student body. This grant reduction was to be implemented over a three-

Table 2.8   *Minimum recommended fees for overseas students in 1980/81*

| | New overseas students (£ p.a.) | | Home students | |
			Undergraduate (£ p.a.)	Postgraduate (£ p.a.)
Universities				
Arts	2000		740	1105
Science	3000		740	1105
Clinical years of medicine, dentistry and veterinary science	5000		740	1105
Non-university	*Advanced*	*Non-advanced*	*Advanced*	*Non-advanced*
Maintained and Voluntary Institutions				
Laboratory and Workshop-based courses	3300	1890	740	595
Classroom-based courses	2400	1380	740	595

year period; by 40% in 1980/81, 40% in 1981/82, and 20% in 1982/83. Thus the new policy had a serious effect not only on individual overseas students, but also on educational institutions themselves. In the past, institutions may sometimes even have derived marginally more income as a result of fee increases for overseas students: but under the new arrangements those who had had high proportions of overseas students in their student body stood to lose a substantial part of their income. Because the Government was unwilling to increase grant allocations in respect of any additional home students whom institutions might attract, such universities and colleges could only balance their budgets if they *either* cut back on their overall activities *or* made good the loss of grant income by high levels of overseas recruitment at the new fee levels.

Debate on the policy

The Government's policy was fully explained to Parliament, particularly in the course of debates in the House of Lords on 12 December 1979 and in the House of Commons on 5 June 1980. Additionally Ministers appeared before two House of Commons Committees, and Government took a further opportunity to elaborate its views through White Papers[9] issued in August 1980 responding to the Committee Reports.

In essence the Government justified its policy on the grounds that there was a need to cut public expenditure and that the subsidisation of overseas students by an estimated total of £127m (of which £102m was for advanced courses in universities, polytechnics and other colleges, and £25m for non-advanced courses) was unjustified when there were other heavy claims on public expenditure. Ministers stated that overseas student numbers had risen very quickly in spite of previous fee rises, and attempts by the previous Government to restrict numbers by means of quota to their 1975/76 levels had been unsuccessful; so unsuccessful, in fact, that universities had been educating 5000 more overseas students than provided for under the recurrent grant (whilst home students were 5000 below target) and the total higher education system had 8600 (17%) more overseas students than provided for. There seemed little justification for subsidising courses which were patronised largely or solely by overseas students, and it had also to be borne in mind that large numbers (about 20%) of overseas students in Britain came from countries with a national income per capita higher than that in Britain. Overseas students in British higher and further education were welcome and if the full-cost fees policy were adopted it would not be necessary to restrict numbers by quota. It was believed that the quality of our system and the strength of demand were such that overseas students would continue to come at the higher fees. Students already enrolled on courses would not be charged the full-cost fees for continuation of their studies; there was provision in the aid programme to assist poorer countries; and the position of refugees would be watched.

The new policy was approved in votes in both Houses of Parliament at the end of the debates referred to above. But criticism came from a variety of sources including Parliament, the education world, student bodies, and overseas countries. In response to government arguments, critics counter-claimed that continued fee subsidies were justified on the grounds that Britain derived substantial educational, commercial and political benefits from receiving overseas students into its education system: these benefits seemed not to have been taken into account by Government, which appeared to have made its decision on purely budgetary grounds. Moreover the basis of the Government's calculation of the amount of subsidy was faulty since it confused marginal and average costs, and furthermore ascribed the cost of research to the cost of educating students. Third, Britain had a moral obligation to its dependencies and to those of its ex-colonies which could not sustain full education systems of their own and had come to rely on British facilities, sometimes with the UK's own encouragement. Gibraltar, Hong Kong, Cyprus and Mauritius were frequently mentioned. Fourth, poor countries and poor students would be particularly badly affected, especially those developing countries who most needed science and technology study facilities (now to be the most expensive) and refugee students. Fifth, the UK sent many of its own students abroad, and in the interests of reciprocity Britain should follow the policies of non-discrimination and low tuition fees pursued by many other countries. Finally, the introduction of the new policy was too hasty, allowing insufficient time for consultation with the interested parties, for much needed study and analysis, or for adjustment by either suppliers or supplied in the overseas student market.

The most formal reactions to the policy were the Reports of the House of Commons Education, Science and Arts Committee, and of its Foreign Affairs Committee. These committees both reported in April 1980. There were also statements by Commonwealth Governments through their representatives in London and at the Commonwealth Education Conference in Sri Lanka in August 1980.

The Report of the House of Commons Education, Science and Arts Committee[10] regretted that there had not been fuller consultation by Government, expressed doubts about the calculation of full-cost fees and concluded that the information apparently available to the Secretary of State was neither sufficient nor up-to-date. The time given to education institutions to adjust was too short. The Committee nevertheless accepted the full-cost calculation as a convenient basis for accounting. They recommended that subsidies for overseas students should be carried on the Overseas Development Administration budget in future; that Government should take steps to improve the statistical analysis of overseas student trends as a basis for better forecasting; and that a wider bursary scheme than the one proposed by Government should be set up as a matter of urgency.

The Overseas Development Sub-Committee of the Foreign Affairs Committee was primarily concerned with the effect of the new policy on overseas aid and development.[11] The Sub-Committee was particularly critical of the lack of a properly integrated coherent policy on overseas student affairs and of the apparent absence of adequate machinery in Government to produce a properly co-ordinated approach. It recommended that these deficiencies be remedied; it urged Government support for investigations of the factual situation concerning overseas students and their costs, both in the UK and in the other OECD countries; it recommended that numbers of students and trainees financed under the aid programme be kept at 1979/80 levels; it proposed special help for poorer countries and for Commonwealth countries and British dependencies with incomplete education systems. It sought a wider fee support scheme, and special help was urged for those British educational institutions which were international centres of excellence. It was recommended that the higher fee levels should not be charged to students already studying in the UK who would be progressing from a preliminary course to a higher one.

Overseas governments and their representatives in London also lodged protests and made representations. Two overseas diplomats appeared before the House of Commons Overseas Development Sub-Committee and eleven governments had made official approaches to the Foreign and Commonwealth Office by mid-March. Later, Commonwealth representatives met under the aegis of the Commonwealth Secretariat and made concerted representations in London. The matter was also put on the agenda of the Commonwealth Education Conference in Sri Lanka in August 1980 which resolved that:

> para 49. Since the Conference apprehends that recent increases in fees for overseas students will cause considerable hardship to those from developing Commonwealth coun-

tries and that the development plans of those countries will be adversely affected, *it is recommended that* governments should consider setting reasonable levels of fees for students from Commonwealth countries.

para 50. *It is also recommended* that governments should consider treating the following categories of students as home students for tuition fee purposes: (a) scholars under the Commonwealth Scholarship and Fellowship Plan; (b) students receiving national awards and those receiving awards from recognised international agencies; and (c) an agreed number of other students from Commonwealth developing countries which do not have adequate educational facilities of their own.[12]

The Government response

In response to the various representations made to it, the Government stood by the general policy, but made five exceptions:

(1)   An overseas postgraduate research scheme was launched to enable overseas postgraduates of high calibre to study in British universities at the same level of fees as is charged to home postgraduates. Sufficient funds were allocated to finance 500 awards in 1980/81 (though the take up of these awards in the first year was below the number available) and the number may rise to 1500 by 1982/83.

(2)   A sum of £5m was made available to universities for 1980/81 to meet transitional difficulties. The bulk of this was handed on by the University Grants Committee to London University where several large postgraduate research institutions specialising in international matters are located.

(3)   Students from European Community member countries would pay home rates of tuition fee, but this would not apply to Greece until the 1981/82 academic year, even though she would be acceding to the Community in January 1981.

(4)   Refugee students would also pay the home level of fees.

(5)   Students from anywhere in the world admitted to UK institutions under fully reciprocal exchange schemes would also pay home rates of fee.

These concessions apart, the Government response to the various submissions to it, in particular to the two House of Commons Reports, was to reject them almost in their entirety. Essentially, with the exceptions mentioned above, the original policy remained intact. Government did agree in the light of the anxieties expressed to make special arrangements to assess at an early date the effect of the new fees on overseas students entering courses in the academic year 1980/81. This was done, and preliminary data became available much earlier than in any previous year. Initial analysis showed that overseas entrants to British universities in October 1980 were about 10% fewer than a year earlier and non-university institutions were more seriously affected.[13] Meanwhile preliminary information from the Universities Central Council for Admissions indicated that overseas applications for admission to undergraduate courses in 1981 were running at around a third below the level of a year earlier.[14]

These indications appear broadly to confirm predictions made in the summer of 1980 by Mark Blaug and Richard Layard that overseas student numbers in the universities would decline by about 10% in the first year. The Blaug-Layard estimates, which also anticipated that polytechnics and the non-advanced sector of further education would encounter an impact more serious than that for the universities, were based on an observation of past trends in the overseas response to fee rises over the period since the mid-1960s.

If Government policies are not changed – and Chapter 8 explores some of the options for change – what trend will overseas student numbers in fact follow? Projection is by its nature an uncertain business and in this case one should note the difficulty of disentangling the effects of fee rises on changing overseas numbers when so many other factors in the equation may also affect the situation simultaneously. Thus on the one hand the effect of full-cost fees on the overseas numbers may be reduced in the short term by the lag effect when policy changes are announced. Experience from 1966/67 (Table 2.6 and accompanying text) suggests that many students who had made plans to enter British educational institutions before the fee rises were announced may still persist with their immediate plans. Thus it is not unreasonable to expect the effect of the fee rises on overseas enrolments only to be seen fully in 1981 and later years.

Another factor is the effect of reclassification of overseas students paying home fees. Since differential fees were first introduced in 1967, there has always been the problem of the precise cut-off point at which a student with overseas origins might become classified as a home-fee-paying student, whether on grounds of periods of residence and study in the UK, of descent from or affinity to UK nationals, or by virtue of immigrant/refugee status. Even after the differential overseas fee was introduced in 1967, it was possible for students to qualify for the home level of fees (and even in some cases for LEA awards to pay fees and maintenance costs) by virtue of their having been in Britain for three years preceding the course; and students under the age of 19 could also pay the home level of fee. Thus Britain has been subsidising the education of more foreign nationals than official figures indicate. With the passage of time the interpretation of the regulations has been changed in a more restrictive direction, notably by Circulars DES 8/77 and ACL 1/78.[15] It was announced in January 1980 that three years' residence would no longer suffice for entitlement to home level of fees. A possible effect is that some formerly home-fee-paying students will move on to advanced courses but will now pay the overseas level of fees, thus causing a rise through redefinition in the recorded numbers of overseas students.

Factors which may on the other hand reinforce the effect of the rise in fees and thus act to depress overseas student admissions still further than might otherwise have happened are

(1) Rising value of sterling and UK domestic inflation. Tuition fees account for only a part of overseas student expenditure. Travel to the UK and living costs while on course may well outweigh in absolute importance the amount of fees paid. For some students an increase in UK living costs of 16% in the twelve months after October 1979, and the appreciation of sterling by perhaps 10% against their currencies over the same period, may have raised their total costs in terms of their own currencies by as much or more than the 1980 rise in tuition fees – in the case of a postgraduate social scientist who paid £1320 in 1979/80 and £2000 p.a. in 1980/81 the fee rise may have been less important over that twelve month period than the cost of living and exchange rate factors. So the decline in student numbers could prove to be greater than an extrapolation of fee levels alone would suggest: and a part of any fall-off in numbers will have to be attributed to these other factors.

(2) Another factor complementary in its effects to the rise in overseas student fees is the cut-back in Britain's overseas aid programme. Even if the scale of financial allocation for the programme were not reduced, an increase in overseas student fees would mean that the amount of money in the Overseas Development Administration's training budget would buy fewer places. The decision actually to cut the aid budget meant that the effect of fee increases was reinforced rather than counterbalanced by concurrent action on the aid side. The Government stated that a significant decline from the 1979

level of aided students and trainees was to be expected in 1980.

(3) Political developments, often unforeseen, may affect the student flow quite considerably. For example, one would have expected a decline in students coming from Iran, even before the Iran–Iraq war; and the war will have affected Iraq also. With an independent majority government in Salisbury, one can also expect fewer refugee students coming from Zimbabwe.

Given time and careful statistical analysis, it would in principle be possible to isolate the effect of full-cost fees from some of these other factors which may turn out to have affected overseas enrolment statistics heavily with the passage of time. All that has been possible here is to point out the obvious dangers of jumping to hasty conclusions when complete figures for 1980/81 are first released.

Notes

1. British Council, *Statistics of Overseas Students in Britain 1978/79*, page 1.
2. *Report of the Committee on Higher Education*, HMSO, Cmnd 2154, 1963.
3. ibid.
4. First Report from the House of Commons Education, Science and Arts Committee: *Interim Report on Overseas Student Fees*, page vi, para 10, HC 552–1, April 1980.
5. *Postgraduate Education: Expenditure Committee Report*, paras 156, 158, HC 96–1, Session 1973/4.
6. *DES Circular 1/77* of 14 January 1977.
7. *Public Expenditure White Paper*, January 1978.
8. World University Service (UK) Conference, December 1978, *WUS News*, Conference report, February 1980.
9. *Government Observations on the First Report from the Education, Science and Arts Committee*, HMSO, Cmnd. 8011, August 1980.
    Government Observations on the Report of the Sub-Committee on Overseas Development of the Select Committee on Foreign Affairs HMSO, Cmnd. 8010, August 1980.
10. HMSO, HC 552–1, 1980.
11. HMSO, HC 553, 1980.
12. *Eighth Commonwealth Education Conference Report* Commonwealth Secretariat 1980.
13. Written Answer to Parliamentary Question. Dr Rhodes Boyson, Parliamentary Under-Secretary of State, DES, to Mr Nicholas Lyell. *Hansard*, 2 December 1980.
14. Universities Central Council for Admissions, *Press Releases 2 and 3* November, December 1980.
15. *DES Circular 8/77* of 18 August 1977.
     DES Circular Letter ACL 1/78 of 27 January 1978.

3. The Economic Costs and Benefits of Overseas Students

by Mark Blaug*

Foreword

On 1 November 1979, the Government announced that overseas students in British higher education would from October 1980 be charged what it called 'full-cost' fees with the aim of withdrawing all state subsidies to overseas students by 1982. There is a standard economic case for state subsidies to higher education students and nothing the Government said suggested that it questioned this case. Why then the objection to subsidising overseas students when there is no objection to subsidising home students?

*This study, commissioned by the Overseas Students Trust and co-financed by the Trust and the Social Science Research Council was undertaken by a research team led by the author and based at the University of London Institute of Education. The other members of the team were John Mace, Sue Owen and Maureen Woodhall. The author of this paper accepts sole responsibility for the paper here presented, while acknowledging the co-operation of his colleagues and of many others (see note of acknowledgements at end).

Social and Community Planning Research, a London-based market survey agency, was engaged to carry out on behalf of the research team a specially designed sample survey of overseas students in Britain, the findings of which are summarised in this book as Appendix A. That survey forms a major data base for the conclusions of this study.

In addition, John Mace, Sue Owen and Maureen Woodhall visited nine randomly selected universities and five randomly selected polytechnics in Britain to collect evidence on the average and marginal costs of overseas students. The student survey and the institutional visits were supplemented by published and unpublished data from the British Council, the University Grants Committee, the Association of Commonwealth Universities, the Department of Education and Science, the Department of Trade, the Overseas Development Administration of the Foreign and Commonwealth Office, the Overseas Students Trust, the United Kingdom Council for Overseas Student Affairs, and World University Service (UK).

In addition to the paper appearing here the study generated a further technical paper by Mark Blaug in association with Professor Richard Layard of the London School of Economics on 'Forecasting overseas demand for higher and further education in the United Kingdom' which is to be published in 1981 in an economic journal.

It can only be because of what I call 'the contributory principle of government expenditure' which states 'Thou shalt not enjoy the services rendered by Government if thou or thy parents have contributed nought to the public exchequer!' This appears to be a widely endorsed norm of public life, although it has so far been violated by National Health Service provisions for tourists and foreign businessmen. Being a norm or value judgement, it is neither true nor false, but it may be reasonable or unreasonable and one could certainly imagine setting it aside on a reciprocal basis between countries. One could also imagine setting it aside if a cost-benefit analysis of overseas students revealed that they bring indirect and unanticipated benefits to Britain as a whole which, in fact, exceed their social costs. In other words, if we could demonstrate, as some have claimed that we can, that the subsidised provision of higher education to foreigners is, so to speak, a profitable export business for the United Kingdom as a whole then, clearly, it would be short-sighted not to subsidise overseas students simply because it appears to violate 'the contributory principle of government expenditure'.

Our task then is to apply cost-benefit analysis to overseas students to determine whether their benefits are in fact greater than their costs. It is worth emphasising that in this study we are concerned only with the *economic* costs and benefits of overseas students to *Britain*. There are political costs and benefits involved in subsidising overseas students, as well as purely educational ones, and we shall have to face the question at the close of our analysis whether it is indeed possible to add *economic* costs and benefits to political and educational costs and benefits. Moreover, there may be objections to treating Britain as the unit of welfare whose net benefits over costs we are seeking to maximise rather than the world as a whole – perhaps the best case we can make for subsidising overseas students is to think of it as a particular species of international co-operation. For the moment, however, we leave all such problems to one side and ask: what are the total economic costs and benefits to Britain of subsidising the higher education of overseas students?

We will argue that the appropriate costs to consider in relation to the question of overseas students are long-run marginal social costs, and we will also show that these have generally been underestimated by most participants in the debates on overseas student fees. The short- and long-run economic benefits of overseas students to the United Kingdom fall principally into four categories: (i) the market value of scientific research which some overseas students carry out; (ii) the contribution which some overseas students subsequently make to British exports; (iii) the contribution which the spending of all overseas students makes to our balance of payments; and (iv) the contribution which all overseas students make to aggregate demand for British goods and services. By way of contrast, we will show that these marginal economic benefits have generally been overestimated by others. Although there is, strictly speaking, no such thing as a single, long-run marginal social cost of one extra overseas student – it will differ by institution, by department, and even by individual course studied – and although some of the economic benefits can only be measured in terms of general magnitudes, not precise numbers, there is little doubt that the smallest, single number we can plausibly assign to the long-run marginal costs of overseas students exceeds the largest possible number we can reasonably assign to the sum of their marginal economic benefits. In other words, it is not possible on strictly economic grounds to make a case for waiving 'the contributory principle of government expenditure', thus subsidising overseas students as we subsidise home students. Whether we should uphold 'the contributory principle of government expenditure' is, of course, a question which cost-benefit analysis as such is powerless to answer.

Costs

Drawing the sample
It seems natural to begin our analysis with the cost side. Much of our evidence of costs comes from a series of visits to a random sample of higher education institutions and we must spend a moment explaining how this sample was drawn.

We decided initially to survey a random sample of overseas students, focusing on full-time students in advanced-level work in either universities or polytechnics, thereby ignoring all those overseas students studying for General Certificate of Education (GCE), 'O' levels and 'A' levels, Ordinary National Certificates (ONCs) and Ordinary National Diplomas (ONDs) and other qualifications below the level of a first degree in polytechnics, further education colleges and the private sector (English language schools, commercial schools, art, drama and music colleges, nursing students and trainees in hospitals, etc.) as well as overseas students in colleges of education and inns of court where the qualifications obtained are roughly equivalent to a first degree. In other words, instead of taking account of all the 86,779 overseas students in public higher and further education in the United Kingdom in 1978/79 (the most recent year for which comprehensive data was available), we concentrated on 37,140 overseas students in universities and 14,375 overseas students taking advanced level work in polytechnics; for other purposes, however, we also refer to 35,264 overseas students in non-advanced work in polytechnics and further education colleges. An overseas student is defined for these purposes simply as any student paying fees at the overseas rate, regardless of his country of nationality, domicility or residence.

Having limited ourselves to 51,515 fairly homogeneous overseas students, we opted for a 5% random sample, or roughly 2600 overseas students, which we hoped to interview face-to-face. The sample was drawn in two stages: first we clustered universities, university colleges and polytechnics into six types, weighted each institution by its proportion of total overseas higher education students, and then selected institutions randomly within each of the six clusters; secondly, we sampled overseas students within each of the selected institutions so as to give each overseas student in advanced higher and further education an equal chance of being selected (see Appendix A for further details). In this way, we simultaneously obtained a random sample of fourteen institutions and a random sample of about 2600 overseas students, each of whom was enrolled at one of the fourteen institutions which we visited. We supplemented the fourteen institutional visits by an additional one to our own institution, the University of London Institute of Education, and derived additional insights from a working party report on overseas student recruitment at the Institute, which was completed just before the writing of this report (August 1980).

So much by way of explanation of our principal source of information for the cost part of our cost-benefit analysis. Let us now ask what it is we really want to know about the costs of overseas students.

Marginal costs versus average costs
If there is one generalisation we can safely make about cost-benefit analysis, it is that the costs are usually easy while the benefits are usually difficult and sometimes almost impossible to measure. Not so in the case of overseas students, however. Here the costs are almost as troublesome as the benefits.

The first question is which costs – average or marginal? If we are asking whether there are too few or too many overseas students in British higher education, as we are in this study, or if for any other reason we are concerned with the efficient utilisation of resources in higher education institutions, the costs we are after are marginal and not average costs. What we want to know is the incremental cost of having one more or one less student and there is clearly no reason why this should coincide with average costs, that is, total capital plus current expenditure divided by the total number of students. On the other hand, if all we are interested in is to save public expenditure on higher education by withdrawing the subsidy to overseas students, the costs we should be looking at are average costs. The Government has not disguised the fact that the decision to introduce 'full-cost' fees for overseas students in 1980/81 was part of a general policy of reducing public expenditure and it calculated this 'full-cost' by dividing total *current* expenditure on higher education by the number of home plus overseas students; in other words, what are called 'full-cost' fees are simply crudely estimated average costs per student. Thus, there is no correct answer to the question: which costs – average or marginal?; it all depends on the motive for asking the question. In any case, it is the relationship between average and marginal costs which gives us all the information we need.

When marginal costs are less than average costs, it follows as a matter of pure arithmetic that additional students will result in a reduction of average costs – the institution is too small to produce graduates at the lowest possible cost per student. Contrariwise, when marginal costs exceed average costs, further growth in student numbers will raise average costs because the institution is too large to yield the lowest possible cost per student. Thus, if there were firm evidence that marginal costs are less than average costs in British universities and polytechnics, government policy should be directed towards expanding student numbers, including overseas students. However, this is true if and only if it cares more about efficiency in higher education institutions than about total public spending on higher education. Likewise, if there were firm evidence that marginal costs exceed average costs, a policy of discouraging overseas students can be justified, not just on budget-saving grounds, but also on grounds of efficiency. It is clear, therefore, that any comprehensive view of the subsidy to overseas students must take account of the relationship between average and marginal costs.

Having raised fees for overseas students in the 1980/81 academic year by 111–177% for advanced-level work, depending on the course and the level in question (see Table 2.5), we could be fairly sure that the number of overseas students would decline in 1980 and indeed in 1981/82. I say 'fairly sure' because the numbers arriving each year in the United Kingdom have shown such a strong upward trend that some observers have even denied that overseas demand is responsive in any way to the level of fees that are charged. Thus, Dr Rhodes Boyson, Under-Secretary for Higher Education, has more than once complained that 'the dog [of higher education] is barking often before it has seen the bone, or even before the bone has been taken away'. No doubt, the dog has barked too often and too loudly in the past and it is true that the number of overseas students in higher and further education rose every year between 1967/68 and 1978/79. Overseas student fees were raised in 1967/68 by a huge 368%, the largest across-the-board percentage increase ever, and this rise was associated with a decline in numbers of 12%; the next increase in fees came in 1975/76 and more increases followed every year thereafter; nevertheless, the total number of overseas students kept growing along a continuously rising trend up to 1978/79 (Appendix Table B.1). Thus, a crude look at the data might suggest that overseas demand is totally insensitive to the level of fees.

However, interpretation of the data is confused by continual changes in the official definition of an overseas student: half of the decline in numbers in 1967/68 was a result of a legal re-interpretation of the concept 'normal country of residence', which shifted students previously defined to be overseas into the category of home students. The definition of overseas students was tightened up in 1971/72, 1977/78 and 1978/79, and these redefinitions went the other way: they counted as overseas students those who would previously have been designated as home students, thus masking the decline in overseas demand. Recent changes in the definition once again work in the same direction, serving to cushion the impact of rising fees on the reported numbers of overseas students studying in British universities and polytechnics.

We show elsewhere (1981, forthcoming) that, appearances notwithstanding, a rise in fees for overseas students, everything else being the same, does in fact cause a decline in the number of overseas students that would otherwise be forthcoming. Moreover, such is the strength of the negative responses to higher fees that we could safely predict that there would be fewer overseas students in British higher education in 1980/81 than there were in 1979/80 despite the likelihood that a further tightening in the definition of the overseas student status will once again produce an artificial inflation in their numbers.

If this prediction is correct,* it follows that we should be concerned, not with the marginal *costs* of additional overseas students, but with the marginal *savings* of fewer overseas students, and the latter is not simply the inverse of the former: the costs of expansion are

---

*The forecast by Professors Blaug & Layard, made in August 1980, has turned out to be substantially correct – Editor.

not matched by the savings of contraction. Besides announcing the impending increase in overseas student fees in November 1979, the Government also placed an effective ceiling on the finance available to support home students in higher education institutions, thereby making its purpose in raising overseas student fees perfectly plain. In other words, from October 1980, higher education institutions would no longer be able to recruit in the home market to fill places left vacant by the shortfall in overseas applications (unless, of course, they were willing to forgo the subsidy on home students). Thus, fewer overseas students in 1980/81 as a result of higher fees would produce vacant places in higher education and therefore under-employed staff. If it were possible to dismiss staff on short notice, there might be considerable savings even in the short run. But over 90% of academic staff in British universities and polytechnics are tenured and, furthermore, only polytechnics are signatories of a National Redundancy Scheme which would allow them to break tenure agreements. It follows that the short-run marginal savings of fewer overseas students in 1980/81 would be nearly zero (even polytechnics cannot invoke their redundancy schemes in less than two or three years).

Although the short-run marginal savings of fewer overseas students are nearly zero, the long-run marginal savings are by no means zero: in time, institutions can lay off part-time staff and rely on natural wastage to reduce their full-time staff numbers; they can also sell off buildings or cut back on their building programmes. The length of this long run required to equate the marginal and average savings of fewer students will vary from institution to institution, and even from department to department within the same institution, because it depends principally on, first, the age structure and normal turnover rate of the teaching staff and second, the actual proportion of overseas students in different courses at different levels.

If overseas students were evenly distributed across institutions, departments and courses, or if more home students could be substituted for fewer overseas students, there would be one set of marginal costs or marginal savings for all students. But as we noted before, home students and overseas students are no longer substitutes and, besides, overseas students are highly unevenly distributed across institutions, across levels of study, and across fields of specialisation. This is a fact of such crucial importance to the question of overseas student fees that we can hardly emphasise it too much. Overseas students constituted only 8% of all undergraduates in universities, polytechnics, and further education colleges in 1978/79 but they comprised 35% of all postgraduates in universities. At one extreme, there are colleges of the University of London – such as the London School of Economics, Imperial College, the School of Oriental and African Studies and the Institute of Education – where the proportion of overseas students, estimated on a full-time-equivalent basis, runs as high as 20–35% (not to mention the School of Hygiene and Tropical Medicine where the proportion is almost 80%). At the other extreme, there are some universities and polytechnics in the North and in the Midlands where the fraction of overseas students may be as low as 3–4%. Apart from being concentrated in postgraduate courses in particular institutions, overseas students are also heavily concentrated in three or four fields of study: at the postgraduate level, they make up half of all the students enrolled in (i) engineering and technology, (ii) agriculture and veterinary science, and (iii) medicine and dentistry; at the undergraduate level, they make up one out of four or five students in engineering and technology (see Table 2.3). Summing it up, we do not go far wrong if we say that the typical overseas student in Britain is an undergraduate student in engineering and technology or else a postgraduate student in either engineering and technology or agriculture and medicine.[1] It is apparent that these are largely laboratory-based courses and therefore more expensive than most, a fact which will prove to be of signal importance to our final conclusions.

Suffice it to say that from now on we shall have to get used to thinking of two sets of marginal costs, one for home students and one for overseas students, and, in addition, to distinguishing between the marginal costs of expansion and the non-symmetrical, marginal savings of contraction. Finally, there is the ordinary distinction between the short run and the long run, being the length of time required to alter the entire scale of operations, which in this case has more to do with inflexibility in the volume of employment offered than with inflexibility in the amount of plant and equipment available. The 1980 'full-cost' fees for overseas students in universities – £2000 for arts, £3000 for science, and £5000 for medicine – were based, as we have said, on crude estimates of the average cost per student regardless of the level of study, and as such clearly far in excess of the *short-run* marginal costs of more overseas students as well as the *short-run* marginal savings of fewer overseas students (the same applies to home students for those few universities falling below their 1979/80 approved targets for home students). What is far less clear is whether that level of fees also exceeds the *long-run* marginal costs and *long-run* marginal savings of overseas students.

Because overseas students are heavily concentrated in particular departments in particular institutions, the marginal costs of more of them, or the marginal savings of fewer, are larger than might at first appear. Everything depends, however, on the magnitude of the change in the numbers of overseas students we are considering. Clearly, there is no such thing as *a* marginal cost or *a* marginal saving of overseas students: marginal costs and marginal savings are not discrete numbers but stepwise functions; the marginal costs of adding 100 students might be zero, whereas the marginal costs of adding 200 students might be considerable; moreover, the marginal costs of adding 1000 students is not twice the marginal costs of adding 500 students; similar remarks apply to the case of marginal savings.

Enough said. To go any further with these questions it is necessary to take a close look at specific courses in specific institutions to see how much excess capacity will in fact be created by stated reductions in overseas demand, and how long it will take to work off this excess capacity by means of natural wastage. Our institutional visits were designed to throw some light on these questions, bearing in mind the generalisation that the greater the excess capacity and the longer the time period required to eliminate excess capacity, the lower are the true marginal savings of fewer overseas students in terms of resources forgone.

Concrete evidence from institutions

In announcing the new set of fees for overseas students, the Government added the proviso that these were minimum recommended figures which individual institutions might wish to exceed. In so doing, they forced higher education institutions to consider the optimum level of fees which they ought to charge. In view of the difficulty of estimating long-run marginal costs, we found that many institutions solved the problem by preparing new estimates of the long-run *average* costs of all students. Although we are less interested in average than in marginal costs, it is worth considering some of these average cost figures as an indicative check on the 'full-cost' fees recommended by the Government.

One university with a heavy concentration of students in pure and applied science made a detailed study of its cost structure in 1978 and estimated the long-run annual average costs of all students at £3700, made up of departmental costs of £3200 and central costs of £500 but excluding capital costs for premises, maintenance and rates. This figures of £3700 was itself a weighted average (by student numbers) of long-run annual average costs per undergraduate of £1610, per postgraduate in taught courses of £3540, and per postgraduate taking research degrees of £5670, thus dramatically revealing the significance of the level of the course at which students are studying.

Another university with a more even spread of students across fields of study produced the following set of annual departmental-plus-central average costs (once again excluding capital costs) in 1978/79 by major faculties without distinction between undergraduates and postgraduates.

Table 3.1 *Illustrative university department-plus-central average costs by major faculties, 1978/79 (£)*

Social studies	1600
Humanities	1800
Mathematics	2000
Basic medicine	3170
Electronics	3550
Biological science	3630
Physical chemistry	4470
Average (weighted by student numbers)	2800

Source: Confidential data

We collected figures on average costs from other universities, all of which were of similar orders of magnitude, suggesting that a 'full-cost' fee of £2000 for arts students comes close to true average current costs, whereas the 'full-cost' fee of £3000 for science students is, if anything, a little less than current costs per student. In this regard it is worth noting that a number of science-and-technology oriented universities have decided to charge more than £3000 for laboratory-based and less than £3000 for non-laboratory-based courses in science and engineering (likewise, they have decided to charge much less for the first and second year of pre-clinical medicine than the £5000 recommended by the Government and slightly more than £5000 for the third and fourth year of clinical medicine).

The new overseas student fees recommended for polytechnics – £2400 for classroom-based and £3300 for laboratory-based advanced courses – are regarded in most of the polytechnics we visited as a reasonable estimate of average costs, possibly a little on the low rather than the high side. A typical set of calculations in one polytechnic of average current costs per full-time-equivalent student taking advanced work in 1978 yielded the results reported in Table 3.2.

| Table 3.2 | *Illustrative polytechnic department-plus-central average costs by major faculties, 1978/79 (£)* |

Social sciences	2371
Humanities	2804
Education	2808
Engineering	2977
Sciences	3155
Art and design	3537
Unweighted average	2729

Source: Confidential data

It is noteworthy that wherever there was any experience with self-financing, commercially priced courses, the fees that were charged were frequently higher than those recommended for overseas students by the DES. We found a number of such self-financing courses, especially set up for overseas students, usually in highly specialised subjects at the postgraduate level, in many of the universities we visited, as well as many courses run by TOPS (Training Opportunity Pilot Schemes) charging full-cost fees in the polytechnics. Fees of £2000 for a six-months' course were not unusual in either universities or polytechnics.

Enough of average costs. What of marginal costs? Only one of the visited institutions – the science-based university referred to above – went so far as precisely to estimate long-run marginal costs (£1800 as against a figure of £3700 for long-run average costs) but all of them had much to say about the relationship between average and marginal costs and between average and marginal savings in both the short and the long run.

Let me explain that all the universities we visited had just completed an exercise for the University Grants Committee (UGC) which made them extremely conscious of the financial implications of fewer overseas students in 1980/81. The subsidy to new overseas students is supposed to be withdrawn gradually over the three years 1980–82 to reach 'level funding' by 1982. 'Level funding' is crudely calculated for each institution by taking the ratio of full-time overseas students in 1979 to all full-time students: if this stands at, say, 25%, the institution's grant is cut by 10% in 1980, 10% in 1981, and 5% in 1982. Universities were asked by the UGC to project the total number of home students plus overseas students currently enrolled who would be continuing their course in 1980 on three assumptions: (i) 'level funding' for all these students; (ii) 'level funding' plus 2%; and (3) 'level funding' minus 5%. This exercise, although not concerned with new overseas students, required universities to project both the number of new overseas students expected in the future and the fees that they would be charged for the simple reason that the projection of overseas students and fees affects total institutional income, therefore total staffing, and therefore the number of home students that can be accepted.

One London University college, with a relatively high ratio of overseas students, calculated these numbers on various assumptions about fees. If fees in 1980 were £2000, overseas students were estimated to decline by 25%; if £2750, they were estimated to decline by 33%; and if £3500 by 42% – and some evidence was collected from both heads of departments and from overseas students themselves to support these assumptions. On the basis of 'level funding' by 1982 and a fee of £2000 for overseas students (adjusted for expected inflation) this college calculated that its cut in grant would by then mean a loss of 10% in academic, administrative and secretarial posts.

All the institutions we visited had undertaken a more or less similar exercise during the academic year 1979/80, although few had projected overseas student demand on various alternative assumptions about fees as in the case of the London college cited above. We were struck by a marked tendency in virtually all the fourteen institutions we visited to reduce their estimates of the expected fall in new overseas students in 1980 as time passed in the academic year 1979/80. When the Government first announced the fee increases in November 1979, a number of vice-chancellors and principals went on record in predicting a fall as large as 70% in the number of new overseas students in 1980. By the time we made our visits (March to June 1980), most of the estimates had declined to 10–50%, the modal estimate being 30%. Considering that fees were going to rise on average by 111% for undergraduates and by 177% for postgraduates, a reduction in demand of 30% would actually be rather modest. As economists would say, the implied price-elasticity of demand, defined as the percentage change in the quantity demanded divided by the percentage change in price, was only around 0·2. Again and again we were told that fees for overseas students represented less than half the cost of studying here and that living expenses in Britain and the overseas value of sterling had gone up so rapidly in the last few years that the relative cost of studying in the United Kingdom had long been unfavourable, whatever the level of fees. Such at any rate were the arguments advanced to account for the low elasticity of the foreign demand for British higher education.

Many institutions believed that the crucial question would be the policy of grant-awarding agencies who financed over 30% of all overseas students in higher and further education. In the universities, the proportion of overseas students financed by an official sponsor was as high as 42% in 1977 (see Table 3.3) but the proportions vary widely among countries. It is clear that the reactions of particular governments, such as those of Nigeria and Iraq, as well as the reactions of ODA and the British Council, will have a considerable effect on the numbers forthcoming and such reactions are even more difficult to predict than the reactions of privately financed students.

Table 3.3   Percentage of full-time university overseas students known to hold a scholarship, grant or other award by countries of origin, 1977/78

Nigeria	69
Iraq	60
India	49
Rhodesia	46
Germany	44
Japan	39
Sri Lanka	39
Malaysia	38
Mauritius	37
Turkey	37
Ireland	36
France	33
USA	30
Iran	29
Singapore	20
Switzerland	20
Cyprus	18
Greece	16
Hong Kong	16
All countries	42

Source: *Association of Commonwealth Universities Yearbook, 1980*, London, ACU, 1980, Vol. 3, pp. 2164–9.

Statistical analysis of overseas demand for British higher education over the last fourteen years suggests a much smaller reaction to the 1980/81 rise in fees than a reduction of 30%. The true figure in the first year (1980/81) is more likely to have been a fall of 5%, building up to a fall of 16–17% in the third year (1982/83). Moreover, we note once again that a stricter definition of the overseas student status in 1980/81 would partly offset even this relatively small decline in actual numbers. This conclusion is subject to one proviso: increases in fees of this magnitude – at least £760 for postgraduates and possibly as much as £3360 for medical students – have never been experienced before and, hence, the past may be no guide to the future, which is simply to say that the casual empiricism of informed observers may this time outguess the statisticians. Certainly, the bulk of overseas students in our survey expressed the view that they would never have come to Britain if fees had been £500 higher than they were (see Appendix A, p. 262).

We were concerned to discover whether institutions were also relaxing their standards of admission for new overseas students in the effort to further offset the decline in numbers. Naturally, everyone we spoke to denied that standards would be allowed to decline but we did receive occasional hints that some departments were now prepared to apply less stringent rules about the appropriateness of foreign qualifications. The question was exceedingly difficult to assess because acceptance rates (number of candidates accepted as a fraction of the number of applicants) differ widely across subject groups and even across individual institutions in identical subject groups, and as much is true of the take-up rate by overseas students of successful applications.[2] Moreover, we arrived in the middle of the annual process of considering applications and before the date at which accepted students agree to take up or to reject the unconditional offer of a place. Thus, only a retrospective glance in 1981 or later will show whether the withdrawal of subsidies to overseas students has had the effect of lowering admission standards.

The polytechnics proved to have much greater difficulties in forecasting overseas demand than the universities. Unlike universities, polytechnics have been operating a departmental quota system for overseas students ever since September 1978, restricting the number of overseas students in a department to the numbers attending in the academic year 1975/76. With the exception of London polytechnics, the quota system was to be dropped once full-cost fees were charged. For polytechnics outside the capital, therefore, the problem was that of predicting the combined effect of three changes taking place simultaneously: first an increase in fees, tending to discourage overseas students; second a change in the definition of the overseas student status, tending to increase the numbers of potential overseas students at the expense of what used to be home students from the point of view of paying fees; and third the elimination of the quota system, which taken by itself would tend to increase the numbers of potential overseas students because most polytechnic courses had larger numbers of overseas students before the imposition of quotas in 1978 than afterwards. To add to the confusion, most polytechnics faced extreme uncertainty regarding their 1980 income as a result of the decision to 'cap the pool' (the imposition of cash limits on local authority pooled expenditure on advanced further education), and this overshadowed their concern over the financial implications of the decision to raise overseas student fees.

In general, we gained the impression that polytechnics were more alarmed about possible changes in the definition of an overseas student than about higher fees as such. Thus, one polytechnic predicted a 10% reduction in overseas numbers if the older and looser definition still applied, but a fall of at least 40% and perhaps as much as 50% if a new tighter definition were to be given legal sanction.[3] Of course, the question of fees and the question of redefinition cannot be entirely divorced: the argument was that if a change in definition vastly increased the number of potential overseas students then the increase in fees would have a dramatic effect. By and large, polytechnics tended to be more pessimistic about the elasticity of overseas demand than universities, sensing perhaps that they faced a somewhat different clientèle than the universities.

One topic on which we gathered as much information as possible was that of the density of overseas students in particular courses. The marginal costs of extra overseas students or the marginal savings of fewer overseas students is clearly more affected by this than by any other factor. This is not to say that a low density of overseas students in particular courses justifies a concern with the marginal rather than the average costs of overseas students. Thus, the Foreign Affairs Committee of the House of Commons declared that long-run marginal and not average costs are appropriate if 'both of the following propositions are true: (a) resources would not become available for reallocation if student numbers declined; (b) overseas students are genuinely marginal on all courses'.[4] But (a) is the exact opposite of the truth and (b) is merely an irrelevant play on the word 'marginal'. The case for paying attention to marginal rather than average costs rests on other grounds. Besides, the more (a) and (b) hold, the less and not the more relevant are marginal calculations. Oddly enough, the Committee went on to note that it received evidence on many courses that overseas students are not 'marginal' but instead comprise 80–100% of the students.[5]

We found an enormous variety of circumstances in the universities we visited and if we can generalise at all, it is to say that the density of overseas students is fairly high in most postgraduate courses in science and engineering, where they frequently comprise 40–50% of the students on a course, and relatively low (5–10%) only in undergraduate courses in arts, humanities and social studies. In no university we visited would an undergraduate course close if no overseas students came and most undergraduate courses had at least a little spare capacity. It appears then that the addition to costs or savings of more or fewer overseas students at this level would not be great. The opportunities for savings appear much greater at the postgraduate level, where indeed half of all the overseas students in universities are to be found. Nevertheless, we found few cases where the abandonment of a postgraduate course in case of a drastic fall in the numbers of overseas students applying was seriously contemplated. The common view was that staff development and 'the educational profile' of the department required that courses be kept open for home students even if only one or two students came. Besides, even if certain courses were closed, staff were too specialised to be usefully redeployed in other departments or faculties; natural wastage could rarely cope with anything but small changes in staff in the right areas; early retirement was expensive and, moreover, the age profile of most departments showed a middle-age bulge; ancillary and part-time staff could of course be laid off but these involved very few numbers; and so forth. All these arguments led to the conclusion, heard almost everywhere, that there was little scope for savings even at the postgraduate level except in the very, very long run.

There are no published and very few unpublished figures for universities on the proportion of overseas students in individual courses. But such figures have been collected by DES for public sector institutions, and one analysis of polytechnics and further education colleges in London and the Home Counties for 1978 provided a graphic picture of the density of overseas students in particular courses: 50% of first-degree courses, 54% of higher national diploma courses, 84% of higher-degree courses and 70% of professional courses have over 25% overseas students; most degree-level courses in chemistry, computer science, economics, engineering and mathematics have over 65% overseas students; and some higher-degree courses in management studies are recorded as having nothing but overseas students. There is little doubt, therefore,

that a drastic fall in the numbers of overseas students in polytechnics of, say, 40–50% would make a large number of courses in
different departments right across a polytechnic non-viable, in the
sense of students numbers falling below the minimum number of
14–16 regarded by DES and the Council for National Academic
Awards as the lowest limit on student numbers in a course. Unlike
the universities, there is also little doubt that in polytechnics such
a decline in overseas students would yield large marginal savings
in two to three years. Polytechnics can lay off staff at relatively
short notice and they have considerable experience with staff re-
deployment schemes.

Even in universities where there is small scope for such short-run
savings, there is little doubt that a drastic fall in the numbers of
overseas students would hit some courses very hard and others not
at all. We asked the overseas students in our survey what proportion
of the students on their course were from overseas: across both
universities and polytechnics, 46% testified that overseas students
were more than half of all the students on their course and 23%
said that overseas students constituted three-quarters of their class-
mates; this tendency of overseas students to be concentrated in
individual courses was of course more pronounced among postgraduates than among undergraduates (see Appendix Table A.1).

There is yet another source of savings from fewer overseas
students which seems to preoccupy polytechnics far more than
universities. Overseas students sometimes require higher teaching
costs, particularly remedial teaching in English or mathematics, and
almost always higher administrative costs than home students. Exchange control in certain countries such as Iran and Nigeria makes
it difficult for many overseas students to pay their fees in time and
this leads to endless litigation with students on the collection of fees.
In one London polytechnic, total unpaid fees of overseas students
in the past have run as high as £50,000 a year and this polytechnic
estimates that at least half of the time of its administrative staff is
taken up with the problems of overseas students – checking qualifications, processing applications for the remission of fees, and chasing
up unpaid fees – who constitute less than a quarter of all students.
A policy of requiring all new overseas students to pay their first
year's fees in advance has worked to reduce the total debt outstanding; nevertheless, this polytechnic estimated that perhaps as much
as half of the total unpaid fees of overseas students in 1979 would
have to be written off.

This somewhat gloomy picture is rarely encountered in the university sector. Many of the university departments we visited expressly

denied that overseas students were particularly demanding of administrative or teaching time. Where there was project work in a taught MA or MSc, there was general agreement that overseas students required more assistance with their projects, particularly when these involved laboratory work. Likewise, it was said that overseas PhDs usually took a longer period of time to complete their theses, that their failure rate was higher and that, in general, they did not receive as good degrees as home students. But all these statements were no more than general impressions: despite persistent probing by the research team, nobody produced hard facts about the differential performance rates of home and overseas students.

Summing up, I think that it is fair to say that overseas students sometimes impose higher teaching and administrative costs than home students, at least in certain institutions. In addition to these extra costs, we must mention the cost of advertising abroad, the cost of circulating information abroad, and the cost of operating fees remission schemes or hardship funds; the latter aggregate to £30–40,000 at many higher education institutions, providing each successful applicant with sums of £2–300 each.

Bringing this discussion to a close, we should add that hardly anything surprised us as much as the vast differences in attitude which different institutions displayed with regard to the problem of overseas students. Some institutions had looked carefully at their students by countries of origin and had monitored overseas applications coming in on the same basis; some had studied the likely effect of the rise in fees on a department-by-department basis; some had surveyed their students to improve their forecasts of likely numbers forthcoming in the future; some had set up development committees which had visited every department to discover how economies could be made and how staff could be redeployed; and a few had engaged in all of these activities. But there were other institutions, and not always those with a low proportion of overseas students, who seemed almost indifferent to the effects of higher overseas student fees and who were unable to provide data on the country of origin, the sources of finance, and the academic achievements of their overseas students. Much of these differences are perhaps explained by the different financial circumstances of individual institutions: 'prestige' institutions with few part-time students, with generous research funding, and with well-established reputations in particular areas were sufficiently secure to withstand the blow of a cut in their UGC grant and were hence more inclined to ignore the problem of overseas students in the hope that government policy would soon change. These were also the type of institutions who declared that they were seeking to increase revenue, rather than to cut expenditure. Examples of action designed to secure this result were additional consultancy work, mounting of new, special courses tailor-made to identified groups of overseas students, and vigorous advertising to attract more overseas students to existing courses. The general impression was that the 'prestige' institutions would be competing more vigorously to attract a greater share of the dwindling number of overseas students.

A single figure for marginal costs

All this adds up to a picture in which almost nothing general can be said about the marginal costs or marginal savings of overseas students. This is hardly surprising because it is bound to be true that differences loom larger than similarities at the level of fine detail in individual institutions and departments. Nevertheless, governments must to some extent set fees across the board and must control the expenditure of higher education institutions without endless attention to individual circumstances. They can hardly avoid, therefore, taking some general view of the average and marginal costs of higher education students, particularly in the long run. Likewise, the application of cost-benefit analysis to overseas students requires us to settle on a single figure for the long-run marginal costs of overseas students, if only for the sake of argument. Moreover, such a single figure has been bandied about in the ongoing debate on overseas student fees and hence cannot be ignored.

The most recent, authoritative study on higher education costs in Britain is by Donald Verry and Bleddyn Davies, *University Costs and Output* (1976), which despite its title includes data on polytechnics. There is a familiar problem about higher education costs, which has to do with the distinction between teaching costs and research costs. Research costs consist largely of special equipment, the pay of non-teaching research assistants, and the time of teaching staff devoted to research. The first two items are usually met out of research grants to higher education institutions and hence are ignored in cost calculations. But the last item is invariably financed out of institutional funds and, moreover, it is typically a major portion of the real cost of carrying out research. The teaching load of academic staff is fixed on the understanding that something like half of their time is devoted to research, which implies that teaching and research are strict complements which cannot be separated from each other. In effect, the extra cost of teaching more students also involves an extra cost of carrying out research, thus confusing the unavoidable and the avoidable costs of an expansion. Although it is not possible in principle to divorce teaching from research costs, what we can do is artificially to break down both marginal and average costs into their teaching and research components in terms of the time that individual staff members spend on the two activities. This is what Verry and Davies did. They asked academics to fill in time-diaries and estimated costs by means of regression analysis, which allows one to calculate the marginal and average costs of more students while holding constant the amount of staff time devoted to research. They showed that *average recurrent* departmental-plus-central *teaching* costs in universities in 1968 varied for undergraduates from £849 in arts to £1435 in the physical sciences, being invariably higher than marginal costs even after adding some £300 for capital costs per student.[6] Their estimates of marginal costs for both undergraduates and postgraduates, once again holding constant staff time devoted to research, and of course capital costs, were as follows:

Table 3.4   *Recurrent departmental-plus-central marginal costs per student in UK universities (except Oxford and Cambridge) by major fields of study, 1968/69*

	Undergraduates	Postgraduates
Arts	310	710
Social science	310	860
Mathematics	350	1470
Physical sciences	480	2100
Biological sciences	550	1580
Engineering	680	1610

Source: R. Layard and D. Verry, 'Cost Functions for University Teaching and Research', *Economic Journal*, March 1975, Table VII, p. 70; see also Verry and Davies, *University Costs and Output*, Table 6.13, p. 194.

All this refers only to universities whereas we are concerned with both universities and polytechnics. I do not wish to enter the highly controversial area of cost comparisons between universities and polytechnics, which remains unresolved to this day, and will therefore assume that cost figures for universities can be read as applying to all higher education institutions. If this assumption is accepted, we may lay down the rough general rule that long-run marginal costs in undergraduate higher education are half of average costs in fields such as arts, social science and mathematics, and two-thirds of average costs in fields such as physics, biological science and engineering; no consistent pattern in the relationship between marginal and average costs emerges at the postgraduate level.[7] It appears, therefore, that British universities and polytechnics are generally too small, at least at the undergraduate level, to minimise tuition costs per student.

In 1976, Tony Flowerdew and Richard Layard updated these Verry-Davies figures by using the Brown Index of University Costs, which had risen from 100 in July 1969 to 266 in January 1976.[8] They estimated the long-run recurrent-plus-capital *marginal* costs of home students in January 1976 at £1750 and noted that this was roughly two-thirds of the *average* cost per student, £2625. Because overseas students were concentrated in more expensive postgraduate courses, however, they calculated that the long-run *marginal* costs of overseas students was as much as £2600, being a cost-weighted average of £900 for undergraduates and £3000 for postgraduates, which by pure chance is just about the same figure as the average costs of all students.* The Brown Index has risen from 100 in January 1976 to 132·1 in November 1978 and 146·6 in November 1979 (the index is no longer calculated for January). Applying the Brown Index to the Flowerdew–Layard estimates thus yields the following figures for long-run *marginal* costs in the academic years 1978/79 and 1979/80:

	1978	*1979*
Home students	£2312	£2565
Overseas students	£3435	£3811

Overseas students are much more expensive than home students not because of any higher teaching or administrative cost involved but simply because roughly a third of all overseas students are postgraduates on laboratory-based science, engineering and medical courses.

The Government has frequently mentioned the figure of £127m as the cost to the Exchequer in 1978/79 of subsidising overseas students in public higher and further education,[9] made up of £102m on 59,625 overseas students in advanced-level work and £25m on 27,154 overseas students in non-advanced work, a category of overseas student which we have so far ignored. These figures seem

* Layard and Flowerdew do not explain the basis of their calculations. However, if we take the 1975 distribution of overseas students between levels and subjects, translating the reported categories into those employed by Verry and Davies, and use these as weights to add up the 1968 costs updated to 1976 by means of the Brown Index, we obtain the figures of £1681 for the marginal recurrent-plus-capital costs of home students and £2877 for the corresponding costs of overseas students, which is roughly the same as the Flowerdew–Layard numbers of £1750 and £2600.

to have been calculated from average recurrent expenditure on both home and overseas students in higher and further education. But if the long-run marginal cost of overseas students in universities and polytechnics is more or less the same as the average cost of all students, the implied subsidy per overseas student in advanced work in 1978 is £2635 (£3435 – £800, the weighted average fee paid by or for overseas students in the academic year 1978/79), amounting to a total of £155m, to which something more must be added for the subsidy per overseas student in non-advanced work. Little is known about costs of non-advanced further education colleges but if we update earlier work in the 1960s, it appears that a figure of £1300 for marginal costs in 1978 is not unreasonable. Overseas students in non-advanced further education paid a fee of £390 in 1978; thus, the subsidy for this category of student is indeed £25m [27,154 × (£1300 – £390)], giving a grand total of £180m for the subsidy on all overseas students in public higher and further education. The Government's smaller figure of £127m ignores capital costs and takes no account of the fact that overseas students in advanced higher education are congregated in the more expensive type of courses.

The notion that long-run marginal costs in higher education are roughly two thirds of average costs and that the Government is consistently overestimating the public costs of subsidising overseas students by appealing to average rather than marginal costs has received wide currency. It seems to have been planted by a Report of the Working Party on the Costs and Benefits of Overseas Students in the UK, which simply applied the perfectly valid two-thirds rule for home students indiscriminately to overseas students where, as Flowerdew and Layard showed, it does not pertain.[10] Since then it has been echoed repeatedly in Parliamentary debates and endorsed by at least one Parliamentary Committee.[11] The Government's propensity to appeal to a crude measure of average costs – recurrent expenditure on higher education divided by the total number of students – has in fact flattered rather than damaged the case for overseas students at the price, unfortunately, of promoting widespread misunderstanding about the true costs of overseas students.

If we must have a single figure for the total long-run marginal costs of overseas students in public sector higher and further education it is £266m, made up of £225m (£3811 × 59,000) in advanced work and £41m (£1500 × 27,500) in non-advanced work. This calculation refers to 1979/80 and our student numbers for that year are estimates only. We emphasise again, however, that the long-run marginal savings of fewer overseas students are not simply the inverse of the long-run marginal costs of more overseas students.

It might well take more than ten years to realise all the potential savings of fewer overseas students. In the next two or three years, any reduction in numbers would reap some savings in the poly-technics and almost no savings in the universities. Even if all overseas students were to disappear tomorrow, it would only be by the 1990s that we would cut gross expenditure by as much as £266m, or net expenditure (gross expenditure less fee receipts) by £200m.

Benefits

I turn now to the benefits side. The economic benefits of overseas students to Britain as a whole may be classified under four headings: (1) research; (2) exports; (3) the balance of payments; and (4) aggregate demand. Let us take each of these four headings in turn.

Value of research

The Report of the Working Party on the Costs and Benefits of Overseas Students, an informal group made up of representatives from the United Kingdom Council for Overseas Student Affairs and the National Union of Students, managed to assign a number to almost all the benefits listed above. To suggest the flavour of their approach, consider the first of the four benefits. They estimate that there were 7500 overseas students undertaking 'full-time research' in 1976 and another 2500 who produce useful research reports as part of their master's degrees.[12] It cost at least £2000 in 1976 to hire a qualified research assistant in a science department. So, multiplying 7500 by £2000, we get £15m for the value of PhD research carried out by overseas students, to which they add £5m for 2500 master's students also doing useful research. The first of the four benefits is thus valued at £20m.

For sheer boldness of conjecture, it would be difficult to top this method of estimating benefits. The questionable aspect of the estimate is not the salary figure but the notion that all overseas PhD students, not to mention overseas master's students, are carrying out research that is commercially profitable, or at least socially useful in the sense that some award-granting body in the UK would be willing to pay a home student to carry it out if no overseas students were available. We touched on this point with all the nine universities we visited and we certainly found science and engineering depart-ments who were employing overseas students on full-time basis in funded research. On the other hand, we sampled 12% of the univer-sities and university colleges in England and Wales and only observed some 200 overseas students employed in full-time research. More-over, our survey of overseas students found only 2% who had earned any income in research posts and an even smaller percentage who had earned as much as £2000 per annum in such posts. 2% applied to 59,625 overseas students in universities and polytechnics in 1978/79 yields a figure of just under 1200. Although this is the crudest kind of check on the Working Party's estimate, it does begin to suggest an element of exaggeration in their calculations.[13]

More to the point, however, it is not self-evident that suitable home candidates are not available for such research posts on the same terms as overseas students. If the argument is that they are cheaper than available home students then we should have multiplied 7500 overseas students in full-time research, not by £2000, but by the difference between £2000 and, say, £3000. I suspect, however, that the benefit the Working Party had in mind was the *unpaid* but nevertheless valuable research work carried out by overseas students, which they then approximated by the going market price of a research assistant. If we could assign a money value to the output of research activities in universities, it would be unnecessary to take this circuitous route to an answer. The difficulty is that there are no other objective measures of the value of research than what the market or foundations and research councils will pay for. It follows that if overseas students are paid for research work there are no hidden unpaid benefits to add into the account.

Let us grant that overseas students are generally paid less than an equivalent home student to the tune of £1000 per annum. If we are correct in estimating the number of overseas students carrying out paid research at 1200, this factor alone yields a benefit of £1·2m. Let us further suppose that of the remaining 6–7000 overseas PhD students, about half are carrying out research that is of value to Britain rather than to the students themselves or their governments. If it would cost £3500 to hire a postgraduate research assistant in 1979, we may add £12m to arrive at a total of £13m for the value of research undertaken by overseas students.

Stimulus to exports

The second benefit is more intriguing and deserves greater space. Here too the Working Party drives audaciously to a firm conclusion. They cite a 1969 Board of Trade study which found that three-quarters of the firms responding to a survey of export-oriented enterprises testified that 'training of overseas personnel' was valuable to their exports. They also cite a number of engineering departments in universities and polytechnics similarly testifying that certain orders for British goods could be definitely traced to ex-overseas students. The Working Party found this evidence to be totally convincing and consequently placed a figure of £35m a year on the bias towards British equipment that derives from having overseas students in the United Kingdom – without however a single word of explanation of how they arrived at this figure.[14]

In exploring this topic, it is worth spending a moment on the suggestive 1969 Board of Trade study, *Exports and the Industrial Training of People from Overseas.* The study was not principally concerned with overseas students but rather with on-the-job industrial training of overseas nationals by British firms across the entire spectrum of skills (craftsmen, technicians and engineers with professional status) for both short and long periods.[15] The Board of Trade Working Party was perfectly frank in conceding that it is impossible to single out familiarity with British equipment in all the myriad forces that influence an export order but they took comfort in the fact that Britain's leading commercial rivals act as if training of overseas nationals is valuable to their own export trade, a view which was supported by 76% of the 300 British firms replying to the mailed questionnaire (response rate = 66%).[16] It is clear that the firms in question were largely providing industrial training for periods of less than six months under arrangements made privately between British and overseas firms. It is true that 19% of the 6000 'overseas trainees' identified in the survey were enrolled in higher education courses, but most of those were for less than a year, and all the rest were receiving in-plant training, not education or training in a formal educational institution.[17] It is also true that 35% of the responding firms believed that a course of formal study in an educational institution was more effective from the point of view of export promotion than a period of on-the-job training, but that is only to say that it is this figure of 35% and not that of two-thirds or 76% that should be cited as confirming the hypothesis that the presence of overseas students tends to stimulate British exports.

At any rate, the Board of Trade study serves to teach the vital lesson that even without overseas students there would still be many ways in which British firms could increase the number of individuals in foreign markets who are familiar with British goods. Moreover, the advantage of doing so via short periods of in-plant training or even briefer factory visits is that the individuals in question can be hand-picked as likely to become in their own country the production engineers and managers of tomorrow, whereas more than half of overseas students all in higher education select themselves and hence it must be true that many will never reach decision-making positions in industry or government which would entitle them to place orders for imports from one country rather than another.

We collected a considerable body of testimony from particular departments in universities and polytechnics concerning individual overseas students who had returned to their own country to man offices of British firms or who had entered local industry and ordered British goods; in a few cases they had returned to higher education in their own country and, having become 'dedicated Anglophiles', proceeded to order British books and British educational equipment. We also visited a number of British-based multinational enterprises, and received evidence from such bodies as the Industrial Council for Educational and Training Technology and the British Educational Equipment Association, all of whom provided a wealth of anecdotal evidence testifying to the positive effects of selling in foreign markets that are well endowed with individuals who had once studied in Britain.* The difficulty with this evidence is that in so many cases these are traditional British markets in Anglophone countries in which the BBC Foreign Language Service and the cultural activities of the British Council may have as great an influence on Anglophilia as a period of overseas study in Britain. For example, Nigeria has always been linked to Britain: many educated Nigerians, including those who have received their entire education at home, speak English, go to Britain for holidays, specialist medical treatment, conferences and short courses, and confine much of their reading to British books and journals; nevertheless, Unesco data show that in 1976 there were three times as many Nigerian students in the United States as in the UK (Appendix Table B.6), and some say that young educated Nigerians are now increasingly orienting themselves towards the United States. Be that as it may, it is difficult if not impossible in such circumstances to single out the effect of exposure to long-term study in Britain and even more the marginal effect of exposing more or fewer Nigerians to the experience of studying in Britain.

The firms we visited did not deny that investment in providing education for overseas students is a long-term investment whose return to British exports cannot be guaranteed but they did insist that the majority of ex-overseas students in all walks of life continue to reflect a preference for British goods and British expertise. When asked, however, whether they preferred to spend a given sum of money on making their own arrangements for in-plant training as compared to the same sum spent out of public revenues on educational facilities for overseas students, the replies were somewhat less favourable to the case for overseas students.

---

* See also Chapter 4, with additional evidence on these points.

As a further illustration of the possible trade-off between training and education for overseas nationals, consider the 1979 submission of the British Council to the Overseas Development Sub-Committee of the Select Committee on Foreign Affairs which formed part of the evidence on which the Foreign Affairs Committee report, *Overseas Students' Fees: Aid and Development Implications*, was based. The British Council conducted a preliminary survey of both overseas students and in-plant trainees financially assisted under the UK Technical Co-operation Programme over the last six years (about 10,000 a year), linking their country of origin and field of study or training to principal British manufacturers of associated equipment. On balance, they found little sign of export orders being systematically related to the education and training provided under the Technical Co-operation Programme, and they noted the general conviction among the companies approached that technical co-operation, education and training should be linked directly to particular sales opportunities in particular markets if it is to play a significant role in promoting exports. Even the Foreign Affairs Committee, while expressing surprise that neither the British Council nor the Overseas Development Administration had ever made a longitudinal study of the career patterns of ex-students on return to their countries of origin, concluded in carefully chosen words that 'our assumption . . . is that there is, in some instances, a connection (however elusive and unquantifiable) between the admission of students and *more particularly, of trainees* and the pursuit of British commercial interests'.[18]

That the connection between overseas students and exports is unquantifiable is perhaps one of the common grounds between all those who have expressed a view on the matter one way or the other. But there are published statistics on British exports by countries of sale in both physical and value (quantity times price) terms, cross-classified by sectors of origin. Unfortunately, the statistics cover only visible goods; invisible exports – foreign payments for British services, such as tourism, insurance, banking, and transport, interest on money borrowed from abroad, payments of profits and dividends on foreign investments, as well as private remittances and public transfers – are not classified by countries. Nevertheless, it is worth asking whether we can discover any systematic correlation between the number of overseas students coming from a particular country and the value of UK visible exports sold to that country x years later. To do so we have to decide how large x is. We experimented with various lags and chose the one that gave the best results. We calculated the average growth rate of overseas students coming to

Britain for every country in the world over a ten-year period and compared these to the average growth rate of British visible exports to the same countries over a later ten-year period. It turned out there was a definite relationship between overseas students and exports. For example, the simple correlation coefficient (r^2) between the growth of overseas students during the decade 1960–70 and the growth of exports during the decade 1965–75 is $+0.37$. This assumes that the lag between overseas students and exports is only five years. Some have conjectured that the lag is at least ten to fifteen years but we found that there were no significant relationships between overseas students and exports when we examined lags as long as fifteen years. Moreover, when we turned the argument on its head and tested the no doubt absurd hypothesis that British exports in one period promote overseas students in some later period, we also found a positive correlation: the growth of exports over the years 1960–70 are correlated with the growth of overseas students over the years 1965–75 with a $r^2 = +0.33$. It appears therefore that the relationship between country-oriented exports and overseas students is not one of cause and effect but is itself a reflection of some third factor, such as traditional British influence in a country.

In the attempt to go deeper, we calculated the country *shares* of the total value of UK world exports and the country *shares* of total overseas students coming to the UK and then compared the two *rankings*, fixing the lag between prior overseas students and subsequent exports arbitrarily at various lengths.

The top 20 importers of UK exports are ranked in Table 3.5. It is immediately obvious that our principal markets, particularly in recent years, are Europe and the USA, and the USA but not Europe is a major sending area of overseas students to Britain. Compare the rankings of the top 20 senders of overseas students, as shown in Table 3.6. In 1972 only Malaysia sent more than 8000 students to the UK, followed by France, USA, Ireland, Iran, Mauritius and Hong Kong sending 3–7000 each. In 1977 only Malaysia and Iran sent more than 10,000 students (Malaysia topping the list with 16,600 students) followed by Nigeria, Hong Kong, USA, Greece, France, Ireland and Switzerland sending 3–7000 each: together these top nine countries sent one-third of all overseas students in the UK in 1977.

It is immediately apparent that there is some sort of loose relationship between exports and overseas students: the USA, France and Switzerland are important export markets for British goods, and they are also large exporters of students to the UK. On the other hand, countries such as Malaysia, Iran, Nigeria and Hong Kong, which are major senders of overseas students, are not major markets for

Table 3.5   Percentage shares of UK exports by value going to the
top 20 countries in descending order, 1961, 1970, 1977

1961		1970		1977	
1. USA	7·8	USA	11·7	USA	9·3
2. Canada	5·9	Germany, Fed. Rep.	6·2	Germany, Fed. Rep.	7·5
3. Australia	5·3	Ireland	4·7	France	6·4
4. Germany, Fed. Rep.	5·0	Netherlands	4·7	Netherlands	6·4
5. India	4·0	Sweden	4·5	Belgium	5·5
6. South Africa	3·9	Australia	4·3	Ireland	4·9
7. Sweden	3·8	France	4·2	Switzerland	4·3
8. Netherlands	3·7	South Africa	4·2	Sweden	3·6
9. Ireland	3·6	Belgium	3·6	Nigeria	3·2
10. New Zealand	3·2	Canada	3·6	Italy	2·9
11. France	3·2	Italy	3·0	Denmark	2·4
12. Italy	3·2	Denmark	2·7	Norway	2·3
13. Denmark	2·4	Switzerland	2·6	Australia	2·3
14. Norway	2·2	Norway	2·2	Canada	2·1
15. Belgium	2·1	Japan	1·8	Iran	1·9
16. Nigeria	2·0	Spain	1·8	South Africa	1·7
17. USSR	1·8	New Zealand	1·6	Saudi Arabia	1·7
18. Switzerland	1·5	Finland	1·6	Spain	1·6
19. Finland	1·4	Nigeria	1·4	Japan	1·4
20. Rest of the world	35·0	Rest of the world	29·6	Rest of the world	27·7

Source: Calculated from IMF, *Direction of Trade Annual* (Washington, D.C., International Monetary Fund, published annually), 1961–5, pp. 282–4; 1968–1972, pp. 103–5; 1971–7, pp. 265–6.

British exports. We can make these comparisons more precise by applying Spearman's coefficient of rank correlation, ρ, to the country ranking orders of exports and overseas students. Spearman's ρ is a standard, non-parametric measure of association between two variables when both are measured ordinally and hence can only be ranked in series.[19] There is the old problem of the appropriate time-lag between overseas students and exports and we solve this difficulty as before by experimenting with various lags of two, five, eight, and even ten years between the academic year in which overseas students studied in this country and the year in which British exports were sold abroad. As a sample of our calculations, we list in Table 3.7 a number of Spearman's correlation coefficients to which we applied a standard t-test to check whether the correlation is significant or not.

Table 3.6   Rank order of top 20 countries sending overseas
students to UK, 1968, 1972, 1977

1968	1972	1977
1. France	Malaysia	Malaysia
2. Malaysia	France	Iran
3. Nigeria	USA	Nigeria
4. India	Ireland	Hong Kong
5. USA	Iran	USA
6. Mauritius	Mauritius	Greece
7. Hong Kong	Nigeria	France
8. Germany	Switzerland	Ireland
9. Sri Lanka	Hong Kong	Switzerland
10. Iran	Germany	Sri Lanka
11. Cyprus	India	Germany
12. Switzerland	Greece	Iraq
13. Greece	Cyprus	Turkey
14. Singapore	Sri Lanka	Japan
15. Iraq	Iraq	Singapore
16. Turkey	Turkey	Rhodesia
17. Rhodesia	Singapore	Cyprus
18. Japan	Rhodesia	India
19. Ireland	Japan	Mauritius
20. Rest of the world	Rest of the world	Rest of the world

Notes: Figures refer to all overseas students in advanced and non-advanced higher
and further education, as well as overseas students in the private sector.
Source: British Council, *Statistics of Overseas Students in Britain*, Table V. p. 20.

Table 3.7   *Spearman's correlation coefficients for rank orders of
UK export shares and overseas students by countries, various years*

1. Overseas students leading by 8 years: shares of exports 1977 and overseas
students 1968/69
$\rho = +0.29$, not significant at 0·10 level
2. Overseas students leading by 2 years: shares of exports 1977 and overseas
students 1974/75
$\rho = +0.57$, significant at 0·01 level
3. Overseas students leading by 2 years: shares of exports 1975 and overseas
students 1972/73
$\rho = +0.46$, significant at 0·025 level
4. Exports leading by 5 years: shares of exports 1970 and overseas students
1974/75
$\rho = +0.47$, significant at 0·025 level

Source: See Tables 3.5 and 3.6.

Spearman's ρ varies between 0 and 1, being 1 when the two rankings coincide exactly and 0 when the second ranking bears no relationship whatsoever to the first. The first of our correlations is low and not significant. Since the lag involved here is as much as eight years, we tried a shorter lead and this gave significant results whatever the years involved even when the lead was as short as two years (correlations 2 and 3). Because correlation is not causality, however, we once again inverted the rankings to test the hypothesis that British exports generate overseas students. Lo and behold, this also produced a significant correlation, not only for a five-year lead of exports (correlation 4) but also for three and four year leads (not shown in Table 3.7). We may therefore reject the simple theory that overseas students stimulate exports and likewise the simple theory that exports stimulate overseas students.

Table 3.6 refers to all overseas students in public and private sector education, whether doing advanced or non-advanced work. Taking

Table 3.8 Spearman's correlation coefficients for rank orders of UK export shares and overseas students in universities by major fields of study by countries, various years

---

1. Overseas students leading by 6 years: shares of exports 1977 and overseas students in engineering and technology 1970/71
    $\rho = -0.582$, significant at 0.01 level
2. Overseas students leading by 4 years: shares of exports 1977 and overseas students in engineering and technology 1972/73
    $\rho = -0.49$, significant at 0.025 level
3. Overseas students leading by 6 years: shares of exports 1977 and overseas students in social, administrative and business studies 1970/71
    $\rho = +0.02$, not significant at 0.10 level
4. Overseas students leading by 6 years: shares of exports 1977 and overseas students in postgraduate engineering and technology 1970/71
    $\rho = -0.513$, significant at 0.025 level
5. Overseas students leading by 6 years: shares of exports 1977 and overseas students in postgraduate social, administrative and business studies 1970/71
    $\rho = -0.044$, not significant at 0.10 level
6. Exports leading by 8 years: shares of exports 1970 and overseas students in engineering and technology 1977/78
    $\rho = -0.49$, significant at 0.025 level
7. Exports leading by 8 years: shares of exports 1970 and overseas students in social, administrative and business studies 1977/78
    $\rho = +0.11$, not significant at 0.10 level

Source: See Table 3.5 and *Association of Commonwealth Universities Yearbook, 1975, 1980*, App. II.

the argument one step further, we conjectured that it was perhaps public sector overseas students in particular fields of study that alone tended to promote exports and so we applied the same procedure to overseas students in universities classified by fields of specialisation. Table 3.8 shows a sample of our results.

Here is a new nonsense result: having overseas students from a country studying engineering and technology reduces the UK's export share four and six years later (correlations 1, 2 and 4); this is not true for undergraduate overseas students studying social, administrative and business studies, a wide category which includes economics, computer science, operations research, management, marketing and business studies (correlation 3), although even here the relationship is negative for postgraduates (correlation 5). To add to the nonsense, correlations 6 and 7 show that exports in one year actually tend to reduce overseas students in engineering, technology, social, administrative and business studies eight years later.

Having strained the argument to the breaking point, we may now sum up. Export penetration of particular national markets is influenced by a whole host of factors: price, transport costs, promised delivery dates, expected probability of meeting the delivery date, provision of spare parts and expected probability of delivering spare parts, maintenance and service guarantees, and, finally, knowledge in the particular country of the technical characteristics of the product in question, particularly if it is not an internationally standardised product. Obviously, everything else being the same, the more individuals in country X have familiarity with a British product, the larger the volume of British exports of that product to X. The problem, however, is that everything else is rarely the same. If the exported good is an internationally standardised product, it is a simple matter for a production engineer in country X to consult sales catalogues for a price comparison. But price is only one element, and frequently a minor element, in the judgement of where to place an order. It is delivery time and particularly the past record of a firm or group of firms in meeting delivery dates which is frequently the decisive factor in placing an order in one exporting nation rather than another. Thus, if a national firm has already penetrated a market and established a good record in meeting delivery dates, it has an inherent advantage over its commercial rivals from other countries in securing a new export order in country X. Besides, it will also have acquired technical, commercial and financial knowledge of market conditions in country X, and this will promote its efforts to push exports in country X even if few of X's citizens have an intimate knowledge of its products or the country from which these exports derive. In short, once a national market is penetrated by British or American or German exports for whatever reason, it tends to stay penetrated by British or American or German exports unless there are large and dramatic changes in price, in delivery dates, and in service guarantees.

Given the complex set of factors that influence the country-composition of exports, it is not easy to determine the significance of the number of individuals in country X that have studied abroad in a particular exporting nation, and there is certainly little warrant to assume, as so many have, that it must play a major role in governing the exportability of British or American or German goods to country X. Obviously, our calculations of the correlation between exports and overseas students can at best provide negative evidence, which they did, but even positive evidence would still have left us with the task of quantifying the marginal effects of more or fewer overseas students on exports. Given more time, it might have been possible to analyse the problem with the aid of multivariate techniques, say, by regressing the country-pattern of particular British export products on price, distance, delivery dates, maintenance provision, past record of exporting (implying knowledge of marketing conditions) and of course the number of higher educated individuals who have received part or all of their higher education in Britain; this technique allows one to single out the role of one factor, holding all the other factors constant. But this is an enormous research task, which goes well beyond current frontiers in the empirical literature on international trade. Besides, the negative evidence from Spearman's ρ gives one little hope that a more comprehensive multiple regression analysis would yield significant results for overseas students.

So far we have addressed ourselves only to visible exports. Lacking data on the country-orientation of invisible services, we cannot calculate correlation coefficients. However, some general remarks on the connection between invisibles and overseas students are in order. Of the various elements that make up UK invisibles, financial and insurance services are the most important by far: together they constitute three-quarters of the surplus on UK private invisible trade, and financial services alone are three times as large as interest, profits and dividends. The classic situation in Britain over the last 200 years has been that the surplus on private plus public invisible trade has more than matched the loss on visible trade. Since the Second World War, deficits in the Government invisible account have eaten into the surplus on private invisibles so as to produce an overall deficit on the balance of payments. In general, invisibles make up around a third of UK's total export earnings minus import payments, a high proportion by world standards, which makes it all the more regrettable that we can say so little about them in relation to the issues before us. Nevertheless, if it were to be argued that overseas students contribute significantly to our surplus of invisibles, it would have to be shown that they are important in generating customers for the services of the City of London, which, as we noted, generates most of the surplus on invisibles. It is not whether overseas students become engineers in their own country but whether they become bankers and shippers that is the vital question for our sales of invisible services. It may be, therefore, that overseas students in social, administrative and business studies are more important to UK trade as a whole than those in engineering and technology who always receive the lion's share of everyone's attention.

We must conclude, therefore, that there is no basis for endorsing and many reasons for rejecting the figure of £35m a year which the Working Party on the Costs and Benefits of Overseas Students placed on the value of the stimulus which overseas students provided to British exports. There is some connection between exports and overseas students, but we refuse to indulge in spurious precision by assigning a number to the connection. Fortunately, it turns out that no reasonable number would make any substantial difference to our basic conclusions. We do insist, however, that the connection is in principle quantifiable, although in practice, as we have seen, it is immensely difficult to quantify. To say, as did the Foreign Affairs Committee, that the relationship between overseas students and 'the pursuit of British commercial interests' is both 'elusive and unquantifiable' is to sweep under the carpet the really critical question. Who is to say that factory visits and short in-plant training courses, geared to particular engineers, technicians, scientists, bankers, ministry officials, etc., might not achieve the same stimulus to British exports at a lower cost than full-time study in a British tertiary educational institution? Governments have to make these decisions all the time and they must do so in terms of some judgement about the quantitative effects of a policy directed at trainees rather than students.

Contribution to the balance of payments

This brings us to the third of the economic benefits of overseas students in the United Kingdom, namely, the net gain in foreign exchange. The Report of the Working Party on the Costs and Benefits of Overseas Students places a value of not less than £50m p.a. on the contribution that overseas students make to the British balance of payments. They arrive at this figure in the following manner: estimating the average annual expenditure of overseas students in 1976/77, exclusive of the fees they pay, at £2000, they multiply the £2000 by the 83,000 students in public sector higher and further education in 1976 to arrive at a total of £166m, of which 30% or £50m is said to be a 'reasonable' estimate of the net gain in foreign exchange from overseas students; no explanation is provided as to why it should be 30% rather than some other percentage.[20]

Before examining the magic figure of 30%, it is worth noting that some of the 83,000 public sector overseas students are here on British scholarship programmes and hence do not spend *foreign currency in Britain*.[21] Their numbers are offset, however, by another 40,000 full-time overseas students in the private sector, many of whom are deliberately equipping themselves with qualifications to progress to higher and further education in public institutions,[22] whose spending makes as much of a contribution to the balance of payments as the spending of public sector students.

The real difficulty, however, is to decide why the *net* gain in foreign exchange should be thought to be 30% of *gross* foreign exchange earnings from overseas students. Clearly, there is an import leakage in the expenditure of overseas students, in the sense that almost everything they buy contains elements imported from abroad. But, surely, this import leakage can hardly be as great as 70% of their total expenditure. The average import leakage of all consumers' expenditure in Britain is around 25%, the marginal import leakage being somewhat higher, and this average is made up of a 70% import leakage for household appliances at one end and a 5–10% import leakage for personal services at the other, with foodstuffs at 40% coming somewhere in between. We can get at the average figure of 25% quickly by taking the ratio of imports to final expenditure (20%) and allowing for the fact that 15% of consumers' expenditure at market prices represent indirect taxes.[23] This quick-and-dirty estimate could be improved by analysing evidence from the Family Expenditure Survey but the extra work involved would hardly be worth the candle. Our survey of overseas students showed that they consume accommodation and services somewhat more, but durables such as cars and television sets somewhat less than adult consumers, so that the average import leakage of their consumption is at most 25% – which is still miles away from 70%. We are driven to the conclusion that, given the logic of the Working Party's argument, they were much too modest: the net gain in foreign exchange from overseas students is 75% of their total spending of foreign currency, so that, given their own logic, they should have arrived at a figure of £124·5m, not £50m.

Alas, it is not so much their arithmetic as their logic that is defective. In counting the net foreign exchange spending of overseas students as a social benefit to Britain as a whole, the Working Party in effect argued that a pound of foreign currency is worth more than a pound of domestic currency. This is an argument which made a good deal of sense in the 1960s when chronic deficits in Britain's balance of payments placed a severe constraint on the Chancellor of the Exchequer's freedom of action. But the bounty of North Sea oil removed the balance-of-payments constraint on Britain's growth potential and the floating of the pound in 1972 made it possible to regard the earning of foreign currency as no better or worse than the generation of domestic purchasing power. In short, we may treat the spending of overseas students as if it were an addition to aggregate effective demand on the same footing as the spending of home students. In that case, however, should we not count that addition to aggregate demand as a benefit to Britain, being nothing more than an 'export' of goods and services to a particular brand of 'tourists'?

Contribution to aggregate demand

The average annual consumption expenditure of some 87,000 overseas students in 1979/80 could not have been much less than £2500 exclusive of fees. But not all of this expenditure constituted an addition to aggregate demand or net value added because raw materials and intermediate products were used up in the production of the goods and services required to satisfy the demands of overseas students. Most of these intermediate products are imports but some are the products of British producer goods industries. Without entering into an elaborate calculation of the cost of bought-in materials in the production of British consumer goods and services, we may surmise that net value added (wages plus profits plus rents) in consumer goods industries is about 65% of gross sales,[24] giving us a figure of £141m for the net addition to aggregate demand generated by the consumer expenditure of overseas students.

Is all of this to be counted as an economic benefit? To answer 'Yes' to that question is to argue that there is heavy unemployment in Britain and that any additional spending is to be welcomed as a way of mopping up unemployment. Once again, however, this is a proposition which would have won general assent in the 1960s. But somewhere in the early 1970s, we entered the era of 'stagflation' in which the traditional Keynesian remedies designed to eliminate unemployment by stimulating aggregate demand serve largely to aggravate inflation. Nowadays the extra spending of overseas students, or the extra spending of tourists in general, may act to absorb some unemployment in labour markets but only at the cost of raising prices in commodity markets.

The dominant view among British macroeconomists in 1981, and certainly that of economists advising the present Government, is that Britain's unemployment problems are caused by constraints on the side of supply rather than on the side of demand: to the immobility of resources in general and labour in particular, to inadequate investment in new equipment, to real wages being too high and real profits too low, in short, to a distortion in the entire structure of relative prices.[25] It is for this reason that the Government is committed to cutting public expenditure, a policy which would make no sense if higher levels of aggregate demand would cure our ills. It appears, therefore, that the question of whether the contribution of overseas students to aggregate demand should or should not be counted as an economic benefit depends critically on the view we take of the nature of 'the English disease' and hence the policies that would cure that disease.

It may be objected, however, that this conclusion holds just as much for exports as for consumer spending. Earlier we admitted that if overseas students do stimulate exports, this is a benefit to Britain that must appear in the cost-benefit equation. But why is it better to sell goods and services to foreigners in Iran than goods and services to Iranians in Britain? It is better, if it is better, because a once-and-for-all increase in exports tends to stimulate investment in the export industries, thus adding to Britain's productive capacity; on the other hand, a once-and-for-all increase in the spending of overseas students for housing, food, clothing, travel and entertainment probably does nothing to improve the utilisation of Britain's resources or to re-align relative prices so as to create incentives for investment.

Even if we agreed on these propositions, and thus on 'what is wrong with the British economy', we would still not be home and dry. Let us suppose that we have made up our minds that the consumer spending of overseas students would to some extent act to reduce unemployment, particularly in the depressed regions of North-East England, Scotland and Wales.[26] But since a large proportion of overseas students reside in the London area where there is relatively little unemployment and where accommodation is already heavily congested, the effect of their spending would also be to raise the prices of consumer goods. In other words, the extra spending of overseas students is a mixed blessing. To evaluate their spending as an economic benefit, we must also decide what cost to attach to inflation as compared to the benefit of reduced unemployment. The question of extra spending by overseas students, or any other group of domestic or foreign consumers, thus involves an objective assessment coupled with a subjective assessment. Whatever the answer to the objective question, different British Governments might, and undoubtedly do, attach different policy weights to the trade-off between inflation and unemployment. The present Conservative Government clearly regards inflation as worse than unemployment and, I dare say, a Labour Government would regard unemployment as worse than inflation. Thus, the present Government would not treat all of the £141m, representing the net additional income generated by the consumer spending of overseas students, as a benefit which offsets the subsidy to overseas students; indeed, they would count little of it as a benefit, partly because they judge that it would be largely inflationary and partly because they deplore inflation more than they welcome reductions in unemployment. A Labour Government might agree that the effect of the spending of overseas students would be largely inflationary but they would count more of the £141m as a benefit because they rate employment effects over price effects.

It is not my task to pre-empt a government's trade-off function between inflation and unemployment. Let us, therefore, rate the contribution of overseas students to aggregate effective demand as greater than zero but less than £141m. We remind ourselves of what we are doing by writing: (£1m–£140m).

Conclusion

The Working Party on the Costs and Benefits of Overseas Students concluded that the benefits of overseas students exceed their costs. Their final calculations for 1976/77, covering all overseas students in public higher and further education, yielded the following:

Total long-run marginal costs (£m)	− 102
Total long-run marginal benefits (£m)	+ 134
Research input	+ 20
Trade effects	+ 35
Foreign exchange earnings	+ 50
Net income from fees after remissions	+ 29
Net benefits over costs (£m)	+ 32

Our calculations for 1979, once again for all overseas students in advanced and non-advanced public higher and further education, reverse these results.[27]

Total long-run marginal costs (£m)	−266
Total long-run marginal benefits (£m)	+(80 to 219)
Research input	+13
Trade effects	+?
Foreign exchange earnings	+0
Contribution to aggregate demand	+1 to 140
Net income from fees after remissions	+66
Net benefits over costs (£m)	−(47 to 186)

Whether we judge the consumer spending of overseas students to add little or much to the inflationary pressures in the British economy, and whether we rate inflation as a more serious evil than unemployment, the fact remains that the net costs of overseas students exceed their economic benefits.

The Report of the Working Party on the Costs and Benefits of Overseas Students in the United Kingdom, with its rosy conclusions of a net social gain of £32m, has received considerable publicity. *The Times Higher Education Supplement* featured it in a full page on the problems of overseas students[28] and the Association of University Teachers sent their 30,000 members a pamphlet in January 1980, entitled *Universities at Risk*, which praised its calculations as the product of 'a high powered working party from a number of organisations in higher education'. It was cited and endorsed by several speakers in an important House of Lords debate on overseas students in December 1979, and it can be read between the lines in a number of interjections on overseas students in the House of Commons.[29] Baroness Young, Minister of State at the DES, seemed to reject the Working Party Report in the House of Lords debate when she declared: 'we have yet to see figures which will stand up to rigorous examination on how one quantifies precisely the benefits that the overseas students bring'.[30] The Foreign Affairs Committee of the House of Commons, in its report on overseas student fees in April 1980, was even more categorical: they reviewed the estimates of the Working Party but concluded: 'we remain sceptical of some of the calculations made – indeed some of them are clearly fallacious'. Nevertheless, the Committee remained persuaded that 'the economic benefits to Britain [of overseas students] are substantial'.[31] I agree but, unfortunately, so are the costs; and the costs seem to outweigh the benefits.

What does it all add up to? We have shown that the long-run marginal costs of overseas students exceed their long-run marginal benefits. This does not mean that the Government is perfectly correct to stop subsidising overseas students because that is not the question we were asking. There are standard economic arguments for subsidising higher education students, having to do with the 'external' effects of higher education and the 'imperfections' of private capital markets,[32] and on the face of it these apply just as much to overseas students as to home students. Government policy is based on the normative judgement that they apply only to British students whose families are contributing with their direct taxes to public revenues. This is what I called 'the contributory principle of government expenditure' at the outset of this report. If we reject this principle categorically, there is no justification whatsoever for charging higher fees to overseas students than to home students and what is left is the question: at what level should all students be subsidised? We can, in principle, apply cost-benefit analysis to answer that question but, obviously, both the costs and the benefits would be very different from those we have discussed in this report.

What we did was to seek an economic reason for setting aside 'the contributory principle of government expenditure' based on the demonstration that the indirect and unanticipated benefits of overseas students to Britain as a whole are greater than their costs. We found that the opposite was the case, which means that we cannot waive the principle on economic grounds. This says nothing about waiving it on other grounds by adopting a global, cosmopolitan approach to the problem of overseas students, thus entering into reciprocal arrangements with some countries where there is a basis for reciprocity and, as for the rest, treating the subsidy to overseas students as a special form of foreign aid. The latter view would perhaps imply full-cost fees for overseas students but generous scholarship programmes for students from selected countries. After all, there are about as many British students studying abroad in the rich, industrialised countries as students from these countries studying here.[33] It is with respect to the third world that we suffer what might be called an 'unfavourable balance of students', with one British student studying there as against ten overseas students studying here. That strengthens the case for not subsidising overseas students indiscriminately and directly subsidising only overseas students from the third world under the foreign aid budget. In this way we would make transparent what is now opaque.

Notes

1. All the figures in this paragraph are drawn from P. Williams and M. Kendall, *Overseas Students in Britain. Some Facts and Figures*, London, Overseas Students Trust, 1979, supplemented by British Council, *Statistics of Overseas Students in Britain, 1977/78* London, British Council, 1979.

2. Past data shows that the acceptance rate is consistently lower for overseas students compared to home students in all subject groups but they vary for overseas students from 7·5% in medicine to 62·3% in science: Williams and Kendall, *Overseas Students in Britain. Some Facts and Figures*, Table 6.

3. See M. Blaug and R. Layard 'Forecasting overseas demand for higher and further education in the United Kingdom' forthcoming 1981.

4. House of Commons, Third Report from the Foreign Affairs Committee. Session 1979/80, *Overseas Student Fees: Aid and Development Implications*, London, HMSO, 1980, § 13, p. ix.

5. Third Report from the Foreign Affairs Committee, *Overseas Student Fees: Aid and Development Implications*, § 14, p. ix.

6. D. Verry and B. Davies, *University Costs and Outputs*, Amsterdam, Elsevier, 1976, Table 4.7, p. 78; a comparison between universities and polytechnics is provided in Table A4.1.2, p. 101.

7. D. Verry and B. Davies, *University Costs and Outputs*, Table 5.6, p. 128; see also the 1978 figures for the science-based university we referred to earlier (p. 55).

8. T. Flowerdew and R. Layard, 'How Much Should Overseas Students Pay?', *Times Higher Education Supplement*, 19 March 1976, p. 11.

9. See House of Commons, First Report from the Education, Science and Arts Committee, Session 1979/80, *The Funding and Organisation of Courses in Higher Education: Interim Report on Overseas Student Fees, Vol. I Report*, London, HMSO, 1980, § 17, p. viii.

10. Report of the Working Party on the Costs and Benefits of Overseas Students in the UK, *Overseas Students: A Subsidy to Britain*, London, London Conference on Overseas Students, 1979, p. 4.

11. Thus, Neil Kinnock, MP for Bedwellty and Shadow Spokesman on Education, argued that the Government should have calculated marginal and not average costs because overseas students 'are, as the Government themselves argue, marginal to the general provision. Marginal costs are a much more adequate means of accounting in these matters and they are between one-half and two-third of average costs', Hansard, 5 June 1980. See also House of Commons, Third Report from the Foreign Affairs Committee, *Overseas Student Fees*, § 15, p. x.

12. Report of the Working Party, *Overseas Students*, p. 4.

13. As a matter of fact, there were just over 5000 overseas students enrolled for a PhD in British universities in 1977: *Association of Commonwealth*

Universities Yearbook 1980, Vol. 3, p. 2171. There are virtually no PhD students enrolled in polytechnics, but there are some full-time research assistants employed in various capacities in polytechnics and further education colleges. Still, the figure of 7500 overseas students in full-time research in 1976/77 seems somewhat too high.

14. Report of the Working Party, *Overseas Students*, p. 5.
15. The same is true of an earlier unpublished report by the Ministry of Overseas Development and the Ministry of Labour, *Survey of Industrial Training of Overseas Nationals* (1965), which surveyed 7000 establishments in manufacturing.
16. Board of Trade, *Exports and the Industrial Training of People from Overseas. Report of a Working Party*, London, HMSO, 1969, § 29–30, p. 8.
17. Board of Trade, *Exports and the Industrial Training of People from Overseas*, Table 3, p. 30, Table 7, p. 32.
18. Foreign Affairs Committee Report, *Overseas Students' Fees*, § 35, p. xvii (author's emphasis).
19. See S. Siegel, *Nonparametric Statistics for the Behavioural Sciences*, London, McGraw-Hill, 1956, pp. 202–13.
20. Report of the Working Party, *Overseas Students*, p. 6.
21. The precise number of these students has been a matter of dispute: the total number of full-time overseas students supported by ODA in 1978/79 was 6000 plus another 4000 on courses lasting less than a year (Foreign Affairs Committee, *Overseas Students' Fees*, § 12, pp. viii–ix).
22. 42% of the overseas students in our survey had obtained lower-level qualifications in Britain before taking up advanced work at a British university or polytechnic (see Appendix A, p. 247).
23. I am indebted to Harold Evans of LSE for clarification on these points.
24. Value added is about 55% of sales receipts in the private market sector. Adding value added by the government, non-market sector (education, health, domestic services to households, etc.) gives us 65% as an estimate of the value-added component of total consumption spending by overseas students: see Central Statistical Office, *National Income and Expenditure 1980*, London, HMSO, 1980.
25. A single reference must suffice to demonstrate that this is now mainstream opinion. A team of American and Canadian economists, headed by R. E. Caves and L. B. Krause, recently examined *Britain's Economic Performance* (Washington, D.C., The Brookings Institution, 1980), a sequel to their earlier study, *Britain's Economic Prospects* (1968). At one point in their analysis, they ask: is there an output gap in the British economy, that is, both unemployed labour and spare industrial capacity which might respond to stimulative demand management along well-known Keynesian lines? And they conclude: '[one] way to test the existence of an output gap is to determine whether increments in monetary demand translate themselves primarily into higher prices, as they will when an economy approaches its full economic potential. An

examination of the output and
money growth in the United Kingd...
results. During the ten-year span, 8¹...
ended up, on average, as price incre...
of money GDP went to inflation du...
proportion soared to 92·0% during the...
increasingly won out over real growth ...
1973, putting the existence of an output ...

26. This is argued by the Department of Ec...
technic, 'The Implications of DES Circula...
Sunderland' Sunderland. Sunderland Polytec... ...ed.

27. Total long-run marginal costs consist of 59,000... ...u higher and
further education at £3811 each and 27,500 in ...-advanced further
education at £1500 each as explained earlier. 10,000 of those in advanced
work are supported out of British funds (see footnote 21 above); thus,
49,000 paid an average fee of £1100 (minus fee remissions in 1979 of
about £2m) and 27,500 in non-advanced work paid a fee of £520, which
yields a rounded figure of £66m for net income from fees.

28. *Times Higher Education Supplement*, 8 February 1980, p. 7.

29. Hansard, *Parliamentary Debates*, House of Lords. Official Reports, Vol.
403, no. 59, Wednesday, 12 December 1979, pp. 1280, 1281, 1288, 1293;
Hansard, *Parliamentary Debates*, House of Commons. Official Report,
Vol. 985, no. 185, Thursday, 5 June 1980, p. 1693.

30. Hansard, *Parliamentary Debates*, House of Lords. Official Reports, Vol.
403, no. 60, Thursday, 13 December 1979, p. 1345.

31. Foreign Affairs Committee, *Overseas Students' Fees*, 15, p. x.

32. These arguments are set forth in the many available textbooks on the
economics of education: e.g. M. Blaug, *An Introduction to the Economics
of Education*, London, Penguin Books, 1970, Chapter 4, and D. M.
Windham, *Economic Dimensions of Education*, A Report of a Committee
of the National Academy of Education, Washington, D.C., National
Academy of Education, 1979, Chapter 4.

33. Unesco, *A Summary Statistical Review of Education in the World
1960–1976* (Paris: Unesco, ED/BIE/CONFINTED 37/Ref. 1, 23 March,
Table 16, p. 47.

Note of acknowledgement
In the course of this study, the team and myself in particular received help
and assistance from a large number of individuals. Sir Charles Carter,
Chairman of the Research and Management Committee of the Policy Studies
Institute, headed a small steering committee, which kept a friendly eye on
our rate of progress and offered valuable advice at critical stages of our
research. Martin Kenyon, Director of the Overseas Students Trust, and
Peter Williams, Professor of Education in Developing Countries at the
University of London Institute of Education, provided continual moral and
intellectual support. I learned a great deal from private discussions with
Richard Layard of the London School of Economics, Donald Verry of

ollege, Roger Dew, Head of Statistics of the University Grants
tee, Kenneth Everard, Education and Training Manager at ICI,
a number of economic advisers at DES and the Department of Trade.
Mary Archer of the Association of Commonwealth Universities kindly made
available recent unpublished data on overseas students.

Sir Alec Merrison and Geoffrey Caston, Chairman and Secretary
respectively of the Committee of Vice-Chancellors and Principals of the
Universities of the United Kingdom, cleared the way for us to approach
universities, and David Bethel, Chairman of the Committee of Directors
of Polytechnics, came to our aid in the same way in approaching
polytechnics. At all institutions, vice-chancellors, principals, directors,
registrars, finance officers, overseas students' tutors and heads of departments were immensely helpful in supplying us with all the data they had
available. Unfortunately, none of them can be named because the information we obtained was entirely confidential. Nonetheless, we wish to express
our deep appreciation for the assistance and encouragement which we
received from a large number of university administrators and academics
who must, alas, remain anonymous. Lastly, we wish to thank Carolyn
Makinson of Social and Community Planning Research for conducting the
survey of students with maximum dispatch and efficiency.

4. Overseas Students and British Commercial Interests*

Introduction – Background to the Enquiry

The companies who founded the Overseas Students Trust in 1961 did so in part because of the connection they believed to exist between British trade and the provision of higher education and technical training in the UK for students from the countries where that trade was carried on. Yet this perception is not easy to support with statistical evidence, and in consequence comparatively little weight has been given to these considerations in the protracted debate about overseas students. As part of its programme of research and enquiry, the Trust therefore decided to gather opinion on the subject, both from its own member companies and from a wider range of British business, all with extensive overseas trading interests.

This is not the first time the link between overseas trade and the training in the UK of overseas nationals has been enquired into. In the late 1950s the old Federation of British Industries sought evidence on the subject from a number of sources, including the Association of Commonwealth Universities, and from UK posts overseas. That enquiry produced no very conclusive results. Then in 1968 the Board of Trade set up a working party consisting of representatives of the government departments mainly concerned (Board of Trade, Department of Employment, Foreign and Commonwealth Office, Ministry of Overseas Development and the Ministry of Technology), the British Council, the Confederation of British Industry (CBI), the British National Export Council and the Council for Technical Education and Training for Overseas Countries. Its task was 'to review the arrangements in the UK for the industrial training of overseas nationals from the point of view of the contribution which they can be expected to make to furthering our export trade'.

Although that was a survey of industrial attachments or in-plant

*In the preparation of this paper, the Overseas Students Trust was assisted by Alan Bartlett, Barbara Preston and Stanley Webb.

training, whereas our enquiry was into the effects of longer-stay study in UK educational institutions, it is noteworthy that the findings of both are very similar. The Board of Trade survey showed 76% of respondents supporting the view that industrial training was 'very valuable' or 'useful' as a means of promoting exports. Our enquiry was not based on a formal survey and questionnaire; but of those companies approached for their view who gave substantive replies, over 80% saw clear benefits to their business of the effect of foreign nationals having studied in the UK.

As to the relative merits of these two types of study abroad in terms of the debate about costs and benefits, they may be seen as complementary, each catering for a different clientele. In fact, the Trust's enquiry excluded industrial training attachments as a subject for comment. Nevertheless, some references were made to it, and in the light of Professor Blaug's discussion of the subject in Chapter 3, it may be worth quoting them in passing. Several firms spoke of the usefulness of industrial attachments, and one expressed the view that the value of UK experience was greater when it had taken the form of practical training in the engineering industry rather than a period of academic study at an educational institution.

By contrast, the largest British oil company, writing from the Gulf, was quite clear that lengthy exposure of individuals to the British educational system was much more beneficial than short exposure. This view was strongly endorsed by Sir Rowland Wright, Chairman of Blue Circle Industries and a former Chairman of ICI, when he said in his address to the Overseas Students Trust colloquium in October 1980 'my own inclination is to set most store on the empathy with things British generated amongst those of influence who have stayed and studied in this country'.

In setting the context of this enquiry, one has to recognise the very real difficulty of assessing the influence of a British education amongst the many factors which may conspire to win orders for the UK or, more generally, to benefit British commercial interests overseas. In the wider frame of UK overseas investment, Anglophilia in Country X could reasonably be assumed an asset: certainly the opposite would be true. But Anglophilia will have been bred and sustained by a variety of elements, of which historical ties, the effect of the BBC Overseas Service, the activity of the British Council, as well as the infusion of UK-educated men and women through the local society will be some. To state this is not, however, to argue that because the last of these is not necessarily paramount – nor for that matter is its proportionate contribution to the development of Anglophilia exactly measurable – it is therefore a factor of no account. In the narrower context of an export order, the same point can be made: price, quality, delivery date, after-sales service will all influence the purchaser's decision. All these factors being equal, then a familiarity with a British product, arising from a period of study in the UK, may tip the scales.

Another difficulty in assessing the trade benefits to the UK of the former overseas student, is the element of lagtime. How long do you allow between the man as overseas student in the UK and the same man as putative buyer or decision-maker in his own country? Our enquiry produced some interesting comments on this, which are quoted later in this chapter.

Field and Method of Enquiry

Early in 1980, the OST decided to seek evidence from abroad through its own members about the value to them of overseas nationals who had studied in the UK. Later, with the help of the CBI and the Department of Trade, a larger enquiry was set in motion. This took the form of a letter from Lord Carr, Chairman of Prudential Assurance (and of the CBI Education and Training Committee) addressed to the chairmen of forty-one companies. A third part of this enquiry was undertaken by the British Council writing to selected posts abroad.

In his letter Lord Carr expressed the view that an important part of the total picture about overseas students would be some form of up-to-date assessment of the benefit to overseas trading operations of the presence in business or government of individuals who had been educated in the UK, and the possible long-term consequence of a reduction of opportunities to pursue professional and other courses in this country. He wrote

> the evidence may be statistical, anecdotal or simply the considered judgement of an experienced businessman operating in an overseas territory, but it could prove very helpful in balancing the mainly academic input to the other [OST] studies. Indeed the House of Commons Foreign Affairs Select Committee recently stressed the importance of an independent commercial view on this subject.

The Trust's member companies and those who replied to Lord Carr, when taken together, include the leading transnational companies based in the UK and constitute, in the range of their operations, the size of their turnover and their worldwide connections, a formidable roll-call of British industry. (They are listed at the end of the chapter.) All but two of the fifty companies approached responded to the enquiry. Of these, six felt unable to offer any useful or first-hand evidence. There were forty-two substantive replies therefore, more than 80% (36) of which spoke of overseas students in terms of the benefits they brought to their companies.

The Carr letter invited comments on the following questions:

(1) What view is taken of the value to your firm's overseas operations of local personnel who have been educated in the UK?

(2) Are such people a factor in your company's relations with the local government, or with your customers or suppliers in the public or private sectors?

(3) Can they and do they affect the attitude of the media towards the UK and therefore your relations with the general public in that country?

(4) Do competing firms from other trading nations adopt a stance in this matter?

This was a speedy exercise, completed in two months, and thus inevitably providing no more than a broad impression. However, many companies in turn trawled their overseas associates and sent a composite view built up from evidence drawn from all parts of the world.

The British Council's simultaneous enquiry went to its representatives in upwards of a dozen countries, asking for evidence on the educational background of their elites. Insofar as this information is indicative of a particular climate of opinion regarding Britain, it has its relevance to this discussion about British commercial interests.

Issues Discussed

The proper way to convey most fairly the views expressed by the respondents to these enquiries is to let them speak for themselves. There are inevitably drawbacks to this method. It may be repetitive unless, as here, it is subjected to intensive editing. One can be accused of pleading a cause by being selective in the choice of quotations. It is obviously 'unscientific', to the extent that it is not based on statistical evidence. On the other hand, the nature of the question at issue is bound to call for personal views based on experience. Indeed, it is first-hand evidence of people who are or have been 'in the field' that must lend the greatest weight and give the most credence to the points that are made. Direct quotation does also provide the subject with an immediacy, a flavour and an authenticity which statistics are bound to lack.

An undertaking was given to maintain the anonymity of the writers quoted, and this has meant the exclusion of some interesting first-hand evidence. But it should be clear from reading the extracts printed and studying the list of companies at the end of the chapter that these are the opinions of Britain's top industrialists and deserve for that reason to be taken seriously. In general, the respondents were chairmen or UK-based directors of the companies; they in turn have sometimes quoted the chairman or managing director of their associated companies overseas, some of whom are expatriates and others nationals of the country concerned.

The extracts could have been grouped according to the continent or country to which they refer, but it seemed more effective for them to be organised round the questions asked in the Carr letter and round certain additional themes which cropped up and were discussed in several replies. These further issues included the question of subsidies once full-cost fees were the norm, the effect of lagtimes in assessing effect, and the value of the English language.

Value of locally employed personnel educated in the UK

In general there was considered to be a very real advantage in having employees with a UK education. Britain's largest manufacturer of motor cars and commercial vehicles, with overseas operations employing significant numbers of staff educated or previously employed in the UK, wrote as follows in response to Lord Carr's enquiry:

> Although the use made of this background must depend very much on the calibre and attitude of the individual there are certainly instances of a greater degree of commitment to the company arising from knowledge of the UK and the company's place in the economy. Communications with expatriates are also facilitated.

A major food and pharmaceutical firm also testified as follows:

> In India and Pakistan education and professional qualifications obtained in the UK are at a very high premium. Many leading employers in these countries will not accept professional staff unless they have them. My own company prefers the recruitment of local middle and senior ranking staff educated in the UK because they have a broader outlook and a better grasp of fundamental principles.

Zimbabweans who have studied in the UK were said by a cement company executive in Salisbury to be in the main well-disposed to the UK and its system of government and general way of life. Moreover, the employment of UK-educated personnel gave outsiders a certain confidence in the standard of work and supervision. In the view of another company trading mainly in Africa:

> We find the Africans who have had university education in other countries than the UK do not fit or even have an adverse influence. This can apply to Eastern bloc universities and to some of the less estimable American universities. A drift in technical education from the UK to other industrialized countries could only harm us in the long term.... It is not so much the smaller number of people so educated as the alternative of other 'undesirable' countries stepping into the breach.

Several companies spoke of the value of British education in the broader sense, of developing liberal attitudes of mind as well as developing technical skills or acquiring knowledge. One china clay company representative asserted:

> Students attach much importance to the reputation of colleges and universities in the UK to allow them considerable freedom to develop as individuals. Might not this reputation still be a helpful influence in our business dealings overseas?

The chief executive of a major multi-national oil group active in the Middle East said that the contribution made by the UK in training and educating overseas nationals is very worthwhile to the individual himself, to his homeland and to the company for which he works on his return there: 'We have a very well-developed base for educational support, and to reduce our activity would quickly erode the benefits which we currently derive.'

These examples make plain the value that British business sets on having UK-educated staff, although it is fair to point out that there were a few companies, largely operating in industrialised countries, who saw no particular advantage in this. Three main reasons were given for the majority view. First, students returning from the UK were widely thought to be more competent and better qualified. Secondly, a British education made for easier communication especially in the fields of science and technology. Thirdly, familiarity with things British meant that they were on a better wavelength with (British) senior management which helped in getting a good working relationship.

Influence of British-educated people on the trading environment
It clearly emerges from the broad spectrum of opinion expressed that almost invariably UK-educated individuals in the middle and

upper levels of government and business have a considerable cultural affection for the UK. This carries over to a basic sympathy towards trading links with Britain, which can be a useful introduction to securing business.

The managing director of an African subsidiary of a major British industrial group stated:

> In some thirty-six years of service with this group of companies and having lived and worked in places as diverse as China, Hong Kong, Turkey, France, Iran and Nigeria, the point is always the same. Businessmen who have spent time in the UK and had education there, no matter how hard-headed, and quite apart from any cultural or social benefits, will always tend to favour the UK, other things being equal, and sometimes when they are not.

His colleague in the Middle East believed that when UK-educated students reached positions of commercial influence they tended to 'prefer the devil they know', thus giving a commercial edge.

It is nevertheless true that other factors must be weighed when commercial decisions are made. It was thought by one oil company, for instance, that the generally pragmatic approach by Kuwaitis to decision-taking is such that 'they are unlikely to give any real weight to old school ties' and the chairman of another worldwide company's Pakistan offshoot commented:

> When it comes to obtaining business, in the ultimate analysis in a price-conscious developing country like Pakistan, which is perennially short of foreign exchange, it is invariably price and delivery that determine whether or not a company gets business. The Japanese, for instance, do extremely well here and I don't know anybody who has been to a Japanese university.

However, the overwhelming weight of opinion was that the presence of UK-educated people in government and local business was a distinct advantage for British trading interests. This was confirmed by a former overseas student with a British cement company in Mombasa, who wrote: 'When it comes to making a decision to purchase equipment, I am more inclined to look for it in the British market. I know exactly where to go and in most cases the names of suppliers are familiar'.

Several other companies commented on the advantages of engineers and other technical trainees growing accustomed to British standards, specifications and so on, which could then give a British firm the edge when quoting for tenders. Such graduates would also be most likely to read British trade directories, and generally be inclined to what was already familiar.

Some companies pointed up the contrast with their dealings with local nationals educated elsewhere. A large electronics firm with overseas connections testified that firsthand experience in dealing with government procurement policy indicated that there was a bias to buy British from those whose educational background was British. Similarly, those who spent their earlier years in France, USA or USSR tended to prefer to do business with the country they knew. An international agricultural group cited the example of Somalia, where officials born in the former British Somaliland (and often educated in Britain) are invariably strongly pro-British, whereas dealings with their Italian-speaking (and-educated) colleagues were often difficult and unproductive. With the end of the colonial era and the 'localisation' of such institutions as Makerere University and the Imperial College of Tropical Agriculture, a British education lasting three years (or a UK head office attachment of similar length) was likely to be of growing rather than diminishing importance.

Companies with business interests in Nigeria, a country with which Britain's trade is worth £1bn a year – more than that with Canada or Australia and the whole of Latin America – contributed a wide-ranging response. An example was the opinion of the chairman of a leading multinational group's Nigerian subsidiary – himself a Nigerian lawyer educated in the UK:

> The benefits accruing to both countries of allowing Nigerians to study in Britain at subsidised fees cannot be quantified in terms of economic advantages on both sides only. One must also look at it from the political and social angles. My contemporaries who studied in Britain at the same time as I did regard Britain as their second home. The friendship cultivated then was very genuine, and this to some extent always affects any decision in favour of Britain. Most of my friends will not buy anything unless it is British because they are used to British products by long usage and therefore rely on the quality of the goods.

A British international chemicals enterprise quoted the chairman of their group of companies in India (their most senior man abroad apart from USA and Australia):

> I cannot help feeling that it will not be practical in an overall sense for Britain to price herself out of the educational market for overseas students in important physical and social science disciplines. The benefits accruing to Britain from the fact that students from abroad receive higher education in her universities can hardly be assessed in a quantitative manner. Even if they were so quantifiable, plain figures would not have brought out the subjective aspects of greater understanding and appreciation

of mutual problems as well as a relative consonance of outlook on things which spring from the educational link.

These subjective aspects are also important from the point of view of commercial interchange between Britain and other countries. Overseas students seek higher training in British universities in selected areas to return to their own countries for application of the skills and knowledge acquired. These latter provide their points of reference, for example when they are in a position to decide between alternative technology sources or when considering the import of machines, intermediates and raw materials.

Thus, taking the Indian case, the fact that a large percentage of overseas students at British universities have come from this country possibly has had something to do with Britain heading the list of countries with which foreign collaboration agreements with Indian industry have been concluded. This in turn is likely to be a favourable backdrop to the recent emphasis which is being put on Indo–British joint industrial ventures in third countries. Thus, in my view there is a positive – though mostly intangible – aspect to the training of overseas students at British universities. This aspect merits full consideration in any analysis of the economics of education in Britain.

The importance of overseas students is also recognised in countries that send comparatively few to Britain. For example, the chairman of the same chemical company's Japanese subsidiary commented: 'Wherever I have met Japanese graduates who have been trained in the UK, there is a very strong sense of goodwill towards Britain and this is seen in many ways in our day-to-day experience.' Then, from West Germany, the head of an oil company wrote:

No obstacle should be put in the way of studying in the UK. In my experience, such studies almost always lead to an Anglophile attitude which exerts an influence in later life. A great deal has been achieved in years past, which must be continued. An increase in student fees can only act as an impediment.

In the view of an executive in Switzerland:

The fact that someone has studied in the UK certainly makes him more likely to take commercial decisions in favour of Britain once these people have gained positions of influence in their respective careers.

The UK Government's decision to raise fees to full cost without warning has inevitably had repercussions on attitudes towards Britain in general. Many Commonwealth countries saw it as an act of discrimination. The view is encapsulated in these remarks by the vice-chancellor of a Ghanaian university, quoted by a British company director:

> One is left with the uncomfortable impression that Britain is turning her back on the Third World and this must be keenly felt by Commonwealth countries. The instinctive turning to Britain by my generation is unlikely to continue if succeeding generations regard Britain as not interested in their welfare.

This sad reaction throws into a sharper relief the widely expressed views about the value of a UK education which are well illustrated by two further extracts from letters to Lord Carr. An oil company's executive in Cyprus wrote:

> Overseas UK graduates absorb during their studies many of the liberal values of the British pluralistic social, economic, political and legal systems. They retain their attachment to these values, and exert a positive influence in the political environments of their home countries.

A similar view was expressed by the chemical company already quoted:

> The young Malaysian educated in the UK obtains not only the best education for the money they pay but also a broadening of the mind that is long-lasting. He becomes a useful ally in business when he returns to his own country. Because he speaks proper English while retaining a command of his mother tongue he is the point of contact between British and local management. The British economy accrues trade benefits as a result. He values affinity with the British as an important factor in business.

Influence of British-educated people on local and national attitudes in overseas countries.
There were interesting responses to the query on this topic raised in the Carr letter, and many reflected a pervasive view about the desirability of a British education. From Malaysia, for example, a plantations executive wrote:

> The enormous goodwill which the UK enjoys derives from the fact that the great majority of the ruling class has received some form of education in the UK or in local schools run on UK lines.

This Anglophile attitude showed to advantage when the former overseas student was a decision-maker in government or concerned with the media. As the head of an industrial company with wide interests in the Far East put it,

Many of my acquaintances at the highest level of Government and business have told me that they do not want super-educated technocrats from MIT etc. – they want British-educated people to maintain the old links, to maintain the British attitude to work and play and not something else. Many of the Malaysian hierarchy and senior businessmen are UK-educated: they send their children to the UK and arrange for private tutoring in the East on a UK syllabus. The 'English' schools in Malaysia contain a majority of Malaysian children. My Malaysian friends tell me that there is a great warmth for the UK and its traditions and general attitude to life. They do not wish to see this link severed or sorely stretched in any way. It is hard to say to what extent the pool of Malaysian students (about 17,000) will decline as a result of increases in fees. No doubt a lot of parents will pinch and scrape to ensure that their children qualify. I am always amazed at the extent to which this happens and the way in which Malaysian students in this country, some of whom must have had a pretty tough time, retain happy memories.

This respect for British education is commented on by the British Council in Italy. Where Britain's academic reputation is high or especially relevant to Italian needs, there is evidence of a clear desire for co-operation, and of the impetus which Italian Anglophilism gives to this co-operation. English is the international language of scientific and economic research, and this leads to a predisposition towards study in Britain. Likewise the Council writing from Japan notes:

> The majority of students who go overseas have always gone and are likely to continue to go to the USA, and we cannot hope to compete in terms of numbers. One could, however, I think, speak of a tendency among the academic intelligentsia to favour Britain.

But are British educational standards any longer good enough to attract overseas students to this country rather than elsewhere? This question was asked by an academic at Khartoum University, who was quoted as saying:

> There is a growing realisation that 'the cuts' are affecting academic facilities in Britain itself. Research and other pioneering activities which were once an attraction to academics and professionals have also been cut back – notably in economics, agriculture and education where Britain once had an outstanding reputation. From our viewpoint, perhaps the most serious consequence of the cuts is the very significant drop in the participation of British industries in academic life in the Third World, and the consequent loss of British influence and trade which that entails.

Third World institutions are no longer content to accept whatever services are offered by the West: they shop around for flexible institution-building packages which can be administered with the minimum of red tape, they look for institutions which themselves have sound facilities to co-operate with.

The stance of other trading nations

Responding companies touched on two aspects of this issue. They noted a tendency, since fees were raised in the UK, for students to turn to other countries, particularly in the English-speaking world. At the same time, some reported positive efforts by foreign companies to use overseas training in their own countries as a competitive weapon. These developments were referred to with a measure of concern in view of many companies' experience that the graduate on his return home tended to favour the country where he had studied.

This general concern was voiced by the Singapore-based executive of a major oil company when he wrote:

It must be driven home to the British Government that a US or Japanese-trained decision-maker in Singapore is less likely to view Britain and her interests in Singapore as favourably as those trained in that country, all other things being equal. Singaporeans trained in the UK, with common language links and greater cultural affinity, indirectly help strengthen the friendship between the two countries.

One bank quoted the example of Ghana, where leaders in many walks of life, 'having spent their student days in London, had developed an intimate knowledge of Britain and particularly favoured British goods and managerial assistance, whereas the newer breed of administrators, who have been educated in countries such as the USA, West Germany and Holland, now direct demands for goods and services to the countries in which they studied'.

The British Council reported that in Saudi Arabia many scientists and medical men had been educated in the UK, whereas most graduates in commerce, management and economics had been to the USA, and this strongly influenced their thinking. In Jordan the huge increases in educational costs in the UK were playing their part in diverting more and more Jordanian school-leavers to the USA and to East Europe, especially the Soviet Union and Rumania for engineering and medicine, which 20,000 of them were currently studying abroad. Only a fifth of Jordan's secondary school graduates could find the university places they sought at home; the rest went overseas. The effect on second rank members of the educational elite seemed likely to grow in prominence.

As to evidence of the activities of foreign companies and countries, the chairman of a British cement company in Nigeria said that industrial competitors were making substantial efforts to attract Nigerian students, and many firms referred to French, West German and also Communist countries' efforts to attract foreign students. It was also pointed out that American educational institutions offer large numbers of scholarships and often they have lower entrance requirements.

One large company with interests in Malaysia quoted the example of a group of civil servants sent some years ago to study in the USA rather than the UK. Those who have now achieved positions of importance were considered to be very much less favourably disposed towards Britain and the British. In the light of this evidence, it was not surprising to read what Britain's largest vehicle manufacturer wrote to Lord Carr:

> All industrialised nations are seeking to enhance overseas trade by every means at their disposal. These certainly include encouragement of education in the home country in order to develop cultural and economic ties.... They then seek to use appropriate local personnel in sales, public relations and labour relations activities as well as in contacts with public sector bodies.

The attitude of foreign companies to this issue is perhaps best summed up in the words of another major exporting company's deputy chairman: 'Casting bread upon the water is a sound policy most unlikely to be ignored by our competitors.' It is instructive to recall that, in its 1969 survey referred to earlier in this chapter, the Board of Trade's working party quoted the same passage from the Book of Ecclesiastes.

Attitude to subsidies

Although the enquiries did not specifically mention fees, it was perhaps inevitable that replies would refer to a subject then so topical. There was a broad consensus of opinion that the effect of the new fees policy could be damaging to British industrial, economic and political interests – particularly in Commonwealth countries – especially in years to come, when the reins of control will have passed to a new generation of decision-takers both in commerce and government who may have studied either in North America or in

Communist countries and who have no ties of friendship with Britain based on educational background.

Nevertheless, included in the responses to Lord Carr's letter were the views of three company chairmen, who expressed understanding of the decision to raise fees to full cost: they did not feel that the benefits of UK education were overriding. The following is representative of this view:

> Our experience confirms that it is helpful to our overseas activities to have foreign nationals educated – and, more important, trained – in the UK. This is not to say that we support the idea of subsidising these students. They will continue to come if they wish to, if they have existing ties, and if the value of the experience is substantial. We doubt if they shop around to find the cheapest country. We should not, however, place ourselves at such a disadvantage in comparison with other countries that we positively drive away students.

However, the chairman of a major electrical group expressed the more typical feelings of anxiety about the long-term effects of the new policy:

> Our people in many parts of the world report widespread dismay at the Government's decision to increase sharply UK university fees for overseas students. It is clear that unless the UK continues to offer competitive education and training facilities, we shall lose out to the Americas, Japan, France and Eastern bloc countries. These countries, with whom we compete internationally, are all subsidising the education of foreign students. Consequently we believe that the whole question must be looked at again.
>
> We believe, however, that the UK approach should be much more selective. Money should be spent on preferentially lower fees for foreign students who are studying subjects which can be of assistance to British exports. We see these mainly being in engineering and science, and only very exceptionally should foreigners studying arts and related subjects be subsidised, and then only if they have outstanding abilities.

Executives with direct, on-the-spot experience of overseas operations also tended towards a view supportive of 'subsidies', as expressed by one group executive recently returned to London to head a worldwide marketing function after a lengthy career spent entirely as an expatriate:

> It has always been my view that the subsidising of overseas students in the UK has been an investment which has yielded considerable rewards, far in excess of the actual cost of subsidy.

A managing director of the Nigerian subsidiary of a major British international group wrote in the same vein:

> In the UK there must be some pressure, particularly when economic conditions are difficult, to feel that UK resources spent on providing education for foreign students is money wasted. I find it hard, however, to understand why anyone could take this view who has had experience of international business. No doubt investment in providing educational facilities is a long-term investment. Sometimes there will be no return and perhaps even a negative one. But for the majority of students there will be good-will and attitudes of mind developed which will directly reflect a preference for British goods and British industry.

How such education should be financed elicited a divergency of views, of which the following are representative samples:

> My own experience overseas tends to support the view that if British students from the Third World are generally unable to attend British universities our trading position in those countries is likely to be eroded. However, one must also recognise that Third World countries are reluctant to allow foreign exchange for educational purposes, so that the solution may well be a much more generous provision of 100% scholarships rather than a subsidised rate of fees.
>
> (the chairman of a large engineering group)

> In general it would be better to encourage able students to be admitted to the UK rather than other countries. If there is to be government financial backing, it should be on a selective basis to ensure that only the most able students, who are certain to return to their own countries, receive this benefit.
>
> (the head of a large building and construction group)

> British educational institutions are being priced out of the market compared with the USA and Germany.... 'Why cannot British aid be channelled into education, not by awarding intergovernment scholarships, but by allocating aid to those desirous of a British education but who cannot afford vastly increased charges? UK educational institutions could benefit both financially and by cross-fertilisation from abroad, and those parents who are prepared for present sacrifices can be encouraged for the future. Culture and commerce often go hand in hand.
>
> (the chairman of the UK Association in Pakistan, who is the CBI representative there)

Lag effects

One important factor in trying to assess the ultimate value to British business of foreigners educated in the UK was underlined by several of the respondents. This is the length of the delay before one can expect to see any effects. The British Council Representative in Japan put it thus:

> It should be stressed again that we are talking about a time-span of 25–30 years, i.e. the length of time it will take a young employee of, say, 25 to rise to the highest managerial levels.

The representative of one large oil company in Abu Dhabi stated, 'It seems that benefits are medium-term and cumulative', while another oil corporation reported from Cyprus about the anticipated switch to study in the USA, France and Eastern Europe: 'The consequences for UK-based business will of course take time to emerge.... In commercial matters, other countries can be expected to benefit as the number of UK graduates in positions of influence diminishes.' A major transport company operating in Southern Africa commented: 'We pursue a policy of recruiting indigenous non-executive directors with some standing in the community, as our UK university-trained people tend to be too junior to have such a standing.'

The British Council Representative in Mexico wrote on this topic,

> The total of British-trained Mexicans is something in the region of 2000. I think we can with some confidence detect the rising up of an age group trained in Britain who are reaching head of department and director level in government and another age group, slightly older, that are reaching the level of Research Institute Director. The first is a group of bright young fairly political animals in the mid-twenties to thirties.

And he went on to remark: 'The situation in Mexico concerning the exploitation of old scholars is probably two years away from ripening and probably eight years from total fruition', having pointed out that the technical co-operation programme under which scholarships are provided only reached a peak five or six years ago.

Nigerian elites are still largely British-oriented, but according to the representative of a major international bank the situation has changed since independence in 1960:

> The downward trend of trade in the 1970s is not unconnected with the lukewarm attitude towards the UK of the new crop of policy-makers in the public sector and the young executives in the private sector of the economy. As strangers to the British higher education system, economy, culture and business traditions, they are not as keen to give priority to fostering of

commercial ties between Nigeria and the UK as with the USA, Canada, and some European countries.

It is common knowledge that most of those who in the past studied in the UK before the introduction of restrictive measures regard the UK as a second home. They formed the cream of the elites and middle class in the pre-independence years and immediately thereafter, before being swamped by the new crops who had studied in other countries and eventually contributed to ringing the death knell to the almost monopolistic commercial ties between Nigeria and the UK.

The value of the English language

The wish to become fluent in English is undoubtedly one of the main reasons that many foreigners come here to study, and such fluency can have definite commercial advantages for Britain. For one thing, English is the international language of science and technology which makes any commercial dealings likely to be smoother, with less chance of misunderstandings. The British Council wrote that in Greece, for example, the younger generation have English as their first foreign language. Britain has the edge over the USA in that it is culturally preferred and English now has the edge over French in that it is considered economically more useful. Both factors need to be cultivated. The English language is the major link between culture and commerce and those working in those two fields do so to mutual benefit.

In addition, it is an acknowledged fact that by and large British businessmen are reluctant to learn other languages to improve their selling prospects. From Mexico the British Council Representative views this with concern:

> What benefit to Britain do returned scholars render? I have never yet met a disenchanted ex-scholar. The immediate economic value to Britain of a Mexican coming to the UK I leave others to assess, but in Mexico we estimate that we are sitting on a gold mine of exploitation. The problem has been harnessing the goodwill. There seems to be some evidence to support the theory that the almost total commerical ignorance of Mexico in Britain is lifting, though there is little evidence that British salesmen are willing either to learn Spanish or use Latin selling methods.

In the view of an official of the Department of Trade:

> There is no doubt that lack of a common language is a serious obstacle to business. It follows therefore that the more English-speakers there are among businessmen and administrators in French-speaking and Portuguese-speaking territories, the better

for our commercial prospects. Encouraging students from those countries to study in the UK is one way of increasing the number of English-speakers in influential positions in the future.

Conclusion

As has been shown, this enquiry took the form of a gathering of opinion. If justification were needed for such an exercise, then a starting point would be Professor Blaug's observation that, though possible in principle, it was 'immensely difficult' to quantify 'the connection between exports and overseas students'; as difficult indeed as would call for 'an enormous research task' going 'well beyond the current frontiers in the empirical literature on international trade'. And this task would still only tackle exports, and visible ones at that, whereas in the event the responses to this enquiry had more to do with the experience of companies located in overseas countries and only to a lesser degree reflected the views of purely UK-based companies selling abroad. Added to that, invisible exports were obviously a major element in the consideration of many companies.

Several companies wrote also of the policy of 'regionalisation'. Where overseas investment now consisted largely of local companies, the policy is to employ local nationals: and one company trading in the East spoke of the smooth rundown of expatriate staff largely being a result of having so many Malaysians educated in the UK. This point of view was echoed by senior industrialists at the OST colloquium in October 1980. One drew attention to expatriate management now coming to an end: because the people running the overseas parts of transnationals were coming more and more from their own region, there was a great advantage if there was an educational link between those who ran the transnational head offices in London and the regional managers and directors overseas. The further point was made that the effectiveness of our transnationals is a UK asset.

With these factors at issue, it becomes important to consider the general climate which would be conducive to the greater success of overseas companies. On the analogy of 'What's good for America is good for General Motors', British business has a vested interest in seeing that the UK's standing is high in foreign countries. It is here that the man or woman who has had a positive experience of study in the UK has a role to play.

It has been the purpose of this paper to set out industry's view on the connection if any between overseas students and British exports, loosely described. Professor Blaug's study ends by putting

'£?' for that connection into his sum of the costs and benefits of overseas students. If the evidence offered by British industry and described in this chapter is accepted, Blaug's £? undoubtedly becomes a positive sum of money, even if no exact figure can be given to it. Our task then is to assess the amount which it would be worth investing in support schemes, in order to capitalise on the perceived advantage to future British trade deriving from the fact of overseas nationals having studied in this country. We then have to ask: who should finance this investment in overseas students – individual firms, industry collectively or official export promotion bodies? Also, on what criteria should the students be selected? These and other questions will need to be asked and answered as part of the attempt to formulate a new policy on overseas students in Britain.

Returning in conclusion to the main theme of this paper, the preponderant view of industry as to the value of overseas students to British trade long-term is well summed up in the following letter to Lord Carr from the Chairman of the UK's largest engineering components firm:

The value to us of our own employees who have received UK education is considerable.... Key personnel overseas have to have concise, often strategically critical discussions with top executives visiting them from the UK and similarly to make optimum use of their own necessarily occasional and brief tours in the UK. In these circumstances the importance of that common ground, difficult though it is to define, which results from experience of the same educational background, is of immense value and this goes far beyond mere fluency in the English tongue.

It is the experience of our top executives who deal frequently with overseas governments and businesses that there is a significant advantage in dealing with those who have had at least part of their education in the UK. This is not to imply that all such are automatic anglophiles – even if they are the reverse, there is a greater confidence of common understanding and grasp of each other's meaning and intention. It is not one-sided – it is particularly helpful to know that *they* know how we think. It is noticeable that such overseas people prefer to deal with the English where there is a choice, and it is felt that this has little if anything to do with preference in the old international trading sense, but to do with a sense of security, of common understanding.

Although these arguments are difficult if not impossible to support with figures, one cannot escape the conviction that a country's trading and commercial attitudes are significantly affected according to the countries in which the decision-makers have received their education and training.

The following companies participated in the survey:

Babcock International
Barclays Bank International
BAT Industries
BICC
BL
Blue Circle Industries
Booker McConnell
British Petroleum Co.
Brooke Bond Liebig
John Brown & Co.
Costain Group
Courtaulds
Delta Metal Co.
English China Clays
General Electric Co.
Glaxo Holdings
Guest, Keen and Nettlefolds
    Group of Companies
The Guthrie Corporation
Harrisons and Crosfield
Imperial Chemical Industries
IMI
Imperial Group
Inchcape Group
International Computers

Johnson, Matthey & Co.
Lonrho
Lucas Industries
Midland Bank
Mitchell Cotts Group
Northern Engineering Industries
Pearson Longman
Pilkington Brothers
The Plessey Company
The Post Office
Racal Electronics
Reed International
Rio Tinto-Zinc Corporation
Rothmans International
Rowntree Mackintosh
Shell International Petroleum
Standard Chartered Bank
Standard Telephones & Cables
Thorn EMI
Tube Investments
Turner and Newall
UAC International
United Transport Co.
George Wimpey

5. Overseas Students: The Foreign Policy Implications

by William Wallace

British Governments have been as reluctant to define policy towards overseas students in terms of political objectives as they were reluctant, before and after the Second World War, to define the overall political objectives of cultural policy – or even to admit that government support for cultural interchange was directly political in its purpose. The inhibitions to more explicit definition of objectives have been similar both in the general and the specific case: ambivalence about the propriety of bringing 'politics' into culture, hesitations over the appropriateness of state intervention in the field, and the pragmatic belief that a case-by-case approach, responding to requests as they are made and needs as they appear, is preferable to any attempt to impose a strategy on disordered reality. 'The British approach to cultural relations', the British Council stated in 1970, 'is not to use them directly to further commercial and political policies or to impress a culture on another nation' – characteristically failing to add what exactly they *should* be used for, beyond the creation of 'an atmosphere of friendly partnership'.[1]

The decentralised pattern of policy-making reflects this settled preference for autonomous and incremental decisions by independent agencies over central direction. The dissolution of the Ministry of Information after the Second World War, with the distribution of its functions among the overseas departments (the Foreign, Colonial and Commonwealth Relations Offices), the British Council, and the newly-established Central Office of Information, owed much to the feeling that it was inappropriate for a democracy to retain what was in effect a ministry of propaganda in time of peace.[2] The 1970/71 Expenditure Committee report on the British Council reflected and reasserted this consensus view. 'The Committee [felt] strongly that cultural relations should be kept as far removed as possible from general considerations of foreign policy.' It noted with disapproval departures from this principle on occasions when the Foreign and Commonwealth Office (FCO) had compromised the

Council's independence, and contrasting their preferred arrangements with the unhappy position in Bonn, where 'the German Foreign Ministry told them unequivocally that they regarded cultural relations as an arm of foreign policy and a matter over which they possessed ultimate control'.[3] It is therefore hardly surprising that definitions of the objectives of cultural policy – or of policy towards overseas students, which (it will be argued below) forms a sub-set of cultural policy as a whole – have been rare and imprecise, or that the public debate about changes of directions should so often appear confused.

To be fair, it is peculiarly difficult to define the objectives of cultural policy or to measure in any precise way how far those objectives are achieved. The Plowden Report's definition, 'to give that impression of Britain and the British people which we would like foreigners to have', begs almost all the awkward and interesting questions:[4] what impression it is possible for government activity of this sort to convey among the mass of other messages and images which other countries are simultaneously receiving, precisely which foreigners it is most cost-effective to influence, and how best to allocate priorities among the various channels for influence within a limited budget. Even with a substantial government budget for overseas information and for cultural and educational interchange, there are severe limits on how far such activities can counteract the impressions which foreign countries receive from the far wider activities of British companies and their representatives, from private individuals from Britain and other countries, from independent newspapers and magazines, independently produced films and television programmes, and so on. At best, the effects of the whole range of government-sponsored cultural activities by a relatively open country such as the United Kingdom can only be marginal, providing a useful marginal benefit when other developments are going well, but able to do little to resist adverse trends.

Matters are, of course, complicated still further by the unavoidably long-term character of the investment. One cannot expect an increased allocation of scholarships for study in Britain to country X to bring either an increase in trade or a gain in political relations within five years, perhaps even within ten – except in new nations where the elite rises rapidly; other factors being equal (which they rarely are), however, the hope is that benefits will thereafter flow for many years. The parallel often made with corporations' prestige advertising is not inaccurate. It is possible to argue that the entire expenditure is unnecessary – though few major corporations would wish to take the risk of abandoning promotion of their overall image altogether. It is impossible to say which part of the advertising effort, exactly, is the most (or the least) effective. Advertising alone cannot reverse adverse independent publicity or make up for poor products or late delivery; but it can help to colour existing attitudes, to make audiences more sympathetic, to alter stereotypes into more exact images.

One immediate – perhaps overwhelming – problem for British cultural policy is thus that Britain's image overseas, as a political model, as a stable and integrated society, and as an industrially and technologically advanced economy, has been deteriorating for reasons far beyond the capacity of any educational or cultural programme to stem. The marked shift in the choice of country of study reported among Japanese students selected by their National Personnel Agency from Britain to France in recent years evidently reflects their overall impression of France as a thrusting and competitive economy with an efficient government apparatus and of Britain as a country in decline. The comment in *West Africa* that the replacement of Britain by the United States as the largest recipient of Nigerian government-sponsored students in 1979/80 'could be attributed to the stagnating British technology, dwindling influence in world affairs and the recent staggering increase in fees for foreign students in Britain' puts the deliberate decisions of British government in proportion.[5] Dr Boyson's comment to the Foreign Affairs Committee,[6] that the absence of any parallel upsurge in British exports accompanying the rapid increase in overseas students coming to Britain since the early 1970s undermines the whole argument that educational interchange helps promote trade, ignores not only the question of time-lags but also the contrary argument that the British economy has not been at its most dynamic during this period, nor its overseas salesmen at their most forceful. It is equally arguable – and equally hard to prove – that without the additional advantages which contacts made through periods of education in Britain have provided, Britain's export performance might have been even worse.

Part of the decline in support for policies which favour overseas students, indeed, lies in the declining confidence which the British elite and population itself has in its own political system and economic strength. Between 1950 and 1958 the total number of overseas students in Britain (according to British Council figures, which included nurses in training) quadrupled from ten to forty thousand, within the framework of a much smaller total student population.[7] The absence of any significant protest against this increase owed much to the widespread acceptance of Britain's global and imperial responsibilities, to popular confidence in the political culture and institutions which overseas students came to share and in the underlying strength of the economy which helped to sustain them. The impetus of the current French cultural and educational drive overseas reflects – and is intended to reinforce – the regained self-confidence of the French Government, administration and electorate, and the vitality of its economy. It would be false to pretend that Britain was in a comparable condition.

In the field of educational interchange, there are further specific inhibitions to the idea and the practice of central and strategic policy direction. The concept of academic freedom and the traditional image of 'the universe of scholars' stretching across national boundaries, with each university contributing to the international intellectual community, are powerful factors. One university principal recently restated this ideal:

> Within twenty years of Edinburgh University's foundation in 1583, students from outside Scotland were already attending its classes and by the beginning of the nineteenth century it was playing host to students from all over the globe. It is a sad time at present when the continuation of this tradition is threatened by the high fees policy. . . .
>
> Universities are and should be in the business of training the best minds as well as they can. Irrespective of geographical origins. . . .[8]

The institutionalised autonomy not only of universities but also of local education authorities limits – as it was intended to – the ability of central government to impose a sense of direction. The contrast with France is often made; though the more subtle difference between Britain and Federal Germany, where a decentralised structure is given a strong sense of orientation from the centre, is less often observed.

Whatever the inhibitions and regrets, however, some overall policy – at the least, some sense of orientation to guide the various ministries, agencies and institutions involved – is now unavoidable. Scarce public expenditure has to be allocated among competing demands. For better or for worse, further and higher education in Britain is overwhelmingly dependent on public funds. The issue posed by the Treasury, of how the spending departments could justify the 'indiscriminate' subsidy to foreign students in terms of competing priorities for educational and overseas expenditure, has to be answered. It is a mark of how misplaced much of the criticism has been that costs and priorities have figured only intermittently in the public and parliamentary debate.

Policy Objectives

From the perspective of public policy, the issue of overseas students must be approached within the context of foreign cultural policy. Universities and polytechnics may have their own distinctive, interests and objectives to pursue; but for central government, the issue is essentially how to assess student interchange among the various instruments available for the pursuit of cultural relations. Bringing foreigners to Britain for periods of study – or, so arranging educational charges and regulations as to encourage them to come – is an activity comparable to, and complementary to, other forms of sponsored visits to Britain: to the dispatch of British lecturers and teachers to institutions overseas; to the provision of British books, equipment, and films to schools and universities in other countries, and to the support of links between them and equivalent institutions in Britain. It is in principle open to question which of these is the most cost-effective means of improving attitudes towards Britain among the educated population of other countries, or of contributing to the improvement of that education; though the problems of attributing costs and benefits are such that any prudent policy will involve some judicious blend of these several activities.

The Central Policy Review Staff (CPRS) defined Britain's overseas objectives broadly into four categories:

(1)   'to ensure the external security of the UK;
(2)   to promote the country's economic and social well-being;
(3)   to honour certain commitments or obligations which the UK has voluntarily entered into or cannot withdraw from;
(4)   to work for a peaceful and just world.'[9]

The House of Commons Expenditure Committee 'regretted' that the CPRS team had not added a fifth objective:

(5)   'to promote the English language and British culture.'[10]

In its turn, the Foreign Office's reply to the Expenditure Committee added two further objectives of its own:

(6)   concern for values and freedoms; 'the standing of this country in the eyes of the world is bound up with our stand on human rights, on how far we can make our values, political, social and cultural, understood'.
(7)   assistance to developing countries.[11]

Cultural policy, broadly defined, serves all but the first of these objectives – though only for the three additional objectives does it provide a major contribution to their achievement. Even the first objective, the insurance of Britain's external security, is indirectly promoted by activities which increase the propensity of foreign governments to listen to British representations and to respect British interests.

Political and economic influence (objectives 1 and 2)
The strongest arguments made for cultural activities as such, and for encouraging students from overseas to study in this country in particular, have in recent years been political and economic: to increase the United Kingdom's influence on and access to other governments, and similarly to increase our influence on and access to foreign companies, institutions and government agencies when purchasing supplies and negotiating contracts. Political influence is one of the most intangible aspects of international relations, particularly in a world in which few of the more important governments are dominated by personalities holding their positions for extended periods and able to impose their decisions without political compromises and bureaucratic modification. In Queen Victoria's time, judicious marriages and successful state visits could carry direct political benefits; invitations to manoeuvres or to shooting parties for the select few might usefully supplement more formal exchanges. In a world of mass societies, it is less easy for governments to pick out and cultivate in advance the politically influential of other countries. They are forced, therefore, to widen the trawl, offering the opportunity of courses or of conferences to a larger selection in the hope that the future leaders will be among their number. So long as Britain wishes to influence the policies of other governments, this will be a necessary part of foreign policy. The impressionability of youth to new experiences makes a period of study in Britain a particularly appropriate means to this end. The issue for policy-makers to decide is how many – and which – countries' policies it is most important for Britain to influence. If we are concerned to exert political influence on a global scale, or to gather votes for British-sponsored resolutions in the United Nations, then the trawl must indeed be very wide. If our political concerns are more limited in scope, then clearly it is more important from this perspective to encourage French students to study in Britain than Malaysians, or Polish students than Vietnamese.

Economic influence and access is as intangible as political; but for a country with faltering competitiveness this is arguably the most valuable gain from overseas students in this country and from other efforts at interchange and exchanges. The CPRS team puts this argument firmly in perspective, as a useful but marginal benefit:

> How much are ... people's decisions affected by their general attitudes? The answer varies greatly from group to group and country to country. As a general rule a rational calculation of where the decision-taker's own interests lie is the most important determinant of decisions. But it cannot be denied that general attitudes have *some* effect.[12]

All the arguments made above apply here about the value of such a marginal advantage in a situation where other factors are relatively equal, but its ineffectiveness where quality, delivery, financial arrangements or salesmanship are deficient. The advantages Britain gains from the position of English as an international language are not insignificant here; it means, for example, that it is possible to expand activities in the Arab oil-producing countries on a Paid Educational Services basis, while the French government is pouring in funds to promote the use of French as a medium for education and commerce in the Gulf. But if Britain is aiming at specific markets, in engineering, heavy electrical equipment, or medical equipment, for example, the value of a period of training in Britain in familiarising potential purchasers with British goods is manifest – provided that their impression of the equipment and its appropriateness is favourable.

How far the provision of education in Britain should be seen more directly as promoting 'the country's economic ... well-being' by contributing – in the same way as tourism – to Britain's invisible export effort is at present a matter of considerable dispute. The public and parliamentary debate after the 1966 decision to introduce differential fees witnessed a number of ingenious attempts to demonstrate that overseas students brought substantial net economic benefit to Britain, through the currency they brought into the country and the support they received from abroad for their living costs while here. Oddly, the imposition of full fees, which would appear to make the case for calculating net economic benefits from students funded from abroad conclusive, has so far provoked fewer attempts to argue this case. The private sector in British education – public and preparatory schools, the University College at Buckingham, independent language schools – has for many years operated on a fully commercial basis, depending heavily on its ability to attract qualified students from overseas. Some British universities and public sector institutions have for a number of years operated specific courses for overseas students or foreign governments on a full-cost basis; many of the undergraduate courses (and arguably also a good few of the graduate) in which overseas students outnumber British have in effect been provided in order to serve the entrepreneurial interests of the institutions concerned. It is on the face of it odd that a government which provides substantial support for the tourist industry, and attaches considerable importance to its invisible earnings, should display some ambivalence on this point. The Select Committee on Education and Science said bluntly that

> the Government must make clear to institutions the extent to which they are expected to behave as an entrepreneurial element in Britain's export effort. . . . This is an area in which there is still widespread confusion.[13]

The Government reply cautiously remarked that

> The guidelines recommended to universities, which set only minimum fees, gave them some scope for an entrepreneurial approach and there is evidence that several are taking advantage of this. The advice given to the public sector of education which laid down the actual fees left less scope in this respect; it is in any case for the local education authorities to consider the extent to which the Education Acts allow them to assume the role of entrepreneur.[14]

Commitments and obligations (objective 3)
The CPRS team made it clear that its third objective was a residual category, referring not to the whole range of Britain's international commitments but to 'certain inherited obligations which are largely irrelevant to the other objectives but from which the UK cannot honourably withdraw – mainly the dependent territories'.[15] Considerations of altruism, and concern for Britain's reputation, necessitate the honouring of these commitments, at least until after the completion of the transition to independence.

The question arises, however, of how long *after* independence these obligations should remain binding. The cultural 'hang-over' from Britain's period as a colonial power remains substantial: evident in the continuing, though declining, links between British universities and educational institutions in the new Commonwealth, in the prominence of Commonwealth countries as senders of students to Britain, in the high proportion of the élite of those countries which has studied in Britain, above all in the position of the English language in education, commerce, finance and diplomacy. Britain therefore finds itself in a very different situation from that of its cultural 'competitors': of having to assess how far to defend a dominant position, how actively to resist the weakening of ties, rather than of choosing how large an effort it should put into conquering new ground.

In the larger new Commonwealth countries – Nigeria or Kenya, for example – considerations of sentiment or moral obligation are easy to subordinate to the more hard-headed factors of political and economic influence. With the smaller countries, many of which lack the resources or the population to support more than a rudimentary structure of higher education, it is perhaps more difficult. It may be natural for the former Caribbean territories to reorient themselves towards the United States and Canada, and for the Pacific territories to turn to Australia and New Zealand – as is already happening. But countries such as Cyprus or Mauritius have less immediately apparent alternatives to a continuing educational link with Britain. How far a British Government would wish to recognise such a continuing 'special relationship' to a group of small former dependencies will depend partly on the importance it attaches to 'the standing of this country in the eyes of the world' and partly on the priority it gives to assistance to developing countries, which will be discussed further below.

The exemption granted to students from European Community countries, it should be noted, is best seen *not* as a consequence of any existing obligations but as a means of promoting other political and economic objectives to which the British Government attaches importance – a more equitable Community budget, a greater recognition by our Community partners of our commitment to membership, and so on.

The promotion of British values (*objective 6*)

The most difficult question – because it is essentially subjective and psychological – is how far it is appropriate for the British Government to exert itself directly to promote its own values and the prestige of its culture as a whole. For economic liberals, this is not an activity in which governments ought to engage at all. For others, such an ambition can only be part of the post-imperial hang-over, the self-centred assumption that Britain has a 'duty' to educate the world to its own superior and enlightened values, without counting the small change of the cost. Anthony Kershaw put the classic case for this 'moral' objective in an adjournment debate on overseas student policy:

But this is not a matter merely of trade and of economics. It is about the English language, the British way of life. It is about what Burke called 'our leadership in equality and in training for freedom which is the peculiar and appropriate glory of England', and which still endures though the Empire has passed away.[16]

French politicians and intellectuals, one suspects, sympathise with this objective more than most of their British equivalents now would. Within the context of a strengthening economy and self-confident political and intellectual elites, a recent report to the French foreign minister summed up the objectives of cultural policy as

> assurer le rayonnement de la France et, par l'échange et le dialogue, son enrichissement dans tous les domaines de l'esprit.... La culture qu'il s'agit de proposer au monde, ce n'est pas seulement le fruit de nos arts et de nos lettres, c'est la science française et nos techniques de pointe, c'est notre savoir-faire dans les domaines de l'administration publique, de l'action culturelle, de l'audio-visuel; c'est notre tradition d'accueil qui fait que de grands créateurs proscrits ou méconnus viennent chez nous recevoir notre protection et consécration; c'est tout ce qui peut conduire Paris et la France à jouer à nouveau, dans un monde transformé, le rôle du carrefour, à être l'un des lieux majeurs de référence et d'expérience dans tous les domaines de l'esprit....[17]

Few British politicians would feel comfortable within current conditions in expressing similar aims. The CPRS team challenge this argument directly. 'The advocates of cultural diplomacy argue that a country's interests can be served by making other countries aware of its values in general, and more specifically of its literature, music, painting, scientific, medical and technological research and its contribution to the humanities and the social sciences. We are sceptical of this argument' – and, by extension, equally sceptical that such activities contribute towards a more peaceful and just world.[18] Yet it would be too simple to dismiss the argument completely: to assume that any attempt 'to teach the nations how to live' is a throwback to Victorian imperialism. Both Labour and Conservative Governments in recent years have attached importance in foreign policy to the promotion and protection of human rights, of political and civil liberties: under Labour, with a greater emphasis on the developing world, under the Conservatives with a greater emphasis on the socialist states of Eastern Europe. The external expression of domestic values is an intrinsic part of any democracy's foreign policy, so long as it retains any degree of self-confidence. We *do* still assume, in spite of all the disappointments of the last fifty years, that a more democratic world would be a more peaceful world, and that our political, social and legal institutions thus offer a model for many other countries.

A peaceful and just world (objective 4)

A related question in cultural policy, most of all with respect to all forms of human contacts and interchange, is how far greater knowledge and understanding among the populations of different countries contribute towards a more peaceful world. One of the underlying assumptions of the nineteenth-century doctrine of free trade was that wider economic and social interchange across frontiers would act as a check upon the aggressive designs of governments by building a sense of international community. This belief still guides a great deal of inter-governmental activity, even as the tightening of entry and immigration regulations in response to the rapid expansion of international travel creates new obstacles to popular movement across international frontiers. Town-twinning, élite conferences, student exchange at all levels, contribute to this widening of popular imagination and deepening of popular understanding: bringing in their wake continuing personal contacts, intermarriage, unofficial international channels which at least marginally blur the simplicity of national stereotypes and the sharpness of national boundaries. The issue here for public policy is how high a priority to place upon international interchange among other educational and foreign policy activities, and how best to promote a balanced and reciprocal flow of students (and others) within an international community which values fluency in the English language, and thus also education in the English language, more highly than English citizens value (for example) fluency or education in Danish, Dutch or Greek – let alone Hausa, Farsi or Malay.

Assistance to developing countries (objective 7)

Agreement is in principle easiest on the relevance of overseas students policy to assistance to developing countries – thus, indirectly, it is argued, promoting a peaceful, stable and just world. The British Council's involvement in overseas students questions had from the outset a substantial developmental side; the Colonial Office gave it the official responsibility for housing and welfare for colonial students in 1950, and presided over a rapid expansion of students from the colonies during the next decade.[19] Much of the debate over overseas students policy over the past fifteen years, inside the Government as well as outside, has revolved around how best to accommodate the demand for education and training from the developing countries without at the same time allowing a flood of students, often pursuing their individual economic advantage, from the richer parts of the world. Suggestions for 'discriminate subsidies', even differential levels of fees, have been floated; the proposal that at least a proportion of the projected savings from the DES budget should be transferred to the ODA is the most recent and, in administrative terms, the most straightforward.

It is not, of course, necessarily self-evident that the best way to meet the needs of the poorer countries for education and training is to take their brightest students out of their own cultures for extended periods, with the risk that they will not wish to return, nor that the education provided in British colleges and universities is the most appropriate for these countries. It is arguable that greater assistance with educational and training facilities in their own countries, supplemented where necessary by shorter visits to Britain for more advanced study, would be more suitable. The Brandt Report pays remarkably little attention to education in 'northern' countries as an aspect of development; and what attention it pays is not uncritical. It notes, for example, that 'in the early 1960s and 1970s well over 400,000 physicians and surgeons, engineers, scientists and other skilled people have moved from developing countries to developed ones' – with Britain being one of the most important receiving countries. This 'brain drain has occurred in part because many students and professionals trained in developed countries have chosen not to return home'.[20] The Report's section on technical assistance urges rather that 'more support should be given to provide the *local* basis for research and evaluation of needs'.[21]

It is also open to question how large a contribution Britain should make to the 'global good' of economic and political development compared to other advanced countries, given its straitened economic circumstances. The Government's *Memorandum* on the Brandt Report emphasises the prior importance it attaches to 'severe corrective action' to reduce the rate of inflation, and its expectation that 'stronger Western economies, such as West Germany and Japan', will take up a larger share of the burden. Educational aid receives only the barest mention, with reference to the poorest countries: 'The Government recognise the particular importance in many of these countries of technical co-operation.'[22]

Nevertheless, the assumption that Britain does have a contribution to make to the process of economic development, and that a significant part of this contribution should be made through the presence of students from less developed countries in British institutions, remains the least questioned of all the aspects of this debate. This is partly, of course, because their presence in Britain does not simply serve developmental objectives, but is also seen as promoting Britain's political and commercial interests.

The International Context

Much of the debate about overseas students in Britain has ignored the international context. The 1966 and 1979 decisions were taken in the domestic context of public expenditure cuts, by the Department of Education and Science in consultation with the Treasury. Other governments were not consulted in advance, and so far as I am aware no information was available to the responsible policy-makers about the policies of other important receiving countries, or about international trends as a whole.

As is evident from the studies commissioned by the Overseas Students Trust, Britain's predicament is shared by a substantial number of receiving countries. Our government – like others – has been struggling with the consequences of the general upsurge in student migration which has resulted from cheaper and easier international travel, the struggle by poorer countries for economic development and by individuals for intellectual advancement and career advantage. Some other governments – such as the Australian – appear to have been relatively successful at evolving and maintaining a coherent policy, even including consultation with the major sending countries.[23] Others have found themselves faced with substantial international or domestic difficulties. The Italian Government announced in 1978 that no more foreign students would be accepted into its medical schools, in the face of severe overcrowding, only to reverse its decision a few days later, after protests from a number of foreign governments. The introduction of new restrictions on foreign student entry to France, in December 1979, provoked strikes and riots at several French universities. Quotas, differential fees and surcharges have proliferated, each receiving government's shifts of policy diverting the flow towards others. In the wake of the recent increases in British fees, the Association of Indian Universities has called for a 'regulatory mechanism' to limit and control the upsurge in students from the Middle East, Africa and Asia which they anticipated would follow.[24]

How much account should Britain take of the attitudes and policies of other governments in formulating policy on overseas students? Which are the foreign governments that we should regard as most relevant to British policy-making? The CPRS discussion of cultural policy and educational aid and interchange looked most often to France and Germany for comparisons. On a number of occasions since the imposition of full-cost fees the spectre has been raised of the flow of students diverted from Britain to East European countries and the Soviet Union. But it is clear from all the Overseas Students Trust studies – and from the student survey (Appendix A) in particular – that for the overwhelming majority of overseas students who come to Britain the English language is a major factor in their choice, and that the alternatives they would look to would be the other developed Anglophone countries: the USA and Canada above all (cited as alternatives by 73% of students in the survey), then Australia and New Zealand (cited by 20%; marginally more, 23%, mentioned other West European countries).

The significance of English as a world language in science, business, finance and in a number of the better-paid professions indeed complicates the context of British overseas education policy almost as much as the historical links of the colonial era. It is enormously to Britain's advantage that English is such a widespread language and its acquisition in such global demand. That enables us to some extent to act as a cultural 'free rider', benefiting from the efforts that other Anglophone governments may make to promote the common language, or operating on a commercial basis where promoters of (for example) French and German feel impelled to subsidise their foreign educational operations. The argument that because other governments maintain extensive programmes, or pursue particular objectives in the educational and cultural field, British Governments should also do so, is not in itself convincing; it becomes convincing only if it can be shown that they thereby gain particular advantages in areas where British interests are at stake and British objectives pursued. And that is peculiarly difficult in all matters connected with cultural policy, as noted earlier. *No* government has yet devised a satisfactory means of assessing the cost-effectiveness of such activities, or of relating scholarships given or studies undertaken to contracts gained or policies reshaped ten or twenty years later.

Uncertainty about effectiveness governs the competition both for political influence and for economic access and advantage. There is of course a prior question, in terms of political influence, of how far a post-imperial Britain should still seek to exert independent political influence outside the North Atlantic area. If, for example, the United Kingdom were to surrender its permanent seat on the United Nations Security Council (an issue tentatively raised by the CPRS Report, which however aroused no sympathy elsewhere), it is arguable that the easier access to Third-World government, which past education in Britain provide, would cease to be so important.

But in a period when 'resource diplomacy' has become part of the vocabulary of foreign policy, when the interaction between political relations and oil supplies is self-evident and the relationship between political and economic relations as a whole is a matter which even the Japanese government is forced to recognise, there remains a need to maintain a modicum of political influence over Third-World governments – for which purpose the informal contacts and goodwill provided by past study in Britain by rising men of influence may help. Britain's interests here are shared by the other governments of the European Community, and in a wider context by the other members of the North Atlantic Treaty Organisation (NATO) and of the Organisation for Economic Co-operation and Development (OECD). Our activities can be seen as part of a 'Western' effort to promote liberal and democratic values and to put across the liberal perspective on international political and economic co-operation, in which the socialist states are the adversary and their efforts to attract overseas students the relevant competition.

It makes sense, therefore, to place the British contribution in the context of the activities of our alliance partners, to ask whether our share is disproportionate and to consider whether a degree of consultation within the procedures of European political co-operation, or within the NATO framework, would not be appropriate. It is, as always, difficult to assess the severity of the 'threat'. We know that socialist governments are active throughout the Third World in recruiting potential students. We know that not many of those who have studied in Eastern Europe or the Soviet Union have yet reached positions of power within the political or economic elites of their own countries. But in many new states the generation trained and educated by the former imperial power is still in control, and there are some suggestions – in Botswana, for example – that the proportion of those trained in the socialist states is much higher among the rising generation. The available evidence suggests that the attractions of study in socialist countries appear markedly less to most aspiring Third-World students, for reasons which include language as well as culture, quality of education and politics; but if the differentials in terms of cost and ease of admission are sufficiently large, the balance of advantages may tip in their favour. From this strictly political perspective, the British share of the total Western effort appears in some respects disproportionate, for reasons of language and of post-colonial ties. If Nigerian and Kenyan elites look more towards the United States for government-sponsored study, and for the private education of their children, where previously they looked to Britain, this may be seen simply as a natural adjustment, when the burden of Western political responsibility is shared more equitably.*

It may be objected that a period of study within the socialist world does not necessarily create attitudes and beliefs favourable to Soviet foreign policy in later life. There have been many reported instances of disillusionment with the socialist system among returning students. But then there have also been examples of Third-World elites who became Communists during their time as students in Britain and France, or of political leaders (such as Dom Mintoff – or Indira Gandhi?) whose experience of Britain has left them at best ambivalent, at worst hostile. It would require very considerable confidence in the evident superiority of Western values and culture to dismiss the impact of study and training in socialist countries on potential leaders of Third-World countries. Our own educational system operates on the assumption that it leaves a lasting and favourable impression on the students who pass through it; the educational systems of the Soviet Union, East Germany, and other East European states operate on the same basis.

The question of political influence *within* the Western alliance is more difficult to assess. The continuing vitality of the 'special relationship' between the United Kingdom and the United States – still valued by successive Conservative and Labour Governments – owes much to the extensive academic interchange, at undergraduate, graduate and faculty level, between the two countries. It is still possible, at least under a Democratic administration, to move around Washington from one graduate of a British university to another; it is worth remarking that both the Deputy Under-Secretary for Defence who was directly responsible for the negotiations on the Polaris replacement in 1979/80 and his Military Assistant had studied at British universities. It is impossible to say how much of the close relationship between the French and German Governments which has become the driving force for European co-operation is attributable to the programmes which the two governments have developed for language teaching, student exchange and joint training. But the absence of any comparable educational relationship with Britain, one suspects, is a not unimportant part of the continuing

---

*I leave aside here the question whether civilian education or military training is the most effective or appropriate means of extending British political influence (with, of course, its own economic spin-off) to many third-world countries. In several such countries British links with the military, through training at Sandhurst, Camberley, Greenwich, and so on, are stronger than with civilian elites. It is arguable that the inculcation of British values within a military context is of particular value to the peace and stability of some troubled parts of the world.

sense – among the British elite as well as among the population at large – of distance from the European continent, and the continuing suspicions and misconceptions on the continent of Britain's intentions and Britain's predicament.

If the competition for political influence is first and foremost with the members of the Warsaw Pact, the competition for economic advantage is first and foremost with our immediate neighbours. It is irrelevant to argue that the Japanese export drive needs little cultural or educational underpinning: the different qualities of the British economy may justifiably require greater support. The relevant analogues here must above all be France, Italy and Federal Germany – economies comparable in size with ours, and not beyond comparison in terms of technical innovation and entrepreneurial drive. The French Government has devoted very considerable efforts to expanding its presence and its influence in Third-World countries, primarily for economic ends: opening new French schools in the Gulf states, offering new scholarship schemes in Anglophone West Africa, sending successions of ministers to and welcoming successive visits from its target states. It is – again – impossible to assess exactly the utility of the educational element within this total effort, or to assess the contribution which governmental activities as a whole have made to the relative success of this drive for exports, as against the quality of the products, the promptness of the delivery, and the attractiveness of the financing arrangements. The distinction between a French Government working to re-establish its language as a medium for trade and technical exchange, a German Government capitalising on its scientific and technical reputation, and a British Government operating with an established linguistic advantage is in any case considerable. The evidence can only be suggestive and anecdotal. The most persuasive, perhaps, is the report from Sierra Leone that the training of thirty or so doctors in Federal Germany has led to a notable shift away from Britain to Germany in orders for medical equipment and drugs. Less persuasive, but not easily dismissed out of hand, is Britain's success in retaining a leading share in such markets as Nigeria, despite the intensifying competition: a phenomenon ascribed by businessmen and officials alike as in part a consequence of the extensive personal ties between Nigerian elites and Britain.

The British position is sharply different in non-Anglophone countries. In Anglophone states, particularly those that once formed part of the British Commonwealth and Empire, the question is posed in terms of the value to be placed on retaining past links or on subsidising exchanges which might take place without financial support, even if in smaller numbers. In Far Eastern or Latin American markets, the question arises as to whether Britain gains from promoting specifically British culture and contacts rather than American or Australian. Several recent responses to the British Council and the FCO have remarked, with an undertone of bitterness, on the futility of doing anything to promote an understanding of English language and culture in the light of the established reluctance of British exporters to acquire adequate Spanish or Portuguese. Here again we are weighing up marginal advantages (and marginal costs) in terms of the initial contacts and access from which a determined businessman can build.

Both political and economic influence, however, depend as much upon a country's total 'image' as upon specific actions and activities. Images, of people, companies, or countries, are built up or reshaped over a period of years by the interaction of a whole series of events and experiences. Access to education in Britain, and the experience of education in Britain, can only be one element in that overall image; the question is how significant an element it may be. The vigour of the reaction of many Commonwealth countries to the decision to increase overseas students' fees owed something to its perception as part of a pattern, in which (as one Kenyan observer put it) it is 'at best a further step in the process of the United Kingdom's withdrawal from global interests, at worst evidence of its short-sighted disinterest in the developing world'. The difficulties which British exporters sometimes face are similarly affected by the adverse image of Britain's economy which has become established internationally – and which has reportedly been reinforced, in a number of individual instances, by observations and experience garnered during study in the UK. It is a matter for political debate and decision well beyond the scope of this paper how much importance a British Government should attach to reversing these interconnected images of British policy and of the British economy and which countries and international regions should be the priority targets of any attempt to reverse them. It may be noted that Britain's closest international partners are in Western Europe and across the Atlantic, as are its predominant export markets. But its imports of raw materials come predominantly from elsewhere, and it would be a brave government which neglected even second-order export markets in a period of sharpened competition and international recession.

Consultation is a painful and time-consuming process, which governments are reluctant to embark on without good cause. It has been suggested above that the British Government would do well to consult, a little more formally, with its partners within the Western world (broadly defined), on the political objectives and obligations of overseas students policy. Given the 'knock-on' effects, outlined in the comparative study in Chapter 7, of changes of policy by individual receiving governments, it would clearly make sense for the major receiving governments to consult each other about their common problems, despite the considerable differences between their patterns of higher education and so between their particular responses. So far as I am aware, policies towards students from third countries have not yet been placed upon the agenda of the European Community's Education Committee, or the Council of Europe's Council for Cultural Co-operation, or the Education Committee of the OECD, all or any of which would appear on the face of it to offer appropriate forums. There is a more particular case for consultation with the other Anglophone receiving states, primarily the United States, Canada and Australia, which all face the acute pressure of demand from such major senders as Malaysia and Hong Kong, and which in some respects form a single 'market' for students from the Third World. As for the many sending governments, it is worth recalling that a substantial number of overseas students in Britain are financed through scholarships from their home governments, and a further substantial number through British aid schemes administered in co-operation with those governments, and that for many Third-World countries these account for all the students they send to Britain. Changes in policy that directly affect their training schemes also affect their overall perception of Britain. Other receiving countries have managed to go through the process of consultation; it should not be impossible for Britain.

Defining Policy
Any attempt to define the outlines of a policy towards overseas students *ab initio* comes up against the awkward obstacles of past history and present commitments. The mythology of the overseas student as the itinerant scholar broadening his mind, or of the poor student training to go back home to develop his country, clashes with the all-too-frequent reality of the career-oriented student migrant. The British system of higher education developed within the context of a global role, with some of its most prestigious institutions heavily dependent on foreign students, in several cases offering courses particularly focused on tropical medicine or oriental languages. The expectations of sending governments are often shaped by their recollections of free access during the colonial period and of additional educational assistance during the transition to independence. If we were starting anew, we would not start from

here; since we are here, however, we have to do the best we can to make facilities and funds match objectives.

A clearer distinction between policies appropriate to the developing world and to other industrialised countries would be useful. With the developing world, Britain (and other receiving countries) is facing an explosion of demand for education, predominantly technical and scientific. Some of this demand is transitory, from countries which have not yet established comparable educational institutions, or which are attempting to press through crash programmes of educational and economic development. Some of it is likely to persist at least as long as Britain remains a more prosperous and more technically advanced country than the home countries from which they come. There is little likelihood within the foreseeable future of balancing the flow. Britain's particular interests in relations with the sending countries are limited and largely economic in character; our policies towards them may justifiably however be seen within the wider framework of Western security, the stability of the international economy and of the international order as a whole, and the desirability of assisting global economic development.

With the industrialised world, Britain is facing a more gradual expansion, in which the balance of flows is relatively even. The demand for education stems from a broader mixture of career advancement, intellectual curiosity, and the desire to travel; the subjects chosen thus spread more evenly across the sciences, the social sciences and the humanities. Britain has particular, and important, interests at stake in its relations with these countries; educational interchange appears as one means among many of furthering them.

A more deliberate policy of promoting student interchange among developed countries would therefore seem to be an important aspect of any rational policy towards overseas students. It would involve a greater recognition of the desirability of widening the experience (and of increasing the language skills) of British students – of paying more attention, that is, to the international understanding of our own potential political and economic elites. Given the obstacles to student exchange within Western Europe presented by different structures of higher education – and the obstacles to faculty exchange presented by different civil service regulations – this would require substantial government involvement, some funding and a good deal of negotiation. For reasons which were only partly connected with education, the British Government exempted students of other European Community countries from the increase in fees; though it has so far taken no other steps to *encourage* educational interchange within the European Community, and reductions in British Council expenditure have fallen on academic interchange schemes here as elsewhere. How far the United Kingdom should consider extending its promotion of educational interchange beyond the European Community is a matter for political judgement. Transatlantic exchanges are extensive enough to need little further encouragement. It is perhaps arguable, however, that such smaller European countries as Norway, Finland, Iceland, and Sweden, are of sufficient importance to Britain to merit the promotion of more selective interchange, or even the provision of limited scholarship schemes.

The question of interchange with the socialist world is outside the scope of this paper. The nature of the exercise is very different: the flow of students is subject in both directions to tight controls; the political and economic interests at stake more complicated. Here there is already a degree of consultation between Britain and its European partners, for political reasons, within the framework of the Conference on Security and Co-operation in Europe; indeed, the political considerations far outweigh the significance for the educational system. It may well be an appropriate objective for the British government to seek to expand such exchanges; but it will take a considerable time to achieve that goal.

With the developing world, the most appropriate policy is clearly one of discriminate subsidy – with the discrimination depending upon political and economic considerations, assessment of the sending countries' needs and our ability to meet them, their relative wealth and foreign exchange position, and their ability to provide equivalent education from their own resources. This has, after all, been the basis of the most directly-controlled area of British Government involvement with overseas students, the series of scholarship schemes operated by the British Council and others. The central failure of the 1980 decision to raise overseas student fees was the failure to link the desire to cut indiscriminate subsidies with the desirability of maintaining and promoting specific subsidies to specific countries.

The exact nature of the subsidies or scholarships offered, the agencies which should administer them, their spread across countries and across disciplines, need not be discussed in detail here. If it is accepted, in principle, that some priority in public expenditure should justifiably be given to the promotion of Britain's political and economic interests in the third world, and to a British contribution to the stability and prosperity of the international order, then a package of well-directed subsidies and scholarships is *prima facie* a more cost-effective way of achieving those aims. The fleshing out of any expanded programme would require a clear sense of geographical and developmental priorities, as well as extensive consideration of the different interests and objectives represented by the Foreign and Commonwealth Office, the ODA and the Department of Trade. The conflict between the obligations a Britsh Government might recognise towards small countries without the capacity to provide a full spread of educational facilities on their own, and without the financial capacities to pay for overseas education on a commercial basis, and the interests a British Government will wish to pursue in relation to large countries with strong financial balances, will have to be faced. But these problems are all in principle soluble within the framework of the Whitehall policy-making process, once the political decision is made and the finance committed.

Alongside the promotion of a wider two-way flow between Britain and other industrialised countries, and the provision of specific grants for students from developing countries, it would also appear appropriate to define policies more closely on the provision of educational services on a commercial basis. The present (1981) Conservative Government is looking to the service sector to take up the slack in employment and in the economy created by the decline of manufacturing industry; the educational sector is a substantial employer, and a source of valuable invisible export earnings actually and potentially. For educational institutions a continuing flow of overseas students may provide a stimulus to maintaining the quality and variety of courses and a welcome source of additional finance independent of government. How far a competitive approach to the overseas students market would require government and educational bodies to have regard in fixing fees to those set by Britain's major competitors is an intricate question, involving nice judgements about marginal costs and benefits; it is perhaps worth noting that in the international market, so to speak, the British level of fees is now twice that of Australia and Canada, and well above levels obtaining within the United States. Whatever attitude is taken towards fees, it might however be appropriate for the promotion of British education overseas to be seen in terms of the direct economic benefits, and thus regarded by overseas posts as a matter of economic as well as of cultural advantage.

Policy towards overseas students, and expenditure incurred under that policy, can make at best only a marginal contribution to the achievement of the foreign policy objectives outlined at the beginning of this chapter. But much politics, much commerce, and much more diplomacy, is a matter of margins. The level of expenditure involved in a package of discriminate subsidies, support for educational interchange, and the promotion of British education as a 'commercial service' represents a relatively small element within the external relations budget – which is where, rather than within the education budget, it belongs. It is for ministers to decide how far the intangible benefits gained justify the expenditure. There is, sadly, little evidence that the issue has been posed to ministers in recent years in any such terms. It is time that it was.

Notes

1. Memorandum by the British Council, *First Report from the Expenditure Committee, 1970/71*, HC–304, p. 3.
2. Sir Robert Marett, *Through the Back Door: an inside view of Britain's overseas information services*, Oxford University Press, 1968, Chapter 11; Sir Ivone Kirkpatrick, *The Inner Circle*, London, 1959, pp. 199–204.
3. HC–304, 1970/71, paras. 24–9.
4. *Cmnd 2276*, February 1964, Committee on Representational Services Overseas 1962/3, para. 27.
5. *West Africa*, 7 July 1980.
6. HC–553, 1979/80, p. 118.
7. A. J. S. White, *The British Council: the First 25 Years*, London, 1965, pp. 102, 144.
8. The Principal of Edinburgh University, reported in *Times Higher Education Supplement*, 30 May 1980.
9. Central Policy Review Staff, *Review of Overseas Representation*, HMSO, 1977, para. 2.31.
10. para 11.
11. *Cmnd 7308*, 1978, paras 3 and 5.
12. Central Policy Review Staff, *Review of Overseas Representation*, HMSO, 1977, para. 14.6.
13. HC–552–1, 1979/80, para. 62.
14. *Cmnd 8011*, 1980, p. 7.
15. Central Policy Review Staff, *Review of Overseas Representation*, HMSO, 1977, para. 2.25.
16. HC Debates 75–6, Vol. 905, cols 1093, 1097.
17. *Les Relations Culturelles Extérieures* (Rapport Rigaud), Documentation Française, 1979.
18. Central Policy Review Staff, *Review of Overseas Representation*, HMSO, 1977, para. 12.22.
19. A. J. S. White, *The British Council: the First 25 Years*.
20. *North–South: a programme for survival*, Pan edition, London and Sydney, 1980, pp. 109–10.
21. *North–South: a programme for survival*, p. 197 (emphasis added).
22. *The Brandt Commission Report*, Memorandum prepared by the Foreign and Commonwealth Office for the Overseas Development Sub-

Committee of the Foreign Affairs Committee, London, HMSO, July 1980.

23. Information provided by the Australian High Commission, London. See, particularly, the ministerial statement on the decision to introduce 'an annual charge on overseas students', Federal House of Representatives, 22 August 1979, cols 441–3.

24. *Times Higher Education Supplement*, 6 June 1980; which also notes that the number of foreign students in India had risen from 14,000 in 1978/9 to 24,000 in 1979/80.

6A. The Needs and Desires of Developing Countries for Foreign Student Facilities

Some Reflections

by Guy Hunter

The Scope of this Paper

Policies directed towards the acceptance and financing of foreign students in British education and training institutions necessarily involve both demand and supply considerations. As to demand what do foreign governments and individuals want from us and – a more doubtful question – what do they need? On the supply side, what should we be prepared to provide? The other studies in this work look primarily at the supply side, after a careful analysis of the size and nature of the *de facto* demand; they consider the various British interests which might justify spending resources on part of this demand, and the capacity of our own institutions to meet it.

This paper will look primarily at the constantly changing course of demand from developing countries (i.e. not from Europe or America). When we are dealing with demand from sovereign governments of developing countries, there can be a question whether, and on what basis, we can look behind the bare demand to the 'need'. Whether we should look seems easily answered, since we have a right to choose how our own resources are to be spent. On what basis we should look poses a more difficult question. Governments must be supposed, as a first presumption, to know their own needs, and they may well support them with evidence from their planning documents. But – and here I trespass just over the border of the other studies – one long-term British interest is to contribute to narrowing the gap between the rich and the poor worlds; and it would not be unreasonable to discriminate in favour of demands which are most helpful to this aim, or against those which are less. Rather different arguments apply to individual applicants.

Accordingly, this paper will look briefly at the nature and history of demand from developing countries, at the achievements and defects of the past record of educational and training co-operation insofar as they may give lessons for the future, and at the probable course of this demand in the coming years.

Types and Sequences of Need and Demand

A significant feature of the developing world is the variation in need and demand, country by country, springing from their different historical backgrounds and development experiences. It is tempting to divide countries by categories of similar needs, although – as will appear – such categories are necessarily rough and full of minor exceptions. It may be helpful to look first at the lower levels of need – artisans, technicians, clerical staff, traders and merchants – a level in which some countries have had a crippling deficiency and others comparative wealth. Demand at the higher level can then be considered.

Lower-level needs

At this level a broad distinction can be made between large geographical areas – particularly Asia, Latin America and Africa. The ancient civilisations of Asia were far ahead of pre-Renaissance Europe – except perhaps in the architecture and wealth of the Christian church – not only in their philosophy, literature and fine arts but in the magnificence of their crafts and manufactures with their superb textiles, metal work, jewellery, ceramics, leather and wood work. It is worth two sentences to remember that it was from Asia, as well as from Greece, Rome and Islam, through wandering scholars, explorers, merchants and artisans, that the rebirth of Europe's knowledge and skills were learned through courts, the infant universities and the Church. As late as 1600 ambassadors from the Court of Elizabeth I were astonished at the state of learning and the practical arts of Mughal India; it has only been since the eighteenth century that science and technology have carried the West so far ahead in economics and power.

If we take the period of rapid decolonisation (1947–65) as a starting point for modern concern, much of Asia had retained its richness at the level of artisans and merchants, diffused from the palaces where they had been originally to serve widespread common needs. Much of Latin America, because of long contact and intermarriage, had this advantage too. But tropical Africa (particularly in the East and centre), when penetrated by colonial power in the nineteenth century, was far behind. Among its multiplicity of local societies, not yet centralised states, without a great accumulation of wealth, both the level and range of crafts and of commerce were thin indeed. This is true also of many small subsistence societies (for example the Pacific islands) scattered in many parts of the globe. We can think of these countries as those in need of most educational help, and they will be considered in more detail below.

These broad geographical divisions are indeed very rough and dotted with exceptions and finer differences. The Belgian Congo, at the moment of independence, had a far better cadre of indigenous artisans and clerks than East or Central Africa, but only two university graduates. East and Central Africa had partly filled the gaps at this level with Asians; Angola and Mozambique with Portuguese; some Francophone West African countries with French *petits blancs*; Anglophone West African countries, with earlier Western influence (including notably Fourah Bay College in Sierra Leone, for higher studies) were also rather better off at the artisan and trading level, partly from their traditional apprenticeship system. In Asia the overseas Chinese filled up the same gaps in some countries, notably in Malaysia and parts of Indonesia. All these local differences implied rather different education and training tasks in each particular case. In brief, the task could be defined by the particular balance between the most urgent needs for development manpower and the existing supply (both stock and flow) of such manpower in any one country at any given time.

It may seem that deficiencies at this lower level do not affect higher education and training and are therefore beyond the scope of this paper. But they have had very considerable effects both in development and in the approach to *all* levels of educational aid or co-operation. First, the concentration of educational aid on academic secondary, undergraduate and graduate courses has been much criticised as widening the gap between an official, usually urban, elite and the mass of (mainly rural) population. Second, in development terms, a lack of trained artisans, technicians and foremen between the graduate engineer or manager and unskilled labour has led to great difficulties in industrialisation. Similarly, in administration, the lack of good middle ranks has led to overwork and under-delegation by a few senior administrators, again with adverse results. Finally, this gap in middle skills may be at least partly responsible for the tendency for development planning to concentrate on large, modern, capital-intensive units, often calling on expatriate experts, rather than on smaller craft, processing, agricultural and commercial development, in which management is first learnt and which uses more indigenous materials, manpower and energy.

High-level needs
Obviously, decolonisation left behind it a very considerable and, in

some countries, sudden demand for well educated manpower to replace expatriates in many branches of administration – in central and provincial government, in a foreign service, in scientific and technical institutions, in police and the armed forces, etc. There was not only this replacement to be found but a considerable expansion of government itself as the new governments launched into exciting new programmes attracting new, and now international, funds. Moreover, in some countries, particularly where 'indirect rule' had been practised, there was a tendency to replace indigenous local rulers (chiefs, emirs, princes, maharajahs, etc.), thought to be contaminated by the colonial ethos, with a growing cadre of new civil servants. This sudden and glittering opportunity for promotion, from school teacher to ambassador, put the enormous premium on education, and if possible education overseas, to which I will refer later.

In some countries (for example, India), where independence had been long foreseen, and to some extent prepared by the colonial power, and where expatriates were, in any case, a tiny number in relation to total population, and the middle tiers of administration were already manned indigenously, this transition was quite easily absorbed. In non-colonial countries (Thailand, Ethiopia, Iran, for example), existing rulers sent their sons to be educated abroad, in order to retain 'the establishment' with an acceptable modern form. But in some, where independence came ten to twenty years earlier than had been expected (either by the country concerned or by the colonial power), the process of replacement and expansion lasted for at least a decade. It was this sudden and very large demand for 'high level manpower' which started the intense demand for places in universities overseas in the 1960s and 1970s. Indeed, it may have been this urgent demand for university qualifications which led to the comparative neglect of the lower levels of training and competence, even where most needed.

Matching Supply to Needs

The countries in greatest need
The countries which inherited at independence the thinnest educational system at higher levels set off, mainly in the 1960s, on an extremely rapid expansion of the whole system – usually starting with secondary schools and aiming primarily at expansion of the university level and retaining some expatriate staff in secondary teaching and as a high proportion of early university teaching. This was the heyday of manpower surveys and projections, and in provision of places in Western colleges and universities. Other inter-

national donors, notably the USA, contributed increasingly to the effort previously carried by the relevant colonial power. This was a period of idealism and optimism about development and aid, and a quite straightforward task for Great Britain, with popular support. The urgency of the governmental demand at secondary and under-graduate levels began to slacken in the early 1970s (except in a few specially disadvantaged countries, mostly small) as the new insti-tutions in developing countries began to pour out their graduates. On the other hand, demand on more specialised courses and post-graduate courses generally continued to increase; and the whole expansion was constantly pushed forward by the personal ambition of students to win the great rewards to overseas qualifications. This was a 'catching up' period in which the difference between countries poor or rich in higher manpower began to narrow, although it remains to this day. It was heavily assisted by the international provision of places for foreign students.

It must be added that the local provision for technician training did not keep up with the more academic expansion. Although many technical colleges were established, the eager demand for a university degree and the ambition of principals drove them upwards to degree-giving status, leaving a gap below them. Moreover, in countries at a very early stage of industrialisation there were few opportunities for the essential practical element, whether by apprenticeship, in-service training, or even sandwich courses or night schools. Inter-national companies did indeed do their best to train – and at some cost, since they were constantly losing their trainees to high govern-ment posts. The provision of places at the middle technical level in the UK particularly for countries in the very early stages of industrialisation, when added to technical assistance in the form of instructors for local institutions, was a significant contribution, despite inevitable differences in UK technology.

Countries richer in basic provision
This category contains not only the developing countries with the higher GNP per capita. It would, for example, also include a country such as India, which has simultaneously great poverty, about 35% literacy and low average GNP, but also possesses the third largest stock of manpower trained in high technology in the world. Part of the reason for this lies, as we have seen, in centuries of development of indigenous manufactures; part in the long association in culture and trade with Britain; part in the long tradition of respect for learning. Apart from its commercial and industrial base and its research capacity, India has created more than

a dozen agricultural universities, which might be a hopeful sign for the rescue of the rural poor. There are reasons other than lack of education for India's poverty.

Long or intense influence from a developed country (Taiwan from Japan; South Korea from the USA; Kenya from British settlement) may be another reason for advance; natural resources (oil in Nigeria) yet another. Whatever the particular combination of circumstances and history this group of countries is not *primarily* or *critically* obstructed in development by shortages of education and training which they cannot provide from their own institutions. Perhaps the Middle East oil-producing countries should have been included in the category of greatest need, since they fall into exactly the opposite case to India – a great shortage of technical manpower and a very high per capita income, enabling them both to import manpower on a huge scale (including Indians) and also to pay for all the places in foreign universities or colleges which they may need. They need skill but not money.

Although the group of countries richer in basic education and manpower does not now have to call on the outside world to aid a vast expansion of their whole educational system, as was needed in some parts of Africa and elsewhere, the very expansion and increasing specialisation of their economies does create a demand for specialised technological education – largely taught courses at postgraduate level; and this demand is likely to increase if their economic growth is not to be checked. Some can afford to pay the full economic price for it, whether by government grants or by families who have grown rapidly rich in the course of this economic expansion. Not all of them, however, are rich in foreign exchange and some, indeed, are among the world's heavy debtors from economies overheated by foreign borrowing; some also face a foreign exchange crisis as a result of the immense rise in energy costs. The recent very steep increase in demand for high level places in the UK reflects this growing demand, and is discussed below.

Some of the countries in this group have, at the middle levels, a continuing domestic and political problem of replacing a considerable and economically important layer of technicians and even administrators remaining from earlier immigration, or fully absorbing them into their culture. Malaysia is an obvious example, in which supply, in terms of places in British institutions, has been very generous. But almost all have experienced very serious poverty, illiteracy and under-employment at the lowest level of all. How far, if at all, overseas training can affect this is an issue dealt with later.

Yet although those developing countries with a richer endowment of skills and training may seem to *need* less overseas assistance, education in every country – developed or developing – is, of its nature, an ever-expanding, never-satiated demand; and in this it is paralleled by 'development'. New needs may be expressed from the changing economy; new ambitions will be constantly expressed by the educational profession itself, conscious of its many deficiencies and of tempting horizons ahead. Even in better-found developing countries, literacy is far from 100% and women's education may lag behind, and, at the higher end of the scale, pressure for more and better research, more specialisation, and endless recommendations for new forms of training keep up the pressure. How far developed countries continue to feel an obligation to spend resources in relieving this pressure will be discussed at the end of this chapter.

A Brief Critique

In broad terms the British effort, both in aid to education and training institutions and in provision for places in Britain, has been a considerable achievement, and earlier colonial effort must here take a full share of the credit. It has helped to equip many countries with a 'modern' educational system as a launching pad into the modern world and to accelerate economic growth. But it has not been without critics, both in the West and in the developing countries themselves; and these criticisms must be taken into account, for the lessons which they may have for our future policy.

The general accusation was (and in some degree still is) that what we gave was unsuitable, in three main ways: academically, technologically and politically. As to the first, we can now forget the old, but true, jokes about teaching Anglo-Saxon (from the London University English syllabus) to students in Uganda, or '*nos ancêtres, les Gaulles*' in Francophone Africa, or an even more alien syllabus. But the accusation that this was not the moment to adopt the full Western academic style in countries weak in resources and hell-bent on economic development sticks rather more deeply. Training in the West, in our earlier stages of development, had a very different look.

Second, it is on the technical side that perhaps the most telling and still valid criticism might be raised. Have we not taught industrial technologies from the West, technologies which are labour-saving and capital-intensive in form, wholly unsuited to the factor proportions and wage-levels of a quite different economic stage? In health services have we not concentrated on fully trained doctors, and aided huge curative hospitals in urban areas, when what was needed above all was preventive medicine and simple services for simple diseases and accidents for the 70–90% rural population at village-level? Many such examples could be given of the handling of both policy and practice, by both donor and recipient governments, of the extremely difficult task of transferring Western up-to-date technology (with its demands on the surrounding economy and even its tacit assumptions and values) to economies in the developing world which are in a very different stage and balance.

The third, political criticism is that the whole educational policy, perhaps originating in developing countries and acquiesced with in the West, accelerated and enlarged the creation of an elite group, and widened the gap between them and the mass of their fellow citizens. As a fact, this is certainly true: it was also inevitable. The numbers with higher education were bound to be limited. Moreover, once the decision to establish a certain type of university had been made, that decision was bound largely to determine the type of secondary education. Perhaps criticism might be better aimed, not at what was done, but at what was *not* done, both at primary level and in offering a far wider range of exits from the secondary level for the majority who would never be scholars, into practical training for work of many kinds in the agricultural economy and in relatively simple industrial skills. This was a question of the balance of resource allocation between the levels: in at least one African country in the 1960s one university place cost as much to provide as 200 places in primary schools. Historically British colonial administration in Africa struck a not unreasonable balance between the extreme reluctance of the Belgian administration of the Congo to educate Congolese beyond the technician level (at that level they were ahead of Anglophone Africa) and development of the university level, which might have seemed premature in view of the fact that colonial administrators and teachers at that time filled the posts which normally required higher education. Considerable effort was devoted by Government, missions and other organisations to training teachers, to establishing trade schools for artisans and to farmer education both through extension and in farmer training centres. But this emphasis was quickly overshadowed, at independence, by the pressure from African governments to 'Africanise' top jobs, and by the political and economic strength of the new elite with its interest in expanding higher education locally and in obtaining places, if necessary at private cost, in higher education overseas. The passport qualification for a job for Africans rose very rapidly from eight years completed primary to Cambridge Overseas School Certificate to a university degree and even a foreign qualification.

In any case, developing countries were determined not to be second class citizens: if they were to enter the dominant world culture they would compete with its best. And, if the tree is to be known by its fruit, the results are far from only negative. The economies and new governments had to be staffed; better that they should be staffed by men and women who had been through the discipline of higher education, even if its content was not tailored to their needs. In fact, quite a few of the graduates from such universities, often with the aid of study in the universities of the West, have come to play a part of great significance in international affairs. In every UN agency there are men and women from the developing world at many levels, including the top. Add to that a host of special committees, research institutions, regional development banks, scientific and professional associations, and it is clear that, compared with the situation barely twenty-five years ago when decolonisation was almost completed, a massive entry into world citizenship by developing countries has taken place – and will certainly increase, and increase faster if the doors of Western learning remain open. There is indeed a danger that too many individuals who have played an outstanding part in administrative and technical leadership in their own country are tempted away by the salaries and conditions in UN and other international bodies. Particularly for small countries, this can be a serious loss.

The task of rescuing the poor does indeed remain to be done; seldom if ever in history since 'primitive communism' has it been the first task. Judgement on the elites depends upon the attitude they take to this responsibility. It may even be true that the larger the educated elite, the more likely that a section of it will be in opposition against those who have abused their position. If the opposition cannot win in the ballot box, they sometimes resort to forceful *coups*.

Present and Future: What level of Response?
In the long perspective the record of a combination of aid to overseas education and training with opportunities for study and training in this country is favourable. Both the educational gap between the developed and developing countries and the gap between the countries better endowed with skilled manpower and those in greater need have been somewhat narrowed in terms of urgent need, if not of numbers. There are indeed some countries which, for various reasons, still require both aid to their own educational and training facilities and, until it is improved, a good number of places within our system. Where such obligations to countries with a special degree of dependence still exist, no doubt their needs should be met, and where necessary subsidised, and in foreign exchange at that.

Among the majority of countries where need is less pressing there are also a number of special cases. For our purposes, Malaysia and Iran are the most notable, since they send much the largest contingents to Britain. The Chinese Malaysians come because of a governmental decision to give priority to Malays in their own institutions. It is at least questionable whether Britain should incur much cost in alleviating the results of this decision. The Iranian influx is presumably a consequence of the intense effort of the late Shah to turn Iran into a high technology Westernised state; in any case the future is now uncertain, and a review will be needed when it becomes more clear. In both cases – and indeed more widely – our response will depend on what view we take of the claims of private student ambition against those of public need.

Apart from these special cases, the probability is that the total application for places is likely to rise. This applies particularly to privately financed students, since there is no reason to believe that the rewards to a foreign university degree are likely to diminish, while the numbers with the necessary qualifications for entry will rise. Certainly, the present policy of charging the full economic cost in Britain is likely to produce a sag in applications for a short time, but the underlying pressure is upwards. Two factors in particular may reduce the pressure on Britain. One is the foreign exchange cost for non-oil countries; the other is the offer of places at less cost in other developed countries. As to the second, it is not necessarily against the interests of developing countries to use countries other than Britain, nor much against British interests if students go to the free world and if we continue to have an adequate mixture of overseas students in our own institutions.

It is probable that governmental (manpower planning) pressure will also increase in technical subjects, as their economies become more diversified and specialised. It might be reasonable to assume that demand for general arts and undergraduate courses would fall somewhat as, first, institutions in developing countries increase their output and, second, the number of unspecialised jobs available decreases. In any case, the *degree of urgency* of need is likely to fall compared to that which led to the high levels of aid or subsidy to fees in the 1960s and 1970s.

British policy and attitudes

It is assumed in this paper that some discrimination between applicants (over and above those which are already applied) is going to be necessary if Britain is to deal with this whole issue in a rational way. A British policy must reflect British interests (short-term or even very long-term), and 'interests' here include some obligations of a rich and highly educated nation. These interests have been listed and discussed elsewhere. They include, first, trade interests; second, political interests, in propagating the values of a free society; third, an interest in enriching our own institutions by the presence of overseas students and scholars, and possibly by their contribution to research; fourth, a narrower commercial interest in selling a product (education) to willing buyers. None of these, therefore, need be discussed in detail here.

But policy towards the development of the Third World – perhaps an obligation in the short term – is both in the interest of developing countries and a long-term British interest; for their economic success and stability are palpably in our interest too. Secondly, the internationalism of learning and the exchange of scholars has been historically and is today a happy obligation to any concept of civilisation, however unquantifiable its benefits may be. These two points must rank among the criteria that we apply in judging our response to demands for educational opportunities from developing countries.

Two possible attitudes

A less committed view   It is possible to take a cool, somewhat uncommitted view of what our future policy should be. It can be argued that we have largely fulfilled our obligations as an ex-colonial power by twenty-five years of aid and co-operation in education and training; and that how developing countries use their growing educational equipment, and what share of their own resources they devote to it, is their affair. The action which would correspond to this view would be to

(1) meet commitments to exceptional countries particularly dependent on our help;
(2) continue positive aid and co-operation with late-comers to independence who may still need the level of expansion which for most took place in the 1960s;
(3) pursue identifiable middle-term British interests in trade;
(4) apply full costs to the majority of applicants for first degree courses, particularly unsponsored students, with a modest number of scholarships reserved for exceptionally deserving cases;
(5) expect the majority of governments to finance, in whole or at

least in part, applicants who are intended to fill a planning requirement; and

(6)   keep an open door to wandering scholars (including refugees).

This view has the minimum degree of dirigism or attempts to influence the educational planning of overseas countries in a direction of our choosing. It accepts an important educational philosophy which would emphasise a free choice of course and an experience which enables the student to make the best of his abilities in his own way. It also implies that the more wealthy families will have the lion's share of available privately financed places; and that some poorer governments may fulfil manpower plans elsewhere.

A more committed view   The heading to this section does not imply a radically different list of types of provision. But it does imply a more positive effort to alter the profile of students accepted in British institutions in a direction which better reflects two factors: first, British interests, including long-term interests, and, second, the interests of development in the third world. It also rests on the assumption that overall economic and social development in the Third World does coincide, as the Brandt Report emphasises, with a very important British interest. Such an effort will require critieria both for choices and appropriate agencies, not all of which are confined to British universities and colleges or to the Department of Education and Science.

Industry and professional institutions

This paper has referred to 'students', which is apt to carry an implication of young people in their first main educational sequence. But, particularly in industry and the professions there are more mature people who have much to gain from a period of foreign experience in their own field. In addition to industrial firms there are a great number of professional associations – of medicine, law, engineering of various types, of parliamentarians, economists and others in many branches of science. Already through these, with the aid of visiting professorships or fellowships, and through foundations and trusts which see international exchanges as a valuable object of assistance, an extremely fruitful exchange of learning and practice is already maintained. It may well be that some additional funding to such institutions could enable this valuable work to be intensified by further selective exchanges of visits and periods of attachment, particularly where overseas members cannot find opportunity for a formal course, or where they need very specialised information or experience.

As to industry itself, much has been done by international companies by bringing their own overseas staff over here for additional experience. Further, a good many leading men in industry are convinced that some period of educational or training experience in Britain for businessmen in developing countries makes them more valuable contacts in trade. It may be that, through the Confederation of British Industry or other suitable means, and with the aid of a moderate fund earmarked for the purpose, much more in the way of fairly short practical attachments and courses could be organised. For, although a first training in engineering or other skills, in a university or technical college overseas may now be quite widely available, the shopfloor experience and actual know-how can still be very hard to obtain in many developing countries, which have not anything like the variety or the number or the specialisation of firms which exists in developed countries. It will be increasingly the topping-up of theoretical training acquired overseas, by practice and by specialisation, which may supplant some of the demand for first degree courses or diplomas. It is recognised that British industry has many priorities other than training foreign students; and that giving shopfloor experience to outsiders can be tiresome and difficult. Nevertheless, if access even to in-service training schemes could be guided and controlled by a responsible industrial committee or trust, something of value might be achieved.

Formal education

I have already suggested that the need to send students for middle and undergraduate level education as such, even if it does not fall off, will have less pressure of urgent manpower need behind it, though perhaps as much or more pressure of private ambition. In guiding the selection of private students who might be exceptions to a full-cost rule some discrimination between countries and as to type of course could well be considered. If in fact demand increases, and if there is some reasonable limit to the numbers of foreign students which our institutions and our Exchequer can manage, this will in any case become necessary. Moreover, there may be some advantage in leaving room and funds for more mature 'students', who probably know more clearly what they need and who may also be able to ride more easily the 'cultural shock' and petty annoyances which are bound to accompany a first plunge into an alien environment.

Education, poverty and aid
The huge gap between the top and the mass of poor people in many developing countries, aggravated by enormous population growth, has been stressed. It is extremely doubtful if this critical issue can be much influenced by any manipulation of the flow of foreign students to the West. In peasant-dominated countries it concerns agricultural effort and structural reform (tenure etc.) for which indigenous training, the social policies of government and dynamic local leadership are critical and to which foreign education can barely contribute. It concerns also, for urban as well as rural poverty, employment and technological policies which again are not expertly known or easily assisted in the West. This is a case for aid rather than formal education, and most probably the kind of aid to very local initiatives overseas which has been best handled by voluntary organisations (Oxfam, the churches, some foundations, and many more). It may well contain a training element, but one which must necessarily take place within the local scene.

Insofar as developing country governments are making a real attempt to tackle these problems, there are a number of teaching and research institutes in Britain which were established in order not to lose the invaluable experience of overseas problems acquired in colonial days, and these have continued to attract senior administrators from the Third World, both on taught courses and for comparative research. Since the effort to drive development down to a point where it really touches the poorer layers of citizens in developing countries is beginning to demand new institutions and new administrative organisations, it is important that this work, which is much more directly aimed at the problems most relevant to Third-World administrators than standard university courses, should not be weakened. It is double-edged, contributing not only to overseas students here but also to technical co-operation staff and consultants. Constantly up-dated knowledge of the changing problems of developing countries and intensive discussion with their active administrators contribute a good deal to friendship and to the esteem in which British competence is held.

A Last Word
Early in this chapter the great accumulation of wealth and power in a small circle of India's rulers in the sixteenth and seventeenth centuries, and the contrast of that to the poverty of the majority of their subjects was mentioned. In fact, over the span of human history since large states developed, this has been, until very recently, the invariable human condition. The effort, in what are now the

modern democracies, to achieve even a moderate equality of opportunity, even a slow narrowing of the gap between rich and poor; to give more heed to the voice of the people and to protect their freedom; to establish a tradition of the rule of law; to legitimise democratic methods of changing rulers – all this took many centuries of effort and cost many revolutions. It was not to be expected that all the new governments of developing countries, from the day when the colonial flag was pulled down, could achieve legitimacy, the peaceful transfer of power or the will to share new power, wealth and privilege much more widely with their citizens. A long period of political experiment, many abuses, great instability were bound to occur as they struggled towards a political solution suited to their time and to their problems. Confused as they have been by outside influences and propaganda and (in ex-colonies) without previous political experience of running a centralised state – since politics had been monopolised by the colonial Power for sixty years or more – and faced with a puzzling choice of alien technology, it is not surprising that their path has been rough or that the spread of incomes and of education should take time.

In face of such countries, the chief obligation of the developed countries is to show a steady patience and goodwill and to share those parts both of their science (in the widest sense) and of their experience with all those who care to use them. In such a perspective an attitude of generous committal, particularly in the sphere of education would seem, to this writer at least, the most appropriate. Certainly, we need not spend resources on those who do not most need them. Certainly, to those countries, institutions and individuals who may contribute in their own country to the battle against world poverty, we should give whatever help we can, whether within our system or by aid to theirs. Certainly, we should contribute especially to the Commonwealth which remains a lively co-operative institution. And, beyond these areas of partial discrimination, we should maintain the principle of the internationalism of learning and of the opportunity to share it.

For all these reasons, we shall need for our purpose a much better co-ordination of our policies, between government departments, between aid and educational provision, and between both with the institutions of industry, of the professions, of the voluntary organisations concerned, and with the representatives of our educational institutions upon which the burden of practical implementation so largely falls.

6B. Study Abroad and Development Policy

An Enquiry

by John Oxenham*

Objective and Approach

The aim of this paper is to enquire whether and to what extent government and private individuals in some developing countries judge that

(1) certain needs in social, economic and political development can be satisfactorily met, only if opportunities for study in industrialised countries such as Britain continue to be available;

(2) meeting these needs will be hindered by recent British policy on the fees to be charged to foreign students, including those from developing countries.

It was hoped to form a sample of countries satisfying the following desiderata:

(1) more than 200 students in Britain;
(2) representation from Africa, Asia and South America;
(3) some representation from other than Anglophone countries;
(4) representation from a range of groups in per capita GNP;
(5) representation from the Organisation of Petroleum Exporting Countries (OPEC);
(6) representation from a wide range of population sizes.

* The assistance of a large number of colleagues was necessary for the preparation of this paper. They are Caroline Alison, Geoffrey Coyne, Rupert Caine, Brian Haughton, Neil Killingbeck, Kevin Lillis, Summit Roy and Jamil Salmi. The British Council through its statistical office and a number of Representatives abroad gave considerable help in getting figures and qualitative information. Richard Jolly and Peter Williams supplied many helpful comments and suggestions. For all this the author remains heavily obliged.

In the event a group of ten countries was achieved, which met all the criteria, except one aspect of the last. It did not prove possible for various reasons to study a state with less than a million population. The smallest country examined was Malawi, which has some 5·5 million people. A very crude index of the importance of this omission can be derived from the fifty states and territories associated with Britain through the Commonwealth and other colonial ties. Thirty of them have populations of less than a million, while twenty have more than a million. If a ratio is calculated of the number of students these countries had in Britain in 1977/78 per 1000 in the age group 20–24 years in their own populations, the smaller (with populations under a million) had an average of 9·1 students, against an average of 2·2 students for the larger. Among the smaller, the ranges were from 0·67 for Tonga to 55·0 for Gibraltar; while among the larger, they were from 0·02 for India to 10·5 for Malaysia (see Appendix Table B.3). The obvious inference is that the smaller developing countries probably need to use foreign educational facilities to a much greater extent than do the larger, for reasons which can be readily conjectured. Their omission from this sample then entails the neglect of the views of a group of some 40–50 states and territories more keenly interested than most in the cost of foreign study.

The ten countries studied were Algeria, Bangladesh, India, Malawi, Malaysia, Nigeria, Tanzania, Thailand, Turkey and Venezuela. The means of study were the national development plans of each of the ten states, together with such reports as were available on requirements and provisions of manpower, supplemented by interviews with eight of the embassies and high commissions concerned. Additional statistics and opinions were gained from the British Council's offices in the countries themselves.

The Context of Study Abroad
Countries are called *developing* in part because there is a presumption that they and their governments have given a high priority to social and economic development. Two prominent features of development policies have been the attempt rationally to plan development and the heavy involvement of the state itself not only in guiding and fostering development, but also in undertaking substantial development programmes of its own.

They are common to all political ideologies and mixtures of state and private effort. That the thoroughness and effectiveness of planning are markedly variable does not matter as much as the fact that the need to plan is acknowledged and attempts to plan are made.

Planning and its implementation are dependent on – among other things – technical expertise. They depend also on the ability of people to administer complex institutions, to evaluate new ideas and to respond to training; in a word, on the competence and quality of a country's human resources. Governments of all shades of opinion have acknowledged this. Accordingly, manpower planning of some sort has become an established area of development planning.

The major instruments for producing the manpower planned have been schools, universities and kindred institutions, so that educational planning has been closely, but not wholly linked to manpower needs. Like the industrialised states, indeed in emulation of them, developing countries have expanded their educational systems very rapidly. Many now spend larger proportions of their national budgets on education than do their industrialised counterparts. In particular, developing states have been and are acutely and explicitly aware that scarcities of professional and managerial personnel hamper their efforts at development. Heavy investments have accordingly been made in institutions to form high level manpower, mainly universities. Other expedients have been tried also, among them study in foreign countries.

Such study sponsored by governments has been marked by three large purposes. The first might be termed gap-filling or the quest rapidly to supply identified deficiencies of expertise through obtaining training at established foreign centres. The second is enhancing the quality of manpower already in place through forms of in-service training conducted abroad. The third is maintaining access to the technologies of the industrialised countries and attempting to prevent the technological lags from widening.

The purpose of recalling these well known facts is simply to establish a presumption that, for governments of developing states, study abroad is a component and deliberate extension of widely agreed judgements and policies on what best produces the high level manpower needed for social and economic development. It may serve other purposes as well, openly or surreptitiously. Nevertheless, the presumption of policy and plan remains. Correspondingly, events which hinder study abroad can be viewed *prima facie* as impediments to social and economic development.

The Assessment of Needs for Study Abroad

All ten states in our case studies conform to the pattern outlined above. All follow policies of considerable state intervention in the economy and hence try to plan their development. Their intentions and programmes are published in periodic national development plans issued by central planning offices. As regards manpower for development, each has a ministry, commission, high level committee or other specialised unit charged with the oversight of manpower needs and provisions, together with a ministry of education, which in some cases is the largest spending unit of the government. Their development plans then contain estimates of the kinds of manpower required, the likely output from the educational and training institutions within the country and the likely shortfalls or surpluses. This is not to claim that all ten states are satisfied, let alone complacent, about the accuracy and reliability of their estimates. Some are more thorough than others and some readily acknowledge imperfections and failures. Nevertheless, all attempt manpower and educational planning.

All ten states see development substantially in terms of industrialisation, agricultural expansion, advancing technology, enhanced physical welfare and improved management. These goals entail an emphasis on scientific and technical manpower, as well as on a basically literate and numerate population. Consequently, along with the expansion of primary schooling professionally oriented education is universally stressed. As part of this approach all have invested heavily in universities, polytechnics, institutes of management and the like.

Concomitantly, self-sufficiency in the possession and generation of skilled manpower is an objective common to all ten, although only one, India, appears to feel comfortably close to its achievement. Despite the investments in educational institutions and the swelling numbers of educated persons, the problem of the 'receding horizon' inheres in the process of economic growth itself: if an economy expands rapidly, its needs for skilled manpower seem persistently to outpace the capacity of its own education and training system to satisfy them. Eight of the states examined have attained economic growth rates in excess of 5% per annum during the period 1970–77, while the three OPEC states have of course enjoyed the additional advantage of plentiful and easily mobilised funds. The ability to invest rapidly in new enterprises has of course underlined the scarcity of specialised skills and the lack of local capacity to produce them readily.

It is in circumstances such as these that governments assess the needs for some of their nationals to go abroad to obtain expertise. All ten share the view that study abroad serves the three functions mentioned earlier. Additionally, of course, it helps build the bases on which the state can construct its own facilities for high level education and training. For a state such as Malawi which is both relatively small and poor, it also provides an option where local facilities would simply not be viable, even if needed. This point would naturally be even more acute in the cases of the very small developing states, whose views are not reflected here.

In regard to filling gaps and enhancing quality, nine of the states envisage *expanding* absolute use of study abroad in at least the short and medium terms, although because of the simultaneous expansion of domestic provision, it will decline as a proportion of the total educational effort. No precise estimate could be located for any of the ten states, however. At the same time, the composition of study abroad will alter from year to year, as states become self-sufficient in particular areas and devote their resources to others. Indeed, it is policy in many to discourage study abroad in subjects which are satisfactorily provided for at home, but the forms of discouragement vary according to the political ideology and circumstances of the government, as will be seen later. In all cases, however, government assistance is not provided for external study, for which domestic facilities are adequate, or which is not judged necessary for national development. In effect, then, study abroad is treated as a residual. It is vital – the Venezuelan authorities used the word *indispensable* – in fact will probably increase, but is essentially transitional.

The bias towards professional scientific and technical studies noted earlier in domestic educational policies is stressed even more in study abroad. It is reflected strongly in the British Council's statistics on overseas students: in 1977/78 almost three-quarters of them were in such fields. A Nigerian has put the view succinctly, 'Knowledge for its own sake must be regarded with suspicion in a developing country, for it undermines the need to use knowledge for a purpose'.[1] For its part, India allows foreign exchange for study abroad, only if what is to be studied is included in a schedule issued to the central bank. A further symptom is the even distribution in UK universities between postgraduate and undergraduate enrolments among overseas students. In our sample of ten states, the overall ratio is 40 postgraduates to 60 undergraduates. However, if the very special case of Malaysia is removed, the ratio inverts itself to 67 postgraduates to 33 undergraduates. For six of the countries, the postgraduates heavily outnumber the undergraduates, for three the numbers correspond with the overall UK ratio for overseas students, about 50 : 50, and for only one, Malaysia, do the undergraduates outnumber the postgraduates – by nearly five to one.

In connection with assessing needs for study abroad, a brief note may be made of the issues of wastage and cultural dependence. On wastage, through the brain-drain for example, none of the authorities interviewed expressed concern nor have their governments introduced measures to control it. In seven of the cases, there were mechanisms for bonding – Thailand and Turkey expect two years in government service for every year of study abroad – or guarantee. On cultural dependence, only two states inclined to regard study abroad as a necessary evil rather than as both necessary and desirable. The remainder declared it a tradition with many merits which should endure, although its current levels may well be reduced, when urgent needs have been satisfied. Similarly, neither our informants nor the governments of the states concerned appeared to attach much weight to the possibility that study overseas might deprive their own educational institutions of their countries' best talents.

The Choice of Countries and Institutions for Study Abroad

To what extent does the attempt to plan manpower and hence study abroad lead governments to assess countries and particular institutions for their suitability? A first step in answering this query is to note that opportunities for study abroad arise from three sources, namely governments themselves, programmes of technical co-operation with industrial countries and private funding. Only when funds are found by themselves do governments have the option of completely selecting countries and institutions for study. Even so, only two governments do this with any strictness. One has arrangements with seven 'acceptable' industrialised states, whereby its students are paid for by itself and placed in institutions appraised by itself. The other eight appear to be content to award scholarships and to leave it to the holders to secure themselves places in 'acceptable' countries and in appropriately accredited institutions. Three governments do, however, strive to monitor the quality of various institutions, in order to be able to advise their students. One does the monitoring through tracing the post-graduation performance of students. By and large the governments appear to have a generalised confidence in the standards of recognised institutions in industrialised countries and so do not attempt to direct their students closely. At least two of them acknowledged that, with the resources at their disposal, such direction would be beyond their capacity. Planning at this level, then, is chiefly indicative.

Similar policies seem to obtain in the cases of scholarships from international organisations awarded under government sponsorship, although here of course the organisation usually influences where the award should be taken up.

Where opportunities for study abroad arise from programmes of technical co-operation, they are almost invariably tenable only in the country of the donor government. The limit of planning open to the developing country is the choice of a co-operator and the specification of the fields which the study should pursue. The co-operator itself usually gives considerable guidance on appropriate institutions, although, as the ODA evaluations suggest, perfect matches between stated needs and courses offered do not always occur even then.

Privately funded students are, as would be expected, left to choose their own country and institution of study. The survey recently commissioned for the Overseas Students Trust (Appendix A) suggests that they do not get much advice or other help in making their choices. Nevertheless, these are restricted by subject of study in four states and by the acceptability of the country chosen in six states. It is perhaps as well to remark that acceptability here refers to political factors, rather than to considerations of manpower development.

The issue of political acceptability raises the question of the non-technical criteria which affect the selection of countries and institutions for study abroad.

The first of these are the historical links between sending and receiving countries. In our sample, the six Commonwealth countries mentioned these as a factor, but they appeared important also for Thailand. They consist not merely of sentiment and, for a minority of influential people, family connections but more solidly also of reciprocal knowledge and understanding – although of course this is a basis which time is eroding. It is important, for instance, that much documentation on the Commonwealth countries is more plentiful and more accessible in Britain than in the sending countries themselves. On the other hand, the facts that in 1975/76 only a fifth of Nigerian students, a tenth of Indian students and only 4% of Thai students overseas were in Britain – three, six and sixteen times as many were in the USA – indicate that other influences are more powerfully at work.

The second criterion not directly tied to subject of study is the language of tuition. Where the language of a receiving country is at least a second or official language of a sending state, the attraction to study there is reinforced. Thai students, for instance, are able to use facilities in the Philippines and India, in addition to more obvious centres such as the USA, Australia and Britain. (Indeed, more Thai students go to those two countries than come to Britain, a fact which doubtless reflects both the level of entry qualifications required and the element of costs, to be discussed in a moment.) Nevertheless, as the numbers of students going to Russia, the two Germanies, Poland and similar countries suggest, the necessity of learning a language which cannot readily be used at home is not an insurmountable obstacle to overseas study.

The third criterion is cost. All ten countries suggest that cost is a secondary factor, but an important one all the same. Where a course is necessary and obtainable from only one source, the price will be paid. But where sources of similar quality are also available, the policy is to choose the cheapest. Three states mentioned that the term *costs* indicates not solely the tuition fee. The duration of a course, e.g. a three-year rather than a four-year degree, and the living costs in a receiving country are also elements which are taken into account when a sending government supports a student out of its own funds. Presumably they are also scrutinised by families and other sponsors of private students.

Despite this evidence of attempts to match local needs with the instruction offered by institutions in industrialised countries, disappointments and absurdities do occur. They arise in part from the limitations of the machinery available to the governments of developing countries, partly from the imperfect information available to aspiring students – Professor Blaug's study (Chapter 3 of this book) illustrates this – partly from inexplicable slips in search and negotiation,[2] and partly from the difficulties of accommodating the circumstances of developing countries in courses primarily designed for industrial ones.[3] Nevertheless, in sum, the selection of countries and institutions for overseas study is broadly consistent with the planned priorities of political, economic and technological development and the consequent needs for high level manpower.

Selecting Students for Overseas Study

In keeping with the notion of planned manpower development, selections for study abroad are not confined to young students preparing for careers, but include a large element of in-service career development for the employees of governmental, parastatal and private organisations. An example may be taken from Thailand again: in 1977, of the 2685 people studying abroad under government sponsorship, 2267 were officials on leave.[4] Similar proportions obtain for Bangladesh, Malawi and Tanzania. Enhancing the quality of people already on the job remains important.

In the case of pre-career study, methods of selection vary. In Turkey candidates must have achieved a certain mark in a national examination; in India and Thailand competitive examinations are held, which are believed to ensure a high calibre of student; in

Nigeria, official advertisements invite applications for bursaries for study at home or abroad in a wide range of subjects and special committees subsequently select the recipients.

Bursaries for officials are awarded in the recognition both that many officers have educational backgrounds which do not meet current standards and that further study should improve efficiency and productivity. Indeed, the ten governments appear to be generous in their allowances for leave to study either locally or abroad. The overseas bursaries tend to be awarded more by nomination than by competition and often follow a plan for career development. Accordingly, they tend to be closely linked to the functions of a particular department. With technical co-operation programmes they are often linked to particular projects. This is not to say that all training or education is applied to the purposes for which it was obtained: the tendency for officials to be moved or promoted to new duties with fair frequency makes it difficult to guarantee this. Neither is it to claim that the bursaries always go to the best available candidates, for it is acknowledged that the proclivity of bureaucracies to give precedence to seniority is not easily resisted. Nonetheless, the evidence indicates an identifiable and firm basis of purposeful-ness underlying the selection of both officials and non-officials for study abroad. (In this connection, it is pertinent to recall the use of bonding by seven of the governments to ensure some return to the state from the studies undertaken.)

The data available seem to suggest that poorer governments tend to concentrate more on in-service upgrading than on pre-career preparation. Bangladesh, Malawi, Tanzania and Thailand appear not to have the means to finance much pre-career study, whereas Algeria, Malaysia, Nigeria, Turkey and Venezuela do. One inference from this is that states oriented to manpower planning tend to accord priority to improving the manpower already in place, before alloca-ting resources to pre-career preparation. If this is indeed so, then raising the costs of study abroad makes manpower development for the poorer governments more difficult in two ways: it may force a reduction in the opportunities for enhancing the quality of official cadres and it may simultaneously delay the possibilities of opening pre-career programmes.

Financing Study Overseas
Whatever the accuracy of the preceding paragraph, the issue of finance affects matters powerfully. The three OPEC states in our sample and Malaysia finance a good deal of study overseas out of their own funds and put little reliance on external sources.

By contrast, one country can at present finance no overseas study and relies wholly on technical co-operation and two others finance smaller volumes than they would wish. Another two finance a fair quantity – Turkey's expenditure on postgraduate study abroad in 1978 was equivalent to roughly half the budget for higher education – but also actively seek outside help to supplement their efforts; while India, judging that its own facilities are well developed and indeed used by considerable numbers of students from other countries, finances some study abroad but officially does not actively seek outside assistance. Apart from India, whose official reason for not using much study abroad is not a lack of financial resources, but rather a sufficiency of domestic educational ones, the association between national wealth and the utilisation of study abroad seems strong. This inference receives some support from Table 6.1, which displays the results of a superficial exercise at correlating the wealth of groups of states with the numbers of their students in the UK in 1977. It will be seen that the correlations, while by no means overwhelming and even a bit odd, are not negligible.

Table 6.1   Product-moment correlations between overseas students in Britain and GNP per capita

Country group	Number of countries	I %S: GNPpc	II %S: GNPpc growth rate
Commonwealth	45[a]	0·40	0·14
Asian non-Commonwealth	18	0·15	0·78
Francophone	26	0·49	0·35
Latin American	24	0·53	−0·21

Notes: %S = Students in UK as a proportion of the total population of a sending country in 1977
GNPpc = gross national product per capita in 1977
GNPpc growth rate = the growth rate of the gross national product per capita between 1970 and 1977
[a]This number includes Australia, Bermuda, Brunei, Canada and New Zealand. Their exclusion affects the correlation only slightly.
Sources: British Council, 1979, *Statistics of Overseas Students in Britain 1977/78*; World Bank, 1980, *Atlas of Population and Income 1979*.

By and large, poorer states appear less able to use study abroad to supplement their efforts at manpower development. If they are judged to be most in need of it, then making study abroad more expensive further diminishes their capacity to avail themselves of it.

All ten states were willing to accept assistance from other governments for study abroad, if it were negotiated through official channels. Nine were willing to accept help from unofficial sources, while one discouraged it. Three of the nine, though positive, were careful about it and kept it under scrutiny. The remaining six appeared to adopt an open stance, welcoming help from any reputable quarter. Only three, Bangladesh, Thailand and Turkey, appeared actively to encourage and seek outside funds, even from unofficial sources; although six judged that the need and demand for overseas study was greater than they could meet. Nevertheless, at least one state, Tanzania, frequently did not utilise all the bursaries at its disposal. The reasons appeared to be mainly administrative. Still, the tendency of the richer states to invest more in study abroad lends support to the probability that demand does outstrip supply.

If such is the case, what are the governments' attitudes to students who go abroad financed by their families or other private sources?

Privately Financed Students
Only one of the ten states, Algeria, appears frankly to discourage private students, but not totally disbar them, from study abroad. It creates procedural difficulties, is reluctant to grant foreign exchange and will not guarantee recognition of foreign credentials. The remaining nine take more positive stances, although they divide into two groups, one of six which put no restrictions on private study by either subject or foreign exchange – one indeed accords private students a privileged rate of exchange, provided they are properly recognised by the ministry of education – the second of three states, Bangladesh, India and Tanzania, which make the provision of foreign exchange conditional upon the subject to be studied.

Such practices are of course consistent with the views mentioned earlier that study abroad was to be encouraged. None of the nine states appears to feel that providing foreign exchange for private students is a serious diversion of resources from development programmes, nor do they judge that graduates from study abroad have on balance an adverse affect on their societies. On the contrary, five states aver that private resources devoted to study abroad are a valuable, even necessary, supplement to the government's. All nine point out that the largest proportions of private students are in fact studying in those same fields in which officially sponsored students also tend to cluster, although perhaps higher proportions of private students are to be found in such areas as business studies, accountancy and the like. That is to say, a substantial overlap between the manpower priorities of governments and the choices of private students is perceived and welcomed.

Further, in six states, foreign degrees and diplomas are acknowledged to carry extra weight, especially with private employers, so that graduates from study abroad are thought to have little difficulty in securing employment. This would seem to argue that they are indeed meeting manpower needs and can legitimately be regarded as helpful adjuncts to government policy.

As regards numbers and proportions of private students among those who study abroad, there appears to be some relationship between them, the population and the GNP per capita of a country. Thus relatively small, poor countries with small sectors of industry and commerce seem to have lower proportions of private students, than those which are either richer or larger with consequently larger – in absolute terms – modern sectors. Failing reliable data, the estimates are:

Country group	*Proportion of private students* (%)
Small, poor – Malawi, Tanzania	35–50
Large, poor – Bangladesh, India, Thailand	60–70
Richer – Malaysia, Nigeria, Turkey, Venezuela	75–90

It should be noted, however, that Bangladesh is a special case. Our information is that almost no private students are financed from sources within Bangladesh itself, but support tends to come from expatriate Bangladeshi communities. This fact helps to explain the concentration – small though it is – of Bangladeshi students in Britain rather than, as in the case of India, in the USA, and may help explain the increasing numbers of Bangladeshis studying abroad.

If these estimates are in any way reliable, they suggest that making study abroad more expensive will reduce the private as well as the government capacity of poorer states to use it.

Views on Recent Rises in British Fees

As the survey of Appendix A substantiates, reasons for choosing Britain as a place to study are diverse. The main one, consistently enough, is the fact that Britain is an industrialised country with much of the expertise which developing countries want their own manpower to possess. It is supplemented by a respect for the quality of Britain's educational institutions, by historical links, by the hitherto low cost of studying here. Nevertheless, eight of the states in our sample pointed out that Britain was after all neither a unique nor even a prime source of the expertise needed. As the examples of India and Nigeria suggested, Britain could be displaced as the main locus for study abroad even for states with strong historical ties, a common language and virtually a common educational system. Hence, states and private individuals attempting to invest their resources optimally must review their judgements on studying in Britain.

Only Malaysia and Thailand felt strongly enough to put their adverse views before Parliament. The Commonwealth governments are reported to have expressed their deep regret at the Ministers of Education Conference in August 1980. Informal intimations both in London and in the capitals of the ten states deplored the decision to raise fees by such a considerable margin, without at the same time making any attempt to recognise, let alone accommodate, the reasoned policies of developing countries.

The predictions were – with two exceptions – that the governments concerned would not alter their general expansionist policies on study abroad, but would certainly seek alternatives to Britain. This would apply even more strongly to private students. Further, the example Britain has set to other industrialised countries may well spur developing states to accelerate their efforts towards self-sufficiency, possibly at the cost of distorting their development priorities.

The two exceptions were Bangladesh and Malawi. In the first, fears were expressed that the incapacity of both state and private sectors to support study abroad and the dependence on aid of Bangladeshis resident in Britain would bring about a further steep fall in the numbers of students outside the country. For Malawi, similarly, the dependence on aid and particularly the British programme of technical co-operation led to the hope that donors would maintain their programmes in terms of *places* for study and not in terms of simple cash.

Information from India tended to substantiate the forecast that developing countries would search for alternatives to Britain. 'A flood' of Iranian students have already applied to transfer from British to Indian institutions and there appears a possibility that, in order to meet these new demands, India will attempt to import British lecturers!

Conclusion

Those who have worked in the government offices of a number of developing countries may well have reservations about the real meaning of words such as *development, development planning, education, manpower planning, high level manpower, implementation, coordination, control, quality* and other such. They may also harbour an envious respect for the skill with which private interests are pursued contrary to public policy, especially perhaps in the fields of education and the development of high level manpower. Such uncertainty notwithstanding, it remains a fact that the ten states studied in this paper do put official store by planning and, with wide variations between them, have made some attempt to give the notion substance. Planning manpower, expanding education and concomitantly fostering study abroad have been part of their efforts to promote and accelerate socioeconomic development. The obvious corollary is that to make study abroad more difficult is to hamper what they see as developmental effort.

Despite considerable investment and expansion at all levels of their own educational and training systems, nine of these states judge that they are not yet able to dispense with study abroad. On the contrary, the economically more successful of them judge that they will need more rather than less of it for the foreseeable future, because they seem to have found that economic growth entails needs for volumes and types of manpower that their own systems cannot produce rapidly enough.

For the longer run, however, they envisage the tailing off of the two currently major purposes of study abroad, namely, filling gaps in their manpower resources and enhancing the quality of manpower already in place. The third purpose, maintaining access to technological advances, is seen as a permanent feature but will be pursued on a much smaller scale than the first two.

None of the ten governments appears seriously concerned about the possible ill effects of study abroad. What controls some of them exercise by way of travel permits, foreign exchange, choice of 'acceptable' countries and institutions, bonding and family guarantees appear to them sufficient. Issues of cultural, ideological and technological dependence, cultural alienation, inappropriate transfers of technology, brain drain seem not to loom large for most: the possible disadvantages are judged to be outweighed by the benefits. Only two governments tend to view study abroad as a necessary evil.

Consistent with the emphasis on planning, governments which are applying resources under at least their partial control, tend to guide the choice of subjects to be studied. Some of course give stronger guidance than others. The governments with more restricted resources tend to give more weight to in-service training or enhancing quality than to pre-career preparation or gap-filling.

All ten governments permit students to be financed from private sources. Only one frowns on such efforts, although others do attempt to influence the choice of subject. Nine judge that the private resources applied to study abroad are a useful supplement to official programmes, and four actively encourage private study. The fact that people who study abroad seem to find employment relatively easily is viewed as confirming the probability that most private study conforms to national manpower needs.

Both governments and private individuals from poorer countries seemed unable to make as much use of study abroad as their counterparts in richer countries.

Not surprisingly, then, the general reaction to the severe rises in the fees for British higher education is strongly adverse. The British Government appears to be contradicting its own official policy of assisting developing countries to become self-reliant. Indeed, it is deliberately making matters more difficult for them.

The unanimous assessment was that both governments and private citizens from developing countries would respond to the British step by seeking to satisfy their needs in countries other than Britain. There was some feeling also that a repercussion of the British example might be the distortion of development priorities. Fearing that other industrialised states might find the lead attractive, developing states might accelerate their domestic programmes to produce high level manpower, possibly at the cost of other, equally important, developments.

Notes

1. B. A. Ogundimo in *Centrepoint*, Vol. 1, no. 1, October 1977, p. 65.
2. See, for example, B. E. Cracknell, R. Stonemann and R. B. W. Haines, *An Evaluation of the Training received by Bangladesh Study Fellows in the UK*, London, Ministry of Overseas Development, 1977, pp. 17f.
3. See, for example, T. Maliyamkono, *Policy Developments in Overseas Training*, Dar es Salaam, Black Star Agencies, 1980, p. 1.
4. J. K. Johnson, *Thailand*, World Education Services, 1977, Appendix C.

7. Foreign Student Flows and Policies in an International Perspective*

by Alan Smith, Christine Woesler de Panafieu and Jean-Pierre Jarousse

Part I   Foreign Students – A Growing Problem for Higher Education Policy?

Introduction: general situation and trends

In 1980 the total number of foreign students worldwide has in all probability approached the million mark, for by 1976 (the year for which most comprehensive data are available) the figure had already reached 800,000 – over three times the 240,000 registered just twenty years ago (see Table 7.3). True, the world's total student population has also shown a threefold increase over the same period,[1] so that at first sight it might appear as though there had been no disproportionate rise in international student mobility.

*The present study is the result of research carried out during 1980 by the Institute of Education of the European Cultural Foundation (Paris/Brussels). Initiated and sponsored by the Overseas Students Trust, the study has also received generous financial and material support from the Commission of the European Communities, the Council of Europe and the German Academic Exchange Service – an indication of the increasing interest being shown in foreign student matters at both national and international level. In addition to the organisations mentioned above, the Institute would like to thank the many other experts and bodies, too numerous to mention individually, in the countries under review, who provided information and advice. This presentation represents a condensed version of the complete study, which besides the elements included here comprises detailed country reports on France, Belgium, Switzerland and the United Kingdom, as well as some seventy-five pages of tables based mainly on Unesco statistics. The Institute hopes to publish some or all of this material shortly. As published in its present form, the study consists of the material in Chapter 7 plus Tables B.4–8 which have for convenience been included in the statistical Appendix at the back of this book. Christine Woesler carried out the analysis of Unesco statistics, wrote the first draft of the main report and compiled a country study on Switzerland; Jean-Pierre Jarousse wrote country studies on France, Belgium and the UK and contributed much to Part III of the main report; while Alan Smith, who directed the project, revised, edited and enlarged the main report, incorporating into it some of the main findings of the country studies.

Thanks are also due to Martine Herlant and Manuel Stocker of the Institute's Brussels Office, who assisted the authors in respect of the data on Austria/Federal Republic of Germany and in revising the tables respectively, and the Institute's secretarial staff for their meticulous preparation of the final manuscript.

Nonetheless, foreign students have been increasingly becoming a problem area for higher education policy in recent years. How many foreign students should be admitted? How many of them should come from which parts of the world? Should measures be adopted to restrict or promote foreign student access in specific sectors? Questions such as these – linked not least to efforts aimed at making higher education more economically efficient and perhaps also to the trend towards higher un- and under-employment of graduates – have become typical of the higher education debate in many industrialised countries.

With this situation in mind, the present study seeks to analyse the quantitative development of student mobility worldwide in the last twenty years, and to identify some of the more significant policy trends of recent years with respect to foreign student admissions. For this purpose, the following twenty-four host countries have been examined, using the only comprehensive comparative data available, i.e. those collated by Unesco, plus additional material specially solicited for the study on a reduced number of countries, notably those marked with an asterisk:

Austria*	Japan
Belgium*	Luxemburg
Canada	Netherlands
Czechoslovakia	Norway
Denmark	Portugal
Finland	Spain
France*	Sweden
Germany* (Fed. Rep.)	Switzerland*
Germany (Dem. Rep.)	Turkey
Greece	United Kingdom*
Ireland	USA*
Italy	USSR

This was no random choice. Our study is concerned with inward rather than outward flows, and in 1976 these countries were playing host to 80% of all foreign students enrolled worldwide. Almost 60% of the world total were registered at higher education institutions in just five of them, namely the USA, France, the UK, the Federal Republic of Germany and Canada. By contrast, students coming *from* these twenty-four countries accounted for less than 30% of the total number of foreign students worldwide in the same year and only nine of the twenty-four countries figure among the world's twenty-one nations which exported over 10,000 students each in 1976.

As Table 7.1 shows, the great majority of foreign students come from developing countries, Asian students alone accounting for some 40% of the world total and, as we shall see later in the study, their growth rates have generally been significantly higher than those for students coming from industrialised countries in recent years.

Table 7.1   Foreign students by continent of origin

Continent of origin	Total 1970	Total 1976	Percentage 1970	Percentage 1976	Average annual growth rate (%) 1970–76
Africa	50553	115077	10·6	16·3	14·7
Asia	195910	280811	41·0	39·8	7·7
North America	61426	79392	12·6	11·3	4·4
South America	26283	42218	5·5	6·0	8·2
Europe	90254	144535	18·9	20·5	8·0
Total	424426	662033	88·9	93·9	
World total[a]	477837	705222	100·0	100·0	6·7

Note: [a]This sum includes 90–95% of the world total foreign student population.
Source: Unesco *Statistical Yearbook*, 1972, 1978/9 editions

Worldwide student mobility, therefore, tends to be characterised by one-way traffic rather than reciprocal flows, or by immigration rather than exchange as the discussion of the phenomenon of 'brain-drain' of scientific and technical personnel from the developing to the industrialised countries has shown:

Statistics of the Federal Labour Agency show more than 82,000 employees from non-European countries (excluding Turkey) putting their work capacity, their knowledge and their skill at the disposal of German firms, hospitals or scientific institutes.[2]

Furthermore, facilitating study abroad is still a far more practicable proposition, not least in economic terms, for many developing countries than a correspondingly rapid growth of higher education provision at home, particularly in that primary and secondary education are often considered to have immediate priority. Thus these countries tend to seek ways and means of curbing the 'brain-drain' rather than curtailing study abroad as such, and the 'search for educational advantage' may therefore correspond both to national policy aims and to those of the individual students concerned, who see study abroad as a means of enhancing their future employment prospects. Therefore in recent years there has been an increasing shift of emphasis towards the economic aspects of study abroad at the expense of the more cultural policy-oriented aspects of the problem often prevalent even into the early 1970s.

Accordingly, whereas most of the publications dealing with 'foreign students' a decade ago tended to treat the subject mainly from a socio-psychological perspective, against the background of the conviction that study abroad was mainly of cultural value and contributed to the development of the cosmopolitan citizen,[3] more recently

> Economic benefits have been substituted for cultural benefits and the role of study abroad in producing the classic cosmopolitan, cultured individual has been subordinated to its role in providing 'needed' skills that can be used by nations at home in the development process.[4]

For the host countries, too, economic considerations have begun to play an increasingly significant role in the discussion on policies to be adopted with regard to foreign student access. The rising cost of higher education provision, the increasing difficulty of meeting demand for places in certain disciplines (notably medicine and pharmacy), rising graduate unemployment and the realisation that certain developing countries, notably those belonging to the OPEC group, had suddenly reached such a level of affluence as to render them less dependent on free higher education elsewhere – all these factors and others besides have led to the introduction of various forms of restrictive measures.

At the same time, attention is increasingly drawn to the vital necessity of maintaining and further developing the international flow of students – again with frequent reference to the international ramifications of political and economic affairs in the modern world. This is particularly true of the relatively meagre student mobility between the industrialised countries which will be discussed in a separate section below.

In general, it may be said that the growing attention devoted to foreign student access is increasingly giving rise in the host countries to a call for more 'reciprocity' in student mobility where this is feasible, or the ascendancy of the view that more of the cost should be met by the foreign students themselves or the authorities of their country of origin. Since this is clearly less practicable with regard to certain countries of origin than others, we are currently witnessing a trend towards a more 'differentiated' approach to foreign student admissions, implying a greater degree of adaptability of higher education provision to both the needs and economic strength of the foreign students' home countries.

The move from 'open' to 'regulative' and 'differentiated' admission policies for foreign students

The diversity of and increasingly rapidly changing regulations pertaining to higher education access for foreign students make it difficult to identify trends common to all the countries under review – all the more considering the relative scarcity of up-to-date comparative material on this topic.[5] Nonetheless, certain tendencies relating to groups of countries may be observed.

As pointed out in the Introduction above, we may say that open, uncontrolled systems of access for all students fulfilling basic admission requirements have in general tended to become less and less usual in recent years, even though, as Cerych has pointed out,[6] increased restrictions on one sector of higher education are sometimes counter-balanced by a slackening of restrictions in others. Particularly severe have tended to be admission restrictions in the field of medicine and allied subjects, and even countries that have largely preserved an open access system, such as Italy and Spain, are now actively considering the introduction of restrictions in this sector.[7]

Foreign student admission policies have not been left unscathed by such developments, and a variety of regulative measures have been introduced. The form that such measures may take, differs considerably. In general, however, they fall into two categories, one or other or both of which may be operated by a given host country at a given time:

(i) a severe tightening of academic or other admission requirements, often linked to a quantified admissions system whereby only a restricted number of students are admitted (*numerus clausus*);
(ii) the imposition or significant raising of tuition fees.

In brief, access is being made more difficult and/or more costly, while an attempt is increasingly being made as noted above to treat different categories of foreign student applicants in different ways. These two approaches to regulating flows – curtailing numbers and imposing fees – should be discussed in a little more detail.

Numerical limitations on enrolments and the tightening of admission requirements and procedures

Numerical restrictions of one kind or another now exist, at least in certain subject fields, in most of the countries under review, and in some, such as the Federal Republic of Germany, Denmark and the Netherlands, various types of 'quota' systems have been developed. Such systems normally affect both 'home' and 'foreign' students, the quota often varying from subject to subject and sometimes according to the origin of the foreign students concerned. In the Federal Republic of Germany, for example, up to 6% of all available places are reserved for foreign students in the fields subject to the highest imbalance between demand for and supply of places, namely the medical and allied fields, while up to 8% are set aside in agriculture, architecture, biology, forestry, home economics, nutritional science, food chemistry and psychology. In Denmark, foreign student quotas are currently set at 10% in medicine and allied disciplines and 20% in the social sciences.

Nationwide quotas are, of course, difficult to operate unless there are structures for nationwide legislation or control. The latter conditions are typically fulfilled in the Federal Republic of Germany where, although the decision to admit or reject the individual foreign student rests with the individual admitting institution, overall admission policy is governed by law and guidelines for the application of restricted admissions for both 'home' and 'foreign' students have been promulgated by inter-state agreement among the 'Länder'.

Where such legislative powers are more limited or where governments choose not to exercise them, quotas may be 'recommended' to institutions and government funding to institutions oriented along the lines of the quotas concerned. This was the case in the United Kingdom when the Government sought in 1977/78 to establish a quota whereby foreign student enrolments would be effectively pegged back to 1975/76 numbers, by corresponding adjustments to the grant to institutions. (Opinions vary as to the efficacy of the measure in the British context, and since policy was changed again before it had had time to take full effect, the matter must remain unresolved.) Similar government strategy has been adopted in Switzerland, where no funding is provided to institutions to cover the costs incurred when foreign students comprise more than 17% of total enrolments in medicine and engineering.

Both Switzerland and Austria have been characterised in recent years by severe restrictions on foreign student access accompanied by attempts to exempt home students from such limitations. In both countries, foreign student admissions are a discretionary matter for the individual institutions, and this has led to marked variations in practice from one institution and subject to another. Thus in Switzerland, the University of Basle was reported as accepting no foreign students whatever in the 1980/81 academic year, and there are no places open at any universities for foreign candidates not resident in Switzerland wishing to embark upon a full course in medicine, dentistry or veterinary science. Local restrictions are common in pharmacy, psychology, and other fields. Similarly in Austria, where criteria for foreign student admission were newly formulated in 1975, the University for Veterinary Medicine in Vienna had a complete ban on new foreign enrolments in 1979/80, while the Universities of Vienna, Graz and Innsbruck adopted similar measures in medicine, certain natural sciences, journalism and psychology, with less severe restrictions in a number of other fields.[8]

The case of Austria is significant for another reason, too, for its policy is now to admit students from countries where numerical limitations are in operation, only in such cases where the candidates would also have been admitted in their home country. At the time of its introduction, this move gave rise to considerable debate, not least in the Council of Europe where it was the factor largely responsible for a reinterpretation of the Council's convention on the mutual recognition of admission qualifications dating back to 1953, and it is interesting that a similar measure was mooted in Italy in 1976/77 before eventually being retracted. '*Numerus clausus* mobility' – the 'knock-on effect' caused by the introduction of admission restrictions in a given country on the situation of its neighbours – has become an increasingly significant phenomenon in recent years, affecting international student flows and, as a result, influencing the formulation of policies and procedures on access. More will be said on this below.

Other countries, too, without actually stifling foreign student admissions at a given institution, have recently been introducing much severer selection mechanisms than hitherto. This is particularly true of France, which, like the two countries just mentioned, has traditionally enjoyed a reputation of being particularly generous about the admission of foreign students. At the end of 1979, the French Government, seeking, as it put it, to maintain the quality of both the foreign students admitted and of the education and services provided for them in France, but clearly also with a view to stemming the rising tide of foreign students discerned over the past few years, passed the so-called 'Imbert Decree'. This, with a certain delayed action effect, gave rise to widespread student demonstrations and clashes with the police during the summer term of 1980. This decree constitutes a marked tightening up of admission procedures. First, it requires that foreign students wishing to study in France pass a French language examination in their home country, thus reinforcing the system of *pré-inscription* (pre-registration) already introduced in 1974. Secondly, prospective entrants must give proof of having a bank account at their disposal containing sufficient resources for each phase of their course. Thirdly, the decree marks a radical centralisation of responsibility in the selection process itself: formerly a matter for each institution of higher education individually, the power to decide on whether or not a candidate from overseas shall be accepted or rejected, and at which institution he or she shall be registered, is henceforth invested in one single central commission chaired by the Director, M. Imbert – hence the name of the Decree – of the Centre National des Oeuvres Universitaires et Scolaires (CNOUS), a government-sponsored agency charged with the provision of social aid for students (university restaurant, work, accommodation and the administration of certain student grants).

The effects of this new French policy remain to be seen, both as regards foreign student enrolment in France itself and possible repercussions (knock-on effect) for neighbouring countries, in particular French-speaking Belgium, whose fee-waiving arrangements, as we shall see, make it potentially highly vulnerable.

In the Federal Republic of Germany, too, centralised procedures have been adopted in respect of admission for foreign students to the so-called *numerus clausus* subjects. The Co-ordination Office for Foreign Student Admissions, established under the aegis of the West German Rectors Office and with a secretariat located at the German Academic Exchange Service Headquarters, differs from its French counterpart, however, in two important respects. First, it is the result of voluntary action taken by the institutions; and secondly, its function is fundamentally distributive, designed to ensure an even spread of foreign students across the country in the particularly over-subscribed disciplines and thereby to make optimal use of the overall quota laid down nationally, whereas the individual institutions are still, formally at least, at liberty to take the final decision on a candidate's admission or rejection. In this sense, one might describe the German system as a half-way house between the purely clearing-house concept of the Universities Central Council on Admissions in the UK and the discretionary powers invested in the new central committee in France.

Regulation via 'market processes': the imposition of tuition fees

A second form of regulative measure on the influx of foreign students is that of the imposition of relatively high tuition fees. This is typically the case in countries such as the USA, Canada, the United Kingdom and Ireland, where fee income traditionally represents a significant proportion of institutional revenue. Such fees are, of course, payable by all students, but recent years have seen the introduction of increasingly sizeable differentials between fees for home and foreign students, whatever definition of the latter is adopted, much as many US state institutions have tended to distinguish between their 'in-state' and 'out-of-state' clientèles.

Government policy in the United Kingdom, in particular, has been directed towards ensuring that foreign students pay for a much larger proportion of their higher education received than hitherto. According to official estimates, the British tax-payers' 'subsidy' to foreign students in higher education in 1978/79 amounted to some £102m, taking into account all recurrent expenditure (less fee income from foreign students) but not capital outlay. Foreign students are now to pay several times as much as home students for the same course, as Table 7.2 shows. As Table 7.2 also makes clear, the new recommendations provide for the important exception that students from other EC countries are to be treated on the same basis as those from Britain (with the difference, of course, that in the case of the latter the fees are generally offset by corresponding provision in the students' maintenance grants), while specific grant award schemes have been introduced to help in the case of certain categories of students from developing countries, more of which exceptions will be said in due course. Nonetheless, the imposition first of a differential and now of a notional 'full-cost fee' for foreign students has given rise to a public discussion of ever increasing intensity. In Parliament itself, the last four years have witnessed no fewer than fourteen debates on the subject.

We have termed the imposition of fees, and in particular differential fees, a 'regulative' measure, in the sense that it is a departure from complete equality of treatment for home and foreign students, and is also to be seen as symptomatic of a more conscious attitude towards the question of foreign student admissions. On the other hand, the policy objectives which such measures are designed to meet, may be diametrically opposed in relation to the desired effect on student flows from abroad. Britain is again a case in point, since whereas just two or three years ago the aim appeared to be one of curbing the influx, it may now be said to be one of even encouraging such an influx providing that the students concerned pay. Trends in the highly fee-oriented USA may provide a pointer here for the way things may develop. There, while on the one hand the conditions of access have in some instances, e.g. in medicine, been made more difficult for students from overseas and the immigration regulations tightened up, renewed efforts are being made in certain quarters to attract greater numbers of foreign

Table 7.2   Recommended tuition fees in the UK for 1980/81 (£)

Level/type of study	Home students and students from other EC Member States	Overseas students		
		Continuing in course already commenced	Starting new course (maintained sector)	Starting new course (universities[a])
Non-advanced further education	216	645	Laboratory/ workshop based: 1890 Classroom based: 1380	
Advanced further education/ undergraduate	740	1165	Lab/ workshop based: 3300	Arts 2000 Science 3000 Med[b] Vet 5000
Postgraduate	1105	1525	Classroom based: 2400	

Notes: [a] The figures for universities are minimum levels and actual fees in particular institutions could be higher. In all cases there will be no set level of fees for postgraduate courses, subject to the proviso that they are not lower than the undergraduate fee for that type of course.
          [b] Clinical years
Source: See table 2.5

students still. Between 1950 and 1976, the proportion of the total student population in the USA enrolled at private institutions of higher education, fell from 50% to just 21·5%,[10] and since the institutions concerned are largely dependent on fee income for their survival, recruitment of foreign students sometimes appears as a welcome means of filling up unused capacity. That this practice is a cause of concern, is clearly evidenced by the recent headline 'Abuses in Foreign Student Recruiting Tarnish US Colleges' Image Abroad',[11] and the Johnson Foundation's Wingspread Conference of 26–28 March 1980 even went so far as to establish an 'Ethics Code to Stem Abuses in Recruiting Foreign Students'.

The signs are that in the UK, the imposition of high level fees had significantly checked the growth in foreign student numbers by 1979, and the early indications are that with the advent of the full-cost fee, a substantial drop in new enrolments may be expected as of 1981/82, unless institutions are prepared to accept a decrease in quality of the students accepted: the UCCA has reported a 43% fall in the number of applications received by November 1980 compared with the same time in 1979.

Furthermore, 'regulation via market processes' may be demonstrated to have pushed the 'product' (study opportunities in the UK) beyond the means of the poorest 'customers': figures assembled by the World University Service[12] point to a marked decrease in the proportion of the foreign student population in the UK coming from countries in the lowest GNP per capita bracket according to OECD classification.

Both the UK and the USA are countries where income from student fees has traditionally been part of the budgetary fabric of higher education. In this respect, the imposition of (higher) fees for foreign students therefore comes as no great surprise. The same holds true for Ireland. In Belgium, on the other hand, the position is significantly different, for whereas – apart from a contribution to cover items such as social security and student activities (around £200 in the 1980/81 academic year at a major university in the private sector) – no significant fees have traditionally been payable, a system was introduced in 1976 whereby certain categories of foreign students are now required to pay considerable sums. Designed to meet the dual objective of checking the influx of students 'escaping' from neighbouring industrialised countries where restrictions on admission had been imposed (*numerus clausus* mobility) while at the same time maintaining the high level of support to students from the developing world, the Belgian measures prescribe payment of fees by almost all students from countries with a per capita GNP of more than $600 p.a., amounting to half the previous year's Ministry of Education grant per student to the institution and in the subject area concerned. In the current 1980/81 academic year, this means anything between £1200 for 'paper subjects' (e.g. the arts and social sciences) at one end of the scale, to over £3300 in clinical medicine. It may be said that the Belgian measures have been successful in achieving their aim, but that their liberal approach towards students from the developing countries (cf. the discussion on policies of differentiation below) may well render the country extremely vulnerable to an influx of (particularly North) African students when the recent French admission reforms, referred to above, really begin to bite.

Towards a differentiated approach to foreign student admissions
All the policy measures mentioned above are indicative of a trend towards a more conscious, regulative approach to the admission

of foreign students in industrialised countries, the main characteristic of which appears to be a greater *differentiation* between various categories of foreign students, whether it be according to their country of origin, their level of study or the length of their stay in the host country concerned. Such policies of differentiation may require several sets of measures at once, dampening the influx of some categories and stimulating that of others. A number of examples may be adduced to illustrate.

For the purposes of discussion, policies of 'differentiation' may be conveniently analysed in relation to two questions: first, what examples may be found of exemption or preferential treatment for certain categories of foreign students where regulative admission measures such as numerical restrictions, high tuition fees, etc. are in operation? And second, what evidence is there of active host country encouragement to stimulate the admission of certain categories of students, notably as expressed by government scholarship schemes? At the same time, an assessment of trends (and of informed opinion on imminent future trends) in the host countries selected for more in-depth examination quickly provides us with the other dimension in this notional matrix, namely the types of positive or negative differentiation which may be observed, these being clearly discernible in terms of foreign students'

  (i)   geographical origin
 (ii)   proposed level of study and length of stay
(iii)   subject of study

And, as we shall see in looking at these types more closely, in relation to the first of the two questions posed above, differentiation measures may involve a combination of more than one such factor.

(i) Differentiation by geographical origin   Differentiation according to foreign students' country of origin is probably the most common type of measure. Where restricted admissions are in operation, for example, it frequently finds expression in preferential treatment for students from developing countries, either by means of a nationwide policy decision (as in the overall guidelines in the Federal Republic of Germany) or practice adopted by individual institutions (as in Austria and again in Germany). But other geographical considerations may also play a role. Thus in Austria once more, bilateral arrangements have been introduced whereby students from Luxemburg, Liechtenstein and the South Tirol region of Italy are treated as home students and thereby effectively exempted from *numerus*

clausus. At multilateral level, the Nordic Council agreement concluded in 1975 provides for reservation of 10% of study places for
students from other Scandinavian countries, while Ministers from
all nine EC Member States have approved (27 June 1980) guidelines
for the admission of students from other Member States comprising
inter alia provision for keeping as many opportunities open to
EC students as possible, even in oversubscribed subjects. Finally,
many countries and/or institutions operate a system providing
preferential treatment for the seemingly ever increasing flow of
refugees seeking shelter or asylum predominantly in the industrialised countries after fleeing one of the world's many areas beset by
natural disaster or political unrest.

Conversely, at the same time, defensive measures may be taken
to curb the growing numbers of foreign students from other parts
of the world. Thus certain institutions in the USA are now reported
to be rejecting a disproportionately high percentage of applications
from Iran, Hong Kong and Taiwan in view of the large student
population from these countries already enrolled, and in the case
of Iran, this trend was further accentuated by political measures
taken in retaliation to the taking of American hostages in Teheran.[13]
Meanwhile in the Federal Republic of Germany, there has recently
been much debate on the question of whether or not to introduce
admission quotas for students from proportionately over-repre-
sented Greece, Turkey, Indonesia and Iran.

The same kind of policy features may also be discerned to some
extent in the case of countries where flow-regulation measures have
been predominantly of a financial nature. The best example of this
is undoubtedly Belgium, whose recently introduced tuition fee
provisions (cf. earlier in this report) effectively maintain free higher
education first for students from an approved list of developing
countries (though now, it is significant to point out, at the expense
of the Ministry of Foreign Affairs/Development Aid budget); second
for those from Luxemburg and for refugees (on the budget of the
Ministry of Education); third for government scholarship-holders
coming to Belgium in the context of bilateral cultural agreements
(at the expense of the Ministry of Cultural Affairs); and finally for
students whose parents are resident and are or have been working
in Belgium[14] (again on the Ministry of Education vote).[15] This list,
it will be observed, effectively discriminates against the vast majority
of students from industrialised countries who, as indicated above,
must pay a notional 50% of the cost of their education, except for
a number of them not exceeding 2% of the number of Belgian students
enrolled in the field concerned the previous year. The reason for

the specific orientation of these measures, as we shall see in the section on '*numerus clausus* mobility' below, becomes clear in the context of statistically well-founded fears that the country might be overrun by German (and, to a lesser extent, Dutch) students seeking to circumvent restricted admissions in their own country, particularly in high cost subjects such as the medical sciences.

No such formalised arrangements according to geographical origin exist in the United Kingdom, the other country which we have looked at in the context of its fees policy, except in the case of students from EC countries. These are to be charged the same fees as home students, though unlike British students they will not be eligible for Local Education Authority or other grants to cover such fees. The effects of full-cost fees are being at least partially offset by preferential grant schemes aimed at students from developing countries, while – conversely – a scheme has been introduced for providing full-cost programmes specifically designed for students from the 'oil-rich' countries and funded by the governments concerned.[16]

(*ii*) *Differentiation by level of study and proposed duration of stay*   As in the case of differentiation by foreign students' geographical origin, many host countries may be increasingly observed to be distinguishing in their admissions policies between foreign students seeking access to a first degree level course and those seeking further specialised training leading to a higher degree qualification.

First of all, it should be noted that the latter is often more costly to the provider, particularly in the case of subjects involving the use of expensive equipment, and it is therefore hardly surprising that until the introduction of a blanket rate of 'full-cost' fees in 1980, recommended UK fees for postgraduates were considerably higher than those for undergraduates. Similarly, Belgian fees are now (1980/81) higher for the clinical section (years 4–7) of medical studies than for the pre-clinical phase.

Conversely, however, there is clear evidence to show that most countries are moving towards a policy of preferential treatment for students entering at further degree level. Thus in France such candidates remain unaffected by the new restrictions imposed, just as they had been exempted from the '*pré-inscription*' measures five years before, and experts in Germany, Belgium and Switzerland, when asked for their views on probable policy trends in years to come, all mentioned an increased emphasis on provision of further degree level facilities as likely. Some Swiss universities are indeed still admitting postgraduate candidates from overseas even where no beginners at all are accepted. In some instances, notably the UK, the proportion of further degree level foreign students is of course already very high (Table 2.3).

If there is an exception to this trend, then it relates to students coming from industrialised rather than developing countries. In their case, too, there has traditionally been a widely held view to the effect that study abroad, except in subjects such as modern languages where it was directly related to the field concerned, was of demonstrable value only at further degree level for the purpose of profiting from research expertise available elsewhere. Recently, however, there has been some evidence to refute this theory and to suggest that in a wide variety of disciplines, mobility during first degree studies may be just as profitable. Thus the response to both the German Academic Exchange Service's newly launched scheme to promote undergraduate study abroad, and to the European Communities' scheme of grants for the development of 'Joint Programmes of Study' (over half of which have so far been at first degree level), has been overwhelming.

Both the schemes just mentioned point to a further type of differentiation of clearly increasing importance, namely that by duration of stay in the host country. In recent years there has been a noticeable trend, likely to become even more pronounced in the future, towards distinguishing for admissions purposes between foreign students whose intention is to carry out an entire course of study in the host country, and those who merely wish to stay there for a limited period of time, usually between three months and one year though occasionally longer, before returning to their country of origin to complete their degree. The latter category, who are widely held to place less strain on host institutions both from a financial and a capacity and infrastructure point of view and who form a particularly significant proportion of the foreign students coming from industrialised countries, are increasingly often being given preferential treatment: as evidenced by the important package of policies referred to above, designed to facilitate equality of treatment in the 'Admission of Students from Other Member States' and approved by the Education Ministers of the Nine on 27 June 1980, and the new 'Rules of Admission for Foreign Students' published in 1980 by the Danish authorities which include similar provisions.

(iii) Differentiation by field of study   Differentiation of admissions arrangements according to foreign students' chosen field of study, has also become a feature in a number of countries of late. Several

examples have already been noted above in passing, so that a little recapitulation is all that is required.

First, differentiation by subject is almost bound to play a role in a situation of restricted admissions in the host country, since some subjects are more disproportionately oversubscribed than others. Thus access is rendered more difficult in the subjects concerned for foreign students also, and a subject-by-subject quota as in Germany or even a zero intake as at some institutions in Austria and Switzerland is the result. Similarly, because of the varying cost of provision, tuition fee-oriented regulatory measures also tend to differentiate between different fields of study, and countries such as Belgium, Ireland and the UK all proceed in this way.

Government scholarship schemes as a vehicle for differentiation policies
In the preceding section we have been looking at the ways in which admissions systems *react* to foreign student flows by making access more or alternatively less difficult for specific categories of applicant. Given that foreign student admissions are, however, often a discretionary matter for the individual higher education institution, or a divided responsibility between institution and government, centrally introduced measures of a 'reactive' nature may often become diluted in their effect.

By contrast, government-sponsored scholarship schemes are a direct expression of the policy-makers' strategy, and at the same time much more closely controllable by government. For this reason, it is worth casting a brief glance at the trends underlying such schemes in recent years, to ascertain the types of foreign student flows that governments appear to be actively encouraging.

Perhaps even more markedly than in the case of the more 'reactive' measures described above, government grant schemes have begun to show clear signs of greater 'differentiation' in recent years, again expressible in terms of foreign students' geographical origin, level of study and chosen discipline. Thus several countries of those selected for more in-depth analysis – notably the UK with its Fees Support Scheme and earlier Overseas Student Fees Award Scheme, Austria with preferential treatment to enable the students concerned to study in otherwise 'closed' disciplines and the Federal Republic of Germany – have been orienting their scholarship policies more towards developing countries. At the same time, particularly Germany but also France and the UK have been stepping up what are known as '*sur place* scholarships' to enable foreign students to study in their home country rather than coming to Europe.

This latter move is also indicative of a more comprehensive view of scholarship policies, whereby students receive their basic training at home but follow more specialised courses in the European host country at a later stage, normally further degree level, and often merely for part of their course of study. Thus experts from almost all the countries under review predicted that the coming years would witness an intensification of grant-aid at postgraduate level, and an attempt to dovetail such aid more closely to the needs of the sending country, e.g. making increased use of bi-national selection panels and by enhancing access opportunities in subject areas of particular relevance to the country concerned.

However, it is not only the interests of the sending countries which have become increasingly taken into consideration of late, but also those of the host nations. The dramatic escalation in the number of scholarships provided for students from the People's Republic of China – the Federal Republic of Germany was said to be awarding no fewer than 500 scholarships in 1980 – for example, is a direct expression of the foreign policy interests of the funding countries concerned, and several host countries are currently seeking to shift some of the burden of scholarship-funding from their own budgets to those of the sending nations.

Taking all these trends, current and emerging, into account, possibly the most significant example of scholarship policy in recent years has been the introduction of the so-called Priority Programme in France, which in one single scheme appears to demonstrate nearly all the trends concerned. The official government announcement of the scheme may serve to illustrate the point:

> The Prime Minister has instructed that a system of scholarships for foreign students be introduced as of 1976, the recipients of which would be working towards a doctorate in a scientific or technological discipline. The programme is to be oriented first and foremost towards students from countries producing important raw materials and sources of energy, or those which constitute potentially important markets for our economy.

Equally evocative is the list of the countries concerned, namely Brazil, Venezuela, Mexico, Egypt, Iran, Iraq, Indonesia, Sri Lanka, South Korea, Thailand, Singapore. Funding of the scheme, under the auspices of which some 500 students have so far received support, is shared between France and the sending country, and selection is extremely severe, being made by a binational panel often including the admissions officer, specially flown out for the purpose, of the institution to which access is being sought. Successful applicants

are provided with intensive language tuition prior to the com-
mencement of their studies, and with special tutorial facilities during
them.

The philosophy behind the Priority Programme is clearly close
to that which inspired the 1980 reform of admissions procedures,
and the government seems likely to continue along the same path,
as indicated by the even more recent Contractual Programmes
scheme negotiated on a bilateral basis in each instance, China, Brazil
and Venezuela being involved in such programmes (similar to the
Priority Programme in their basic conception) so far.

Coherent policy or pressure of events?

As we have seen in the foregoing sections, recent years have been
characterised by a growing awareness of the 'foreign student
question' and by a considerable number of regulatory measures in
most major host countries. Generally speaking, there has been little
consultation between the countries concerned, let alone a conscious
attempt to co-ordinate the measures involved.* Rather each country
has reacted to the specific situation in which it found itself, adopting
measures in line with its own perceived requirements and related
more or less to its own principles of educational planning. In some
cases (e.g. high-level fees in the UK, admission quotas in the Federal
Republic of Germany), this has taken the form of a logical extension
of accustomed practice, in others (introduction of significant fees
in Belgium, imposition of central selection and distribution in
France) it has meant a noticeable departure from traditional practice
and has indeed introduced elements which may well in the long term
exert an influence on policy with regard to the host country's own
students also.

Furthermore, the intensity of the consultation process prior to
the introduction of the measures concerned, has tended to vary
widely from country to country as has the extent to which the results
of such consultation have been taken into consideration. In the UK,
for example, the changes in fee levels over the past few years, and
in particular the move towards full-cost fees as of 1980/81, have been
accompanied by frequent parliamentary debates, deputations, hear-
ings, conferences and consultations with the bodies involved.
Whether the opinions expressed during this process have more than
marginally affected the measures eventually introduced, however,

---

*The European Community agreement of June 1980 does, it is true, constitute
an exception, but it relates only to the flow of students *among* Member States, not
to a common policy on access for students from other parts of the world.

is debatable. In France, on the other hand, almost the entire admissions procedure and access policy on foreign students have been altered at the wave of a ministerial wand without any such consultation process having taken place. Moreover, the measures themselves have, it is widely believed, been based on the results of two reports, one for the Auditor-General in which foreign students play a peripheral but for this small sector of policy important role, the other for the Prime Minister and more specifically devoted to foreign student admissions, neither of which has been made access-ible to the general public.

Reflections such as these, and also the apparent spontaneity with which measures have been introduced in a number of countries, gives rise to the question as to whether one may properly speak of a 'policy' with regard to foreign student access to higher education at all. Are governments and/or institutions not merely reacting as best they can to the pressure of events, rather than taking a step back from the demands of the moment to have a more unimpassioned look at the question as a whole in all its long- as well as short-term ramifications for foreign, economic, trade and development policies as well as those related more specifically to education? Or how else was it possible for the British government, for example, to seek the imposition of a voluntary quota designed to cut foreign student numbers back to their 1975/76 level, only to abandon this approach two years later for one which in effect must encourage institutions to accept as many as possible, provided they can find ones who are willing and able to pay?

When viewed through the looking-glass of international com-parison, however, the conclusion to be drawn from this first part of our analysis of the measures introduced in various countries and of those likely to take effect in the foreseeable future, is that we are indeed witnessing a more conscious approach to foreign student access, which is beginning to deserve the mantle of 'policy', and that despite many variations in detail a number of common trends are emerging.

First, we have noted a general move away from what may be loosely described as 'open' access (meaning admission for all who fulfil the basic requirements) to a more differentiated approach describable in terms of the factors we have identified. Secondly, one may discern an increasing awareness of the interrelationship between inward and outward flows. This is particularly in evidence within a clearly delineated geographical area such as the European Com-munity, where considerable efforts have been made in recent years to stimulate intra-Community student flows of the desired kind.[17]

on a multi-lateral,* bilateral† and indeed unilateral‡ level. But it is also reflected in the desire to regulate the outward flow from developing countries as well as the inward one into the industrialised nations, by intensifying discussions with the sender countries, seeking to dovetail higher education provision more closely to their real needs and stepping up the proportional allocation of funds for 'sur place' scholarships.

Finally, there can be little doubt that we are also seeing a shift of emphasis towards foreign student measures designed to further more effectively the interests of the receiving countries, scholarship schemes again being the clearest but not the only expression of this trend.

We do, therefore, feel that it is becoming increasingly appropriate to speak of a 'foreign student policy' in a number of countries. And although, like so many policies, it is partially and in this case indeed largely conditioned by 'pressure of events', it is worth noting before turning to an analysis of the flows which demonstrate that pressure most clearly, that the pressure has come not simply from the foreign student flows themselves but rather from a multiplicity of factors.

Above all, of course, the measures introduced have been triggered off largely by the deterioration in the economy of so many of the host countries, with its inevitable repercussions for access and higher education provision policies for all students, including those from abroad. Other factors, however, have also played a role, and in particular what might be described as the changing shape of higher education in the industrialised countries themselves. As Barbara Burn recently put it,

> higher education systems in Western Europe have undergone sweeping changes in the last decade and ... these changes affect international student exchanges[18]

First, there are the demographic factors, which suggest that because of the fall in the birth-rate in almost all European countries since the mid-sixties, the increasing demand for higher education will, it is predicted, only continue until the mid-eighties and then tend to fall. With this in mind, and in view of the rising cost of higher education provision, the tendency has been to adopt relatively short-term measures to bridge this intervening period, the most

---

* e.g. the EEC's Joint Study Programmes scheme and the Ministerial agreement on common measures of June 1980.

† e.g. the many Franco-German scholarship schemes.

‡ e.g. the German Academic Exchange Service's (DAAD) Integrated Study Abroad scheme which, however, is not restricted to the EC countries.

obvious result being restricted admission for both home and foreign students as outlined above.

Secondly, reference must be made to the changes which have taken place in the composition of the student population itself in the industrialised countries. As Cerych and Colton have recently pointed out,[19] rising new enrolments, despite falling total numbers in the size of the traditional higher education entrance age-group cohorts, indicate a dissociation between the secondary and higher education sectors which have hitherto been considered as directly related to one another in quantitative terms. Adult education classes, distance study facilities, sandwich courses, part-time study, alternative access routes for those not holding formal higher education entrance qualifications and an increase in the proportion of hitherto under-represented social groups such as women and the children of manual workers – all these are symptoms of and factors contributing to the democratisation of higher education in many industrialised countries. But the 'new' groups of students now participating in higher education, whether because of their origins in social groups less oriented towards international mobility or simply through being tied by family responsibilities and/or a full- or part-time job, are often less inclined to opt for a period of study abroad, and this can scarcely fail to have a negative effect on student mobility within Europe.

A third factor is that of rising graduate unemployment. At a time when the labour market seems unable to absorb even the graduates from a given host country itself, that country may be less willing than usual to open its doors to foreign students who, when they graduate, may exacerbate the job situation still further. Increased selectivity, or at the least a tightening up of visa restrictions and other formalities, are the result.

In other ways, too, the precarious labour market situation impinges on student mobility. For while on the one hand it is held that students tend to want to study longer in order to obtain higher qualifications and thereby enhance their prospects (or merely to 'park', temporarily avoiding the search for the first job), there is also much evidence to suggest that many students wish to complete their courses as quickly as possible in order to enter the job market before this deteriorates still further. For students in this latter frame of mind, and in particular those from highly industrialised countries for whom study abroad generally constitutes an enrichment rather than a dire necessity, a period of study abroad must often appear as an unwelcome prolongation of their course without sufficiently tangible recompense. (That this feeling is in many cases a misapprehension is borne out by empirical evidence to the effect that meaningful study experience abroad tends to improve employment prospects; but feelings, subjective as they are, often die hard.)

Part II   Foreign Student Flows 1960–80 – a Review of Trends in Twenty-Four Host Countries

Introduction: problems of international comparison
Of the many problems which present themselves when it comes to analysing foreign student statistics, two are so particularly severe that they should be mentioned at the outset as a caveat: inadequate availability of data and lack of comparability from one country to another.

Our comparative statistical analysis of the twenty-four host countries chosen for review has been rendered extremely difficult by the *dearth of available figures*. Eurostat statistics[20] refer only to the Member States of the European Community, and the OECD does not produce comparative statistics on foreign students at all. Thus the only internationally collected and collated statistics are those produced by Unesco and published in its *Statistical Yearbooks*. Unesco, too, has produced two studies on *Statistics of Students Abroad*, relating to the periods 1962–8 and 1969–73 respectively,[21] but these relate to outward rather than the inward flows with which we are primarily concerned in the present report. Another relevant publication is that produced by Unesco's European Centre for Higher Education (CEPES) in Bucharest entitled *Statistical Study on Higher Education in Europe 1970–75*.[22]

For the purposes of the present overview, we have therefore taken as our basis the most comprehensive international statistics available, namely those contained in the Unesco *Statistical Yearbooks*. These have, however, served as raw material only, since all the tables contained in the statistical Annex to the present report have been newly produced and assembled, not least to facilitate the compilation of time series.

Nonetheless, the deficiencies of the source should be recognised: the latest Unesco statistics, contained in the *Statistical Yearbook 1979/80* relate only to 1976, and since 1972 the data base has been reduced: distribution of foreign students by subject area and by sex have been dropped. Furthermore, data for certain countries (for example the German Democratic Republic, the USSR, Luxemburg, Sweden and the Netherlands) show considerable gaps. The following Unesco data are available for all twenty-four countries:

- number of foreign students compared with the total student population (1960–76);
- distribution of foreign students according to country or continent of origin (1960–76);
- distribution of foreign students according to subject of study, compared with the same distribution for the total student population (1960–70);
- distribution of foreign students by sex, compared with the same distribution for the total student population (1960–70).

As well as more up-to-date figures on these categories, a really exhaustive analysis would need at the least to be able to draw on data of the following kind:

- distribution of foreign students by country of origin *and* field of study, in order for example to detect significant *numerus clausus* mobility flows;
- total new enrolments of foreign students, in order to be able to detect most recent tendencies more clearly;
- distribution of foreign students by type of institution (if possible also by sex);
- distribution by term, year or level of study;
- duration of stay of foreign students in the host country, which would permit an evaluation of their distribution according to full course or temporary mobility;
- distribution of foreign students by social background, in order to be able to make sound comparisons with developments in the student population as a whole and the effects of the changing composition of the student population on international mobility.

In the time and with the resources available for the present study, it has naturally not been possible to plug gaps as extensive as these. Nonetheless, the attempt has been made to procure more comprehensive statistics from national sources, in particular with regard to Austria, Belgium, France, the Federal Republic of Germany, Switzerland, the United Kingdom and the USA, with a view to presenting a more complete, up-to-date and exact analysis of foreign student trends in the countries concerned.

The second major problem confronting a study such as this is the frustrating *lack of comparability* in the data available.[23] Given the considerable differences between the educational systems of the countries under review, this is in part unavoidable. But other more objective categories are equally vague, for example the question as to whether data for a given year refers to the academic, calendar or fiscal year. Unesco statistics are based on the following principle:

> The years stated indicate the calendar year in which the academic year begins. Consequently, for those countries where the academic year overlaps to a greater or lesser extent with the following calendar year, the year 1973, for example, should be read as academic year 1973/74.[24]

Another source of misunderstanding is encountered when trying to compare the foreign student body with the student population as a whole. Figures for the latter normally relate to the whole of tertiary level education, the distinction being drawn between 'university type' and 'non-university type' institutions/courses, though the definition of these types varies again from country to country.* As far as the definition of what constitutes a 'foreign student' is concerned, some countries follow strictly nationality-based criteria while others prefer to go by residence. Unesco opts for the following:

> A foreign student is defined as a person enrolled at an institution of higher education in a country or territory of which he is not a permanent resident.[25]

The residential criterion is particularly favoured in the UK and Canada, though in Britain the precise definition of the criterion has changed repeatedly in connection with the decision as to which

---

*The Unesco definition of 'Higher Education Institution' is the following; (a) universities and equivalent institutions (degree-granting); (b) teacher-training at the third level in non-university institutions (teacher-training colleges etc.); (c) other education at the third level in non-university institutions (technical colleges etc.).

'As far as possible, the figures include both full-time and part-time teachers and students. Evening courses providing recognised third-level education are included, as stated in a note to this effect. Although as a general rule these figures do not cover correspondence courses, they do include them in certain well-defined cases (indicated by a note) in which such courses provide recognised third-level education. In point of fact, these are courses leading to the same diplomas as intra-mural studies.

'It should be noted, however, that the criteria applied for determining the three types of education may not be exactly the same in each of the countries and territories covered. Moreover, following reforms in the educational system, a number of non-university institutions in a given country may be attached to universities or recognised as equivalent institutions from one year to the next. This will tend to impair international comparability and the breakdown by type of institution must therefore be used with caution.' (*Statistical Yearbook 1975*)

A similar definition can be found in the *International Standard Classification of Education*, Paris, Unesco, March 1976, p. 7.

groups of (foreign) students should pay what level of fees. (The present definition is that of a student enrolled at an institution of higher education in the UK who has been ordinarily resident in the UK for less than three years at time of entrance.)[26] This state of affairs and the country's highly diversified system of tertiary education, has – as the Overseas Students Trust has pointed out[27] – given rise to variations in the figures on foreign students in the UK. But the concept of nationality as the guiding principle is no less fraught with shortcomings, even though it has been adopted by most countries and has administrative advantages for the host nations. For what of the students whose parents are immigrants or migrant workers? And that these constitute anything but a negligible quantity in many host countries will be demonstrated clearly later on in this report.

As far as at all possible, we have tried to ensure genuine comparability in the figures relating to foreign students on the one hand and the total student population on the other. Thus in cases where the data available on foreign students relates only to universities and equivalent institutions (Belgium, the Netherlands, Canada, Japan and Switzerland), the Unesco figures for the total student population have been modified in like manner. It has not, however, been possible to iron out deficiencies in comparability caused by the frequent changes of definition in the national statistics provided to Unesco. Thus French figures for 1970 are only very approximate, while those from 1973 onwards are based on much more detailed information. The USA recently changed the categorisation of immigrant students; Canada included 'half-time' students in its 1973 and 1978 figures, but not in others, while in the UK full-time students only have been counted. Belgium, too, changed its classification system in 1976.

All these comments and caveats should therefore be borne in mind when reading the following statistical analysis of foreign student trends since 1960. However, they also constitute a finding in their own right: one of the main conclusions to be drawn from our report is the demonstrably urgent need for more international consultation on foreign student statistics.

An overview of trends in the total enrolment of foreign students since 1960
Table 7.3 provides a general view of inward flows of foreign students in the past twenty years; and Appendix Table B.4 elaborates the data for the twenty-four survey countries. As may be seen the number of students studying abroad rose by almost three and a half times

Table 7.3   *Foreign student population: general overview*

Year	World		Twenty-four countries of survey		Five most important host countries[b]	
	Total[a]	%	Total	%	Total	%
1960	237503[a]	100	148925	62·7	120592	50·7
1965	349393[a]	100	246556	70·6	189457	54·2
1970	508810[a]	100	368363	72·4	253846	49·9
1976	800000[c]	100	618863	77·4	461573	57·6

Notes: [a] This sum represents 90–95% of the world total foreign student population.
[b] USA, Canada, France, the Federal Republic of Germany and the United Kingdom.
[c] This sum is an estimation, constructed from known data for fifty countries (705,222); plus Brazil (25,642 foreign students in 1974), USSR (30,563 foreign students in 1971) and Lebanon (20,857 foreign students in 1969).

Source: Based on Unesco *Statistical Yearbooks*.

between 1960 and 1976. Even back in 1960, over 60% of all foreign students were enrolled at institutions in the twenty-four countries under review in the present report, and this had risen to almost 80% by 1976. This reveals a clear tendency to greater concentration of foreign students in a relatively small group of highly industrialised countries. Indeed, almost 60% of the world's total foreign student population is now enrolled in just five countries, namely the USA, Canada, France, the Federal Republic of Germany and the UK, this group's 'share' having risen by around 10% since 1960. Given that another 16% are studying in what may be termed the 'middle' group of seven further receiver countries, namely the USSR, Italy, Belgium, Japan, Switzerland, Austria and Greece, the process of concentration becomes more manifest still: three-quarters of the world's foreign students are enrolled in just twelve countries.

To a greater or lesser extent, the host countries to which foreign students are increasingly turning share a number of important features, notable among these being their comparatively high level of industrialisation, correspondingly well-developed higher education provision in the so-called 'hard sciences' (medicine, natural sciences, engineering) which, as we shall see later, are in especially high demand among foreign students, and comparative 'accessibility' of their language of instruction. Thus the relatively low proportion of foreign students going to Japan is presumably attributable in large part to that country's language, which makes it well nigh inaccessible to the majority of foreign students, and this same factor, allied to the relatively small size of the countries concerned and hence their higher education capacity, appears to hold true for other highly industrialised countries such as Denmark, Finland, Norway, Sweden and the Netherlands towards the lower end of the host country scale based on total foreign student numbers. Greece, too, is only an apparent exception, since 60–70% of its foreign students come from Cyprus. Political factors also appear to play a role in determining the strength of flow; otherwise countries such as the USSR and the German Democratic Republic might be expected higher up the list of 'receivers'. The fact that they are not, also suggests that despite the bilateral and multilateral agreements (e.g. the equivalence agreement of 1972) between them, student mobility among the Eastern European countries is still at a fairly low ebb.

*The development in foreign student numbers relative to total enrolments**

The fact of receiving a particularly large number of foreign students does not, of course, of itself imply that this foreign student contingent represents a significant impact when viewed in terms of its proportion of the entire student body. Thus of the top five receiver countries, only Canada (largely a result of a distortion of figures because of the high immigrant percentage), France and (if viewed with British and not Unesco data) the UK have foreign student contingents of close to 10% or above, whereas the figure for the USA is more like 2%. Other countries with smaller numbers in some instances show much higher percentages, notably Austria, Belgium, Greece, Luxemburg† and especially Switzerland.

Despite the fact that foreign student numbers have more than tripled since 1960, Appendix Table B.4 shows that their overall percentage has fallen slightly worldwide. A closer look at the selected host countries, however, reveals differing tendencies. In one-third of the countries, the percentage of foreign students has risen significantly, namely in Belgium, Denmark, France, Greece, Italy, Luxemburg, Canada and the USA. In a further third, it has remained roughly constant: Finland, the German Democratic Republic,

---

*The available information is summarised at Appendix Table B.4.

† The high figure for Luxemburg may be because a large number of students seek entry to the one (now two) year courses in natural sciences at the Centre Universitaire which may then be recognised as partially fulfilling course requirements in pre-clinical medicine, particularly in the Federal Republic of Germany. If this supposition is correct, it would be another example of the international ramification of *numerus clausus*. In any case, the total *number* of foreign students enrolled in Luxemburg is, of course, extremely low (70).

Japan, Norway, Portugal, Sweden, the UK* and the USSR. Finally, it has fallen noticeably in a third group of eight countries, namely Austria, Czechoslovakia, the Federal Republic of Germany, Ireland,† the Netherlands, Spain, Switzerland and Turkey. As Appendix Table B.4 shows, a particularly marked rise has taken place in France and Canada, an equally significant fall on the other hand in Austria (where foreign students accounted for a third of all enrolments back in 1960), Switzerland and – to a much lesser extent – the Federal Republic of Germany. The fact that in all three of these last-mentioned countries numerical restrictions on entry were introduced progressively over the period under review has clearly had its effect on foreign student enrolment figures.

In order to interpret the above-mentioned trends adequately, however, it is necessary to examine the growth-rate of the host countries' *own* student population over the same period, since – as noted above – the years since 1960 have witnessed a vast expansion of higher education in most parts of the industrialised world. Thus in a country such as the Federal Republic of Germany, in which this process of expansion and democratisation has been particularly marked, it is not surprising to encounter a falling proportion of foreign students relative to the total student population, and this is also true of countries such as the German Democratic Republic, Norway, Spain and Turkey. Denmark, where the Nordic Council measures to promote intra-Scandinavian mobility appear to be taking effect, Italy (substantially a result of the rapidly growing contingent of Greek students‡), and Greece (similarly a result of a large influx of Jordanian and Greek Cypriot students) are more individually explicable examples of countries with a comparatively high growth rate of foreign students relative to that of the student population as a whole.

Given the dramatic increase in the home student population of all industrialised countries between 1960 and 1976 and the tendentially negative effects which the changed social composition of this

---

* However official British figures differ from these Unesco data and show that the percentage in the UK is also rising significantly, if less quickly (see Table 2.1).

† The fall in the Irish figure is almost entirely due to a dramatic drop in the number of students from the UK enrolled there, the British contingent accounting for by far the largest group of foreign students at Irish institutions.

‡ The following figures show the growth-rate of foreign students in Italy with and without Greek students, taking 100 as the 1964 index:
all foreign students: 1964 = 100, 1970 = 602, 1975 = 1021, 1976 = 1627
without Greek students: 1964 = 100, 1970 = 273, 1975 = 305, 1976 = 424.

is likely to have had on mobility, the normal expectation might have been for a very substantial fall in the percentage of foreign student enrolments. That this has not taken place, suggests that in real terms international student flows, and in particular those from developing to industrialised countries, have actually increased in importance in real terms during the period under review.

Most recent figures, specially collected from national sources for the present study, appear to confirm this view. Thus the 1978/79 foreign student figures quoted for the USA by the Institute of International Education in New York (263,938) showed an increase of 12·1% on the previous year, and the provisional 1979/80 figures (286,343) are another 8·5% higher. As for the major European countries, Table 7.4 suggests that the trends referred to above remain valid.

Thus while at French universities the index for foreign student enrolments rose from 100 to 127 in the four years concerned, compared with 100 to only 104 for French students, foreign student enrolments in Germany showed slower growth-rates than those for German students in every type of institution, including the universities. Figures for new enrolments, however, are beginning to show the effects of the regulative policies described in Part I above. Thus in Austria, for example, there has been a marked slowing down, and this has been even more in evidence in France, where new foreign student enrolments had reached 22·4% and 28·2% of the total new enrolment figure by 1974/75 and 1975/76 before the effects of the *pré-inscription* measures sent it tumbling (1967/77, 17·9%; 1977/78, 16·4%; 1978/79, 17·6%).

*Foreign student flows by geographical origin: some general comments**

After focusing our attention in the section above on the countries in which foreign students choose to study, we must now take a closer look at where the students come from. For this purpose, the geographical composition of the foreign student body in nine countries – Austria, Belgium, Canada, France, the Federal Republic of Germany, Italy, Switzerland, the UK and the USA – has been analysed over the period since 1960, as has that of all the twenty-four countries under review in respect of their most important countries of origin. In the space available in the present version of our study, it has not been possible to reproduce all the detailed time-series tables produced, though the commentary in this chapter draws on their results. Instead, the synoptic table (Appendix Table B.6) has been

* The available statistical data is summarised at Appendix Tables B.6 and B.7.

Table 7.4   Total foreign student enrolments in selected European countries since 1975/76

Host country	1975/76 Home	Foreign	Total	1976/77 Home	Foreign	Total	1977/78 Home	Foreign	Total	1978/79 Home	Foreign	Total
Austria	62292	8753 (11·4%)	77045	74387	8939 (10·7%)	83326	80553	9138 (10·2%)	89691			
Belgium	73572	9788 (10·5%)	83360	76386	10396 (12·0%)	86792	78287	11062 (12·4%)	89349	78318	11320 (12·6%)	89638
France	711195	85578 (10·7%)	796773	715011	96409 (11·9%)	811420	722877	104503 (12·6%)	827380	736861	108471 (12·8%)	845332
Germany (Fed. Rep.)	788022	47281 (6·0%)	835313	822656	48580 (5·6%)	870236	862056	51252 (5·6%)	913308	893724	52173 (5·5%)	945897
Italy	717382	18921 (2·5%)	736303	728205	28390 (3·8%)	756595	730959	27136 (3·6%)	758095	740255	26648 (3·5%)	766903
Switzerland	42510	10113 (19·2%)	52623	44113	10085 (18·6%)	54198	45475	10423 (18·6%)	55898	46934	10676 (18·5%)	57610
United Kingdom	456800	47900 (9·5%)	504700	459600	55900 (10·8%)	515500	451700	58400 (11·4%)	510110	450000	58000 (11·4%)	508000

Sources: Austria: Bundesamt für Statistik, Wien.
Belgium: J. P. Jarousse, *Foreign Students in Belgium*. Paris, Institute of Education, European. Cultural Foundation, 1980 (mimeograph).
France: J. P. Jarousse, *Foreign Students in France*. Paris, Institute of Education, European Culture Foundation, 1980 (mimeograph).
Germany: Figures provided by the German Academic Exchange Service, Bonn.
Italy: D. Fazio, 'L'Università Italiana: Situazione e Problemi', *Universitas* I/1 (April–June 1980), pp. 10ff (19).
Switzerland: C. Woesler, *Foreign Students in Switzerland*, Paris, Institute of Education ECF 1980 (mimeograph).
U.K.: J. P. Jarousse, *Foreign Students in the UK*, Paris, Institute of Education ECF 1980 (mimeograph).

developed, placing the nine host countries in relation to the thirty-five leading 'exporter' nations for the year 1976.

In addition, some specific countries or areas of origin have been singled out for special attention as examples of particular trends in foreign student flows, notably those linked to the movements of migrant workers, refugees and students from the oil-rich countries.

Looking first at the development in foreign student numbers according to their continent of origin (see Appendix Table B.7), one is struck by a number of phenomena.

First, many host countries are characterised by a foreign student population coming very predominantly from one continent, region or country. Thus 51·5% (in 1973 only 43·6%) of all foreign students in France are African (1979/80 figures), and of these, 60% come from the Maghreb countries of North Africa alone. The foreign student body in Japan, Turkey and Greece is completely dominated by the Asian contingent, and even for the highly multi-racial USA the provisional 1978/80 figures from the Institute of International Education show 55% Asians. Austria (55% in 1977/78), Switzerland (69·8% in 1978/79), Belgium (40% in 1978/79), Italy (67% in 1978/79) and Denmark, meanwhile, all show similarly high concentrations of Europeans. In some instances, one individual country of origin even predominates, as Table 7.5 shows.

Table 7.5 Main country of origin in selected host countries

Host country	Country of origin	Percentage of total number of foreign students		
		1964	1970	1976
Greece	Cyprus	72	66	63
Italy	Greece	37	47	59
Japan	Korea (Dem.)	49	49	57
Portugal	Brazil	72	45	39
Turkey	Cyprus	46	35	31
Austria	Germany, Fed. Rep.	39	29	25
Denmark	Norway	—	14	22
Switzerland	Germany, Fed. Rep.	24	20	21
Canada	UK	7	10	20

Source: Based on Unesco *Statistical Yearbooks.*

Other host countries, on the other hand, are characterised by a foreign student population composed mainly of contingents from two continents. Thus in 1976, of students from abroad the Federal

Republic of Germany had 40% Asians and 40% European, the Netherlands 35% Asians and 42% Europeans, Portugal 47% South Americans and 28% Africans. Canada shows an even greater equilibrium, with roughly 30% of its foreign students coming from North America (USA), Europe and Asia respectively, while the three Eastern European countries included in our survey, i.e. Czechoslovakia, the German Democratic Republic and the USSR, all have foreign student populations of mainly European and Asian origin.

Dramatic changes in these patterns are, not surprisingly, the exception. However, Denmark's figures show an increase in the proportion of European students from 54% to 74% over the period 1970–76, African students accounted for almost 50% of the foreign students in France in 1976 compared with only 30% twelve years before, and the rising percentage of European (= Greek) students in Italy has caused a corresponding fall in the proportion of Asians and Africans. In the UK, on the other hand, the proportion of the Asian student population relative to all foreign students in the country has risen by 10% in the past decade, standing at around 50% by 1976 (Iran and Malaysia alone accounting for half of this number), and in Belgium the percentage of African students rose from 23·5% in 1970 to 32·8% in 1979 – even before any possible 'knock-on' effect following the recent French reforms began to make itself felt. Of the falling patterns, the increasing reluctance of British students to study in Ireland saw the latter's percentage of European students fall from 70% to just 30% between 1970 and 1976, and the South American element in Portugal's foreign student population has been falling quickly, though not in Spain, where this phenomenon was much more true of students from North America between 1970 and 1975 – partially, it seems, a consequence of the end of the war in Vietnam.[28] None of these changes, however, has served to alter the predominantly 'South to North' orientation of flow.

Examples of some specific geographical types of student flows

Students from OPEC countries   Hitherto in this report we have used the term 'developing countries' without distinguishing in detail between the very different types of country which the term covers. Such a distinction has, however, become more and more necessary in recent years in view of the dramatically rising GNP of several countries concerned, notably the oil-exporting states.

The extent to which the rising flow of students from OPEC countries can affect foreign student enrolment is revealed perhaps most clearly by statistics relating to the USA. According to the data contained in the Institute of International Education's annual publication *Open Doors*, the proportion of the foreign student population in the USA made up by students from OPEC countries has risen from 10% in 1954 to 30% in 1978, and since 1974 their growth-rate has been particularly dramatic: from 1977/78 to 1978/79 the number of OPEC students increased by 21·2% compared with only a 7·9% increase in non-OPEC foreign students, as Table 7.6 shows. A closer look at the individual OPEC countries reveals that the increase is due to rising numbers from Nigeria, Saudi Arabia, Venezuela and above all Iran, which accounts for 60% of all OPEC students in the USA. These figures give rise to at least two questions. Firstly, is this trend reflected in figures for other host countries? And secondly, is this increased mobility due solely to economic or also to political factors?

Table 7.6   Number of students and annual percentage increase for foreign students from OPEC countries, non-OPEC countries and all countries, in the USA, 1976/77–1978/79

Country grouping	1976/77 Number of students	1977/78 Number of students	1977/78 Percentage increase	1978/79 Number of students	1978/79 Percentage increase
OPEC	52040	73550	41·3	89120	21·2
Non-OPEC	151028	161959	7·2	174818	7·9
All foreign students	203068	235509	16·0	263938	12·1

Source: Open Doors 1978/79, p. 11.

As to the first of these questions, the analysis of six other major host countries contained in Table 7.7 reveals that marked increases in the proportion of OPEC country students relative to the total foreign student population have occurred only in France and the UK. Canada shows a slight increase, though the OPEC proportion is still very small, the situation in the Federal Republic of Germany has remained extremely constant, while the proportion of OPEC students has actually fallen in Austria and Switzerland compared with 1970. Though there has been a significant rise in the number of OPEC country students going abroad, therefore, their flows have been clearly towards a few specific host countries.

Similarly, the rise in OPEC figures generally seems linked to those of very specific countries of origin (Algerians to France, Nigerians to the UK and Canada, etc.), so that the factor 'OPEC' often

Table 7.7   *Students from OPEC countries in selected host countries, 1970 and 1976*

Host country	Canada		Austria		France		Germany (Fed.)		Switzerland		UK	
Year	1970	1976	1970	1976	1970	1976	1970	1976	1970	1976	1970	1976
Country of origin												
Algeria	35	106	—	17	1002	6970	30	448	77	130	31	662
Ecuador	13	22	1	2	27	125	77	84	8	8	4	20
Gabon	8	48	—	—	391	847	3	10	1	3	1	4
Indonesia	81	260	91	49	14	110	1201	3543	30	44	62	338
Iran	93	387	900	881	503	2469	2805	4118	213	225	550	3775
Iraq	24	70	58	49	79	349	369	221	7	8	570	1541
Kuwait	—	1	—	—	13	27	4	4	4	5	39	214
Libya	4	5	—	—	27	118	136	63	2	4	119	157
Nigeria	212	788	20	47	92	101	316	671	—	15	937	3690
Qatar	—	—	—	—	—	1	—	1	—	—	3	30
Saudi Arabia	7	9	52	46	20	272	177	38	8	6	147	262
United Arab Emirates	—	2	—	—	—	16	—	1	—	—	4	39
Venezuela	51	139	14	26	64	678	64	122	37	33	137	535
OPEC Total	588	1837	1136	1117	2232	12083	5182	9324	387	481	2504	11017
Total foreign students	22263	52087	8573	10696	34877	96409	27769	54080	9469	12204	24606	55927
OPEC percentage	2·4	3·5	13·3	10·4	6·4	12·5[a]	18·7	17·2	4·1	3·9[b]	10·2	19·7

Notes: [a] This figure rose to 14·7% in 1978/79 according to J. P. Jarousse, *Foreign Students in France*, Paris, Institute of Education ECF 1980 (mimeograph).
[b] 1978/79: 4·2% according to data provided by the Swiss Federal Office of Statistics.

Source: Unesco *Statistical Yearbook*, 1972, 1978–79 editions.

becomes intertwined with others. For example, the increase in the numbers of Algerian students going to France may be partially seen in the context of the general increase in North African numbers referred to above, the 'OPEC factor' finding expression only in its marginally faster growth-rate (index 1974 = 100; 1979, Algeria = 182; North Africa as a whole = 169).[29] In particular, the rising OPEC numbers are a consequence of the dramatic increase in Iranian students going abroad in the past few years. Table 7.8 shows the proportion of OPEC students accounted for by Iran:

Table 7.8   Iranian students as a percentage of students from OPEC countries

Host Country	1964	1970	1976	1978
USA	40	42	45	51
United Kingdom	15	22	34	n.a.
Germany (Fed. Rep.)	61	54	44	n.a.
France	36	23	23	24
Austria	77	79	79	n.a.
Switzerland	64	55	47	n.a.
Canada	13	18	21	n.a.

Source: Based on Unesco *Statistical Yearbooks.*

Table 7.9   Iranian students in the USA, 1964–79

Year	Total	Index	Average annual growth rate	% of all Iranian students abroad	% of all Asian students in USA
1964	3719	100	9·5	40·3	9·2
1970	6402	172	24·0	49·0	9·0
1976	23310	627	39·4	60·6	21·5
1978	43340	1210	n.a.	n.a.	n.a.
1979	51870	1394	19.7	n.a.	32.9

Source: 1979 figures kindly supplied by the Institute of International Education (IIE) ahead of publication.

In 1976, no fewer than 40,000 Iranians were already enrolled overseas (just over one-fifth of the country's then 194,000 total student number), making Iran the world's most prodigious 'exporter' of students (though receiving just 686 in return). In the twelve years from 1964–7 alone, the Iranian student population abroad more than quadrupled (1964, 9283; 1970, 13,575; 1975, 33,021; 1976, 40,422), with particularly rapid growth-rates in the USA, Canada and the UK and a large contingent also in the Federal Republic of Germany. Again, such an increase may scarcely be attributed solely to OPEC wealth, but also to a multitude of other social and political factors.

The USA, in particular, has witnessed an astonishing influx of Iranians over the past decade and a half, as Table 7.9 shows. Whether or not the change of regime in Iran will alter this pattern, remains to be seen, both with regard to the Iranian students' own motivation to study in the States and the latter's willingness to receive them: in the short term, the taking of American hostages led to a number of retaliatory steps in certain states designed to exclude Iranian students from American institutions – a move which received a mixed reception in the USA itself.

Refugee flows

A country's intellectuals may be regarded as a seismograph of political unrest, for they are usually amongst the first refugees to leave. Some of them seek residence in other countries, sometimes using registration at a foreign university as a means to this end. Of course, the movement of students linked to flows of refugees is not a true case of mobility in the accepted sense of the term, since the students concerned do not leave their country of origin of their own free will but are constrained to do so by the pressures of political upheaval, and since they often have no intention or possibility of returning to their home country after studying abroad.

Nonetheless, and even though the total numbers of 'refugee students' are not particularly substantial when viewed as a straightforward percentage of the worldwide student population, they may have a noticeable effect on foreign student flows in specific cases, and their overall growth-rate over the past few years has often been dramatic. For example in the first six months of 1980, no fewer than 70,000 sought refuge/asylum in the Federal Republic of Germany, compared with just 5000 in 1963.[30] It therefore seems appropriate to mention this phenomenon briefly in our present context.

Though, as we have noted in Part I above, most industrialised countries do operate a 'preferential treatment clause' for refugees in their various admissions policies for foreign students, few governments have really developed a coherent and consistent policy with regard to educational, including higher educational, provision for such students. Usually the decision to accept and help refugees is taken on an ad hoc basis, by each country separately and from crisis to crisis. The statistical categorisation of the students concerned is also arbitrary and lacking in precision. One reason for this is probably that fear of retaliatory measures or being refused re-entry to their home country at a future date causes many people in this situation to think twice before officially requesting political asylum and the status of a political refugee. This may, for example, account for the fact that whereas only 95 Chilean students were registered in the UK in 1972, this figure had suddenly risen to 356 by 1977 and to 467 by 1978.[31]

These and many other student flows in connection with the movement of refugees would require much more thorough political and statistical analysis than is possible in the context of the present report. Let us, however, consider one example, however briefly, namely that of Vietnam. Because of the uncertain statistical position during the Vietnam war, data for the former North and South Vietnam have been added together. In 1964 only 3000 Vietnamese students were registered abroad. By 1976 this figure had risen to almost 17,000, 90% of these studying in the twenty-four countries we are reviewing, as Table 7.10 shows.

Table 7.10   Vietnamese students abroad, 1964–76

Host country	Total			Percentage		
	1964	1970	1976	1964	1970	1976
Worldwide	3320	4881	14927	100	100	100
USA	399	1118	8910	12	23	60
France	2612	1057	3241	79	22	22

Source: Based on Unesco *Statistical Yearbooks.*

The most important host countries are thus France and the USA, but here we see the effect of political developments (and economic opportunities) on student flows of this kind: whereas in 1964 80% of all Vietnamese students abroad went to France, this proportion had dropped to just 20% by 1976. Conversely, the proportion studying in the USA rose from 20 to 60% over the same period. The French withdrawal from Indo-China and the increased involvement of the USA could scarcely be more clearly reflected.[32]

Migrant workers and their impact on foreign student flows   Whereas in the previous section we have been dealing with a form of mobility due to political causes, another of the recently emerging forms is due more to economic motivation, namely registration at host country institutions of students whose parents moved to that country as migrant workers. Such mobility, it should be recognised, is not really to be regarded as *student* mobility at all in the strict sense of the term, since the students remain in the host country both before and after their period of study, and it is interesting to note that as far as the EC states are concerned, legally binding regulations providing for the treatment of such students on an equal basis with those of the host country (in the shape of Resolution 1612 of 1968) were introduced a full decade before Ministers agreed on the less far-reaching set of common principles for the admission of all other categories of students coming from other Member States, in June 1980, as referred to above.

Nonetheless, the phenomenon should not be neglected in the context of the present study, for it has had an undoubted impact, both statistically and materially, on foreign student flows. Children or relatives of migrant workers are only identifiable statistically in host countries whose definition of 'foreign student' is based on nationality rather than residence, but in several countries they appear to account for fairly substantial proportions of the foreign student population. Thus an estimated 25% of all foreign students in France are said to have been permanently resident there in 1978/79. If these students are deducted from the total foreign student population, the latter than accounts for only 9% instead of 12% of the total student body. In the Federal Republic of Germany the children of migrant workers resident and in many cases born in Germany and possessing a German higher education entrance qualification are nonetheless treated as foreign students. As such, they come under the quota regulations referred to in Part I above and may well in certain circumstances be in a more advantageous position than many of their German counterparts when seeking admission to a 'hard core *numerus clausus*' subject. Unpublished figures generously provided by the Federal Ministry of Education and Science show that 35% of the foreign students from other European countries (including 70% of those from Austria and the Netherlands), 12% of those from Africa, 28% of those from America and 11% of those from Asia are estimated to have had their permanent residence in the Federal Republic of Germany in 1977. In Switzerland, a survey carried out at the University of Zürich in 1975 revealed 29% permanent residence of foreign students' parents in that country,[33] and the picture appears to be little different in North America. In 1973, the last year in which immigrants were included in US foreign student figures, some 17% were estimated to be in this category, and according to Canadian authorities the remarkable explosion of foreign student numbers there, notably from the UK, is very largely attributable to the same factor – the coming of higher education age of the children of the waves of immigrants who entered Canada in the 1950s and 1960s. If these figures, relating after all to five of the world's leading receivers of foreign students, hold even partially true for a significant number of others, then this would mean that the level of 'real' student mobility in the world has tended in the past to be substantially overestimated.

To demonstrate in more detail the influence which migrant worker flows can exert on the levels recorded for foreign students in a given host country, the example of the Federal Republic of Germany may be cited. In 1975 there were almost four million migrant workers in Germany (= 6% of the total population). Among these, the 1·2 million Turks (1976) formed the largest proportion, and it is in relation to the Turkish contingent that the effect on higher education admission figures may be most clearly perceived.

Thus between 1970 and 1976 alone, as Table 7.11 shows, the number of Turkish students in Germany more than trebled, rising during this period from fourth to first place in the country of origin 'league'. By 1976, almost half the 11,000 Turkish students abroad were enrolled at German institutions, compared with a third just six years before, and the proportion of Turkish students relative to the total foreign student population of the country had almost doubled.

Table 7.11   Turkish students in the Federal Republic of Germany (*total and as percentage of total foreign student population in FRG*)

Year	Total	%	Index
1964	1404	5·5	100
1970	1415	5·1	101
1975	4208	8·9	300
1976	4756	8·8	339

Source: Based on Unesco *Statistical Yearbooks*

More recent figures provided by the German Academic Exchange Service for the present study, indicate that the trend has continued since. For whereas in the years from 1975/76 to 1978/79 the number of new foreign student enrolments rose by an overall 10·5%, the figures for three countries – all three belonging to the major countries of origin of migrant workers employed in Germany – were three times as high: Turkey 36%, Yugoslavia 35%, Italy 31%.

There can be little doubt that as the younger age groups of migrant workers begin to reach higher education admission age, and as their level of schooling improves,[34] this trend will be accentuated still further. Thus almost 25% of the 4,000,000 migrants in Germany in 1975 were aged 14 or under (8% of the total age group cohort in the country) but only 362,500 children from migrant worker families were counted in regular schooling in 1974, and 2% of these were at post-compulsory level.

Intra-European mobility: general situation and trends   Despite all exhortations to the contrary, whether by politicians or university rectors, by national or European organisations, the level of intra-European student mobility is generally held to be at an unsatisfactorily low ebb – 'Mobility between Rhetoric and Reality', as Schulte recently put it.[35] The reasons advanced include the lack of readily available information on study opportunities in other European countries, the absence of arrangements for recognition of students' academic work carried out while abroad, the language barrier, lack of financial resources to cover travel, higher living expenses and increased tuition fees, the increasing bureaucratisation of higher education (including the fear of losing the so sought-after place in a *numerus clausus* subject by opting for a period of study in another country), the fear of prolonging studies unnecessarily and thereby encountering an ever less favourable situation on the job market, and many more.

It cannot be the purpose of the present study to examine all these factors in detail, much less to provide a comprehensive investigation into European mobility and possible cures for its ills, though other recent work carried out by the Institute of Education of the European Cultural Foundation should be referred to in this context.[36] In accordance with our present terms of reference, our aim is rather to examine the accuracy of the view that intra-European mobility constitutes in international terms a negligible quantity, and to investigate in a little more detail some of the main characteristics of intra-European student flows, beyond the migrant worker mobility already referred to.

Statistics show that only 30% of European (and by this we mean those from the continent of Europe rather than the Unesco definition of the term) students studying abroad go to other European countries, and although in Belgium, Denmark, France, Spain and the UK the number of students from other European countries increased between two and threefold between 1960 and 1976, this was quite in line with the overall increase in the total foreign student population over the same period.

As a proportion of the total foreign student population, European students have remained at a fairly constant percentage in Belgium, the Federal Republic of Germany, the Netherlands, Austria and Switzerland, i.e. in countries which even in 1964 (around 40%) had a high percentage of Europeans among their students from abroad. A rise in the percentage of Europeans has taken place only in Denmark (from 54 to 74% between 1964 and 1976) and Italy (from 37 to 64%), while the percentage has fallen noticeably in Ireland (from 70 to 31%), France (from 23 to 18%) and the UK (from 15 to 12%) over the same period. Leaving aside Italy and Ireland as special cases due to the influx of Greek* and the exodus of British students respectively, it may be said that in countries where the proportion of European students was already low in 1964, this proportion has tended to fall still further because of the increase in students of Asian and African provenance.

For purposes of comparison, it is interesting to note that the number of European students enrolled at higher education institutions in the USA rose from 10,000 in 1964 to around 16,000 in 1976; with a further rise to around 22,900 according to provisional IIE figures for 1979/80. For the nine countries of the European Community, the Office National des Universités et Ecoles françaises reported figures for the 'balance' of student 'exports' and 'imports' Europe/USA from which Table 7.12 has been derived.

Figures for European students in Canada show a much more dramatic rise. From 1500 in 1964 they had reached 16,000 in 1976, their proportion of the foreign student population in Canada rising from 15 to 32% over the same period. As noted above, however, these figures are highly influenced by immigrant worker flows and do not therefore represent an active 'change of option' on the part of European students resident in Europe.

These figures from the USA and Canada hardly substantiate the often voiced view that while intra-European mobility is stagnating, ever more European students are opting to cross the Atlantic.[37]

---

*With over 30,000 of its students abroad, Greece is the world's third largest 'exporter' of students (after Iran and the USA). Almost 55% of these now go to Italy (1964: 12%), and only another 13% (1964: 30%) to the Federal Republic of Germany – a dramatic change of flow presumably due to a multiplicity of causes, notably geographical proximity, the absence of admission restrictions and comparatively low cost of living.

Table 7.12   Student 'trade balance' between the 'Nine' (members of the European Community) and the United States, 1975

Country	To/from United States	To/from the Nine	Total
Belgium	− 424	− 1768	− 2192
Denmark	+ 116	+ 277	+ 393
France	− 1813	− 3581	− 5394
Germany, Fed. Rep.	− 1228	− 2406	− 3634
Ireland	+ 99	+ 146	+ 245
Italy	− 507	+ 1853	+ 1346
Luxemburg	− 50	+ 1878	+ 1828
Netherlands	+ 463	+ 1947	+ 2410
United Kingdom	− 102	+ 1710	+ 1608
United States	—	+ 3446	+ 3446

Note: + = net outflow; − = net inflow.
Source: Lettre d'Information de l'ONUEF no 10, June 1977.

Mobility within the European Community[38]   Given the particular relationship between the nine Member States concerned, student flows within the European Community deserve closer analysis as one important element within European mobility as a whole.

As Table 7.13 opposite indicates, some 26,000 students from other Member States were enrolled at higher education institutions throughout the Nine in 1976. Because this represents an increase of almost 100% over 1970 in comparison with the 60% increase of foreign students worldwide over the same period, some improvement in the comparative level of intra-EC mobility may be said to have occurred. And as it was only in 1976 that the Community's Action Programme in the field of education, and with it a number of concrete measures such as the Joint Study Programmes Scheme,[39] moves to provide for non-discrimination compared with host country students etc., were introduced, further improvements over the coming years are hopefully to be expected. National policies will have a vital role to play in this process.

Exaggerated expectations do not, however, appear well-founded, at least in the short-term. For in five of the nine Member States, the proportion of students from other Member States relative to the total foreign student population is down at between 4 and 8%. Only in Belgium, Ireland and the Netherlands, where the figure is around 30%, does the proportion become really significant, and

1970

Country of origin	Host country									
	Belgium	Denmark	France	Germany	Ireland	Italy	Luxemburg	Netherlands	UK	Total
Belgium		7	280	151	5	34	n.a.	151[a]	35	663
Denmark	8		63	108	1	11	n.a.	20	54	265
France	469	44		1399	6	205	n.a.	39	120	2282
Germany, Fed. Rep.	428	94	941		11	155	n.a.	156	312	2097
Ireland	15	0	43	23		9	n.a.	4	15	109
Italy	461	18	457	423	5		n.a.	31	124	1519
Luxemburg	370	0	473	462	0	1		2	210	1518
Netherlands	547	24	124	700	15	24	n.a.		112	1546
UK	159	66	827	444	1898	141	n.a.	93		3628
Total	2457	253	3208	3710	1941	580	66	496	982	13693

Note: ᵃData from 1969

1976

Country of orgirin	Host country									
	Belgium	Denmark	France	Germany	Ireland	Italy	Luxemburg	Netherlands	UK	Total
Belgium		8	680	451	4	105	n.a.	148	105	1501
Denmark	12		140	237	2	17	n.a.	16	71	495
France	1230	105		2357	18	294	n.a.	70	1360	4434
Germany, Fed. Rep.	738	293	2092		20	490	n.a.	299	718	4650
Ireland	18	13	132	73		8	n.a.	13	598	855
Italy	1448	33	1339	1066	5			28	276	4195
Luxemburg	811	0	758	682	0	11		6	49	2317
Netherlands	1276	57	333	1460	6	34	n.a.		201	3367
UK	22	184	2004	1161	213	189	n.a.	113		3886
Total	5555	693	7478	7487	268	1148	25	693	2378	25725

Source: Based on Unesco *Statistical Yearbooks*.

Ireland can scarcely be counted in this context anyway in view of the fact that the vast majority of its EC students come from just one country, namely the UK. And among the large receiver countries, a closer inspection of the UK figures shows that not a single EC Member State figured in the top eighteen countries of origin of foreign students in Britain until Germany managed to secure seventeenth place in 1978/79 (Table 2.4).

On the other hand, the percentage of students from other Member States of the European Community relative to the total number of *European* foreign students, is in most cases very high, as Table B.8 in the Statistical Appendix shows. Only Denmark, with its special ties with Scandinavian partners, and Italy, as a result of the influx of Greeks, are exceptions here.

Looking now at the outward student flows *from* EC Member States, it may be noted from Table 7.14 that on average, more than one in three go to another Member State of the Community, the UK (20%) being the only country falling below this mark, probably due in large part to the high recorded 'statistical' level of British students in Canada as discussed earlier.

Table 7.14   Students from the European Community in other Member States, 1976

Country of orgin	Students abroad	Students abroad in another Member State	Percentage
Belgium	2137	1501	70
Denmark	1081	495	46
France	10236	4434	43
Germany, Fed. Rep.	12937	4659	36
Italy	13750	4195	31
Ireland	1877	855	46
Luxemberg	2684	2317	86
Netherlands	3664	3367	92
United Kingdom	19370	3886	20

Source: Based on Unesco *Statistical Yearbooks.*

Table 7.13 (p. 207) reveals that reciprocal student flows exist only between France and the Federal Republic of Germany (both in 1970 and 1976). Quantitatively important two-way flows, though with a more or less marked imbalance in one direction, characterise links between the UK and Germany, Ireland and the UK, Belgium and

Germany. The Netherlands and Luxemburg are sizeable 'exporters' of students to other Member States without receiving many in return, a phenomenon explicable in the case of Luxemburg in terms of the absence of a fully developed system of higher education in that country.

Considering briefly the intra-Community flows in the context of Member States' overall relations with other countries, it is interesting to note that most are substantial 'net importers' of foreign students worldwide: France 'imports' ten times as many students as it 'exports', Belgium seven times as many, Germany five times as many, Denmark and the UK three times as many, and Italy twice. Ireland and the Netherlands send slightly more students abroad than they receive, and only Luxemburg (for the reason mentioned above) substantially more, 90% of the latter country's students abroad going to other EC Member States (mainly France, Belgium and Germany).

Insofar as they play a role as 'exporters' the EC countries, as we have seen, do not by any means send their students exclusively to other Member States. Thus most British students abroad are enrolled in the USA (and Canada). Their German counterparts go mainly to France, Austria and Switzerland, students from France predominantly to Belgium, the Federal Republic of Germany and the USA, and those from Italy to France, Belgium and Germany within the EC but also in significant numbers to Austria (2000 or 15% in 1976, presumably largely from S. Tirol), Switzerland and Canada beyond it. Strangely, the USA figure of 700 suggests that the States are not a particularly frequented destination for Italian students.

To summarise, then, one may say that on the basis of statistics up to and including 1976, student mobility within the European Community, though on the increase, does not play a significant role for most Member States when viewed in the context of their overall roles as host countries to students worldwide. An at once strong and reciprocal flow appears to exist only between France and the Federal Republic of Germany, which are bound by a cultural agreement involving significant injection of funds over and above the mere fact of being EC partners. And apart from Luxemburg and Ireland (both for particular reasons) and the Netherlands, students from Member States appear to move as readily to neighbouring countries outside the Community as to those within it.

Since these results suggest that other bonds essentially linguistic and geographical, are at play in conditioning student flows within Europe, the following sections seek to examine certain typical flows between other specific groupings of Western European countries.

Mobility between the Federal Republic of Germany, Switzerland and Austria The facilitating effect which geographical proximity added to commonality of language can have on student flows, is demonstrated by figures on the mobility of students between Austria, Switzerland and the Federal Republic of Germany. Though Austria and Switzerland are far smaller countries than France and the UK, and not all Swiss Cantons are German-speaking, the total volume of traffic between these two countries and the Federal Republic of Germany is actually greater (9541 students in 1976) than between the latter, France and the UK (8696), as Table 7.15 shows.

Table 7.15   Student mobility between the Federal Republic of Germany, Switzerland and Austria

| Country of origin | Host Country | | | | | |
| | Austria | | Germany, Fed. Rep. | | Switzerland | |
	1970	1976	1970	1976	1970	1976
Austria	—	—	1271	2573	211	357
Germany, Federal Republic	2475	2633	—	—	1843	2593
Switzerland	116	198	835	1187	—	—
A. Total from other countries	2591	2831	2106	3760	2054	2950
B. Total foreign student population	8573	10696	27769	54080	9469	10204
A as % of B	30·2	26·5	7·6	7·0	21·7	24·1

Source: Based on Unesco *Statistical Yearbooks.*

According to these figures, almost four times as many German students go to both Austria (2633) and Switzerland (2593) as to the UK (718); more Austrian students go to Germany than French ones, and more Swiss than British to Germany. Even between the two smaller countries, from Austria to Switzerland, the flow is as strong as from France to the UK. In 1976 one quarter of all foreign students in both Austria (26·5%) and Switzerland (24·9%) came from the two other German-speaking countries under review, and 7% of those in Germany did so – a higher proportion than the French and British students together. And though this proportion has fallen very slightly in Germany and rather more noticeably in Austria since 1970, it has been tending to rise still further in Switzerland. The same language, the relatively similar educational systems, the existence of mutual recognition arrangements and low travel costs all play a role in stimulating such flows, and indeed in some subjects it has become almost a tradition for German students to spend a period of study in one of the other two countries. Ten years ago, before the advent of *numerus clausus*, such mobility was relatively straight-forward, and even now the figures suggest that the tradition continues. Indeed *numerus clausus* mobility has served to trigger off new flows.

Mobility between the Scandinavian countries　Much of what has just been said also applies to the conditions governing flows between the Scandinavian countries – geographical proximity, linguistic accessibility if not commonality, historical tradition and so on. Furthermore, the Nordic Council passed a resolution in 1975 designed specifically to promote intra-Scandinavian student mobility, providing for mutual recognition of studies, reservation

Table 7.16　Student mobility between Scandinavian countries, 1976

Country of origin	Host country					
	Denmark	Finland[a]	Norway[b]	Sweden[a]	Iceland[a]	Total
Denmark		10	72	80	9	171
Finland	70		33	729	1	833
Norway	723	7		234	22	986
Sweden	306	55	89		12	462
Iceland	342	7	48	56		453
Total	1441	79	242	1099	44	
Total foreign student population	3227	529	1147	2723	120	
%	45	15	21	40	37	

Notes:　[a] Data from 1975
　　　　　[b] Data from 1978 (Source: Ministry of Education)
Source:　Based on Unesco *Statistical Yearbooks*

of quotas in *numerus clausus* subjects and the like. Agreements such as these naturally need time to have an impact, but whether or not this is already happening, Table 7.16 indicates a high proportion of intra-Scandinavian flows.

True, the actual numbers of foreign students in these countries are very low – the language barrier is daunting compared with the more widely taught languages such as English, French or even German – but all the countries concerned with the exception of Finland (also an exception linguistically) have extremely high percentages of their total foreign student population from other Scandinavian countries.

And there are indications that the Nordic Council resolution will indeed have the desired results: from 1975 to 1976, the number of foreign students in Denmark almost doubled, and this increase was due almost entirely to a rise in intake from Norway, Iceland and Sweden. In the Danish case, this again highlights the existence of other ties which Member States may have besides that of membership of the European Community, and ones which in terms of student mobility are often more telling.

The knock-on effect: numerus clausus *mobility in Europe*   At the beginning of the present section devoted to student flows between European countries, it was mentioned that they tended on the whole to be relatively weak and that exhortations to the contrary had proved largely in vain. In one important respect, however, recent years have seen a significant and spontaneous development of such flows, namely of students seeking to find study opportunities in neighbouring countries when confronted with restricted admissions at home.

A number of examples of this kind of '*numerus clausus* mobility' may be cited, notably the exodus of German students in the direction of Austria, Switzerland, Italy and Belgium, the last-named country also being increasingly inundated with Dutch students in like manner. The restrictive measures adopted in the 'threatened' countries (and mooted in Italy also) as described in Part I above, have been the result, and that the measures were called for appear clearly from such statistics as those in Table 7.17. That the new tuition fee regulations only appear to be having a fairly marginal deterrent effect, is presumably attributable to the predominantly high income-bracket of the students' parents concerned.

Initially, the Federal and regional authorities in the Federal Republic tended to resist the defence mechanisms introduced by Germany's neighbours. Subsequently, however, the principle seems

Table 7.17   *Students from the Federal Republic of Germany enrolled in Belgium*

Year	Total	Medical sciences	Percentage of total
1970	189	109	58
1976	382	243	64
1977	683	562	82
1978	729	610	84
1979	609	489	80

Source: J. P. Jarousse: *Foreign Students in Belgium*, Paris, Institute of Education, European Cultural Foundation 1980 (mimeograph).

to have been widely accepted by the governments of the European states that no country should be obliged to accept students who could not have been admitted in their country of origin, for this is one of the pillars on which the EC Ministerial agreement of June 1980 is based. As for the university bodies themselves, it is interesting to note that the Franco–German Rectors Conference, for example, has gone clearly on record as deprecating the increase of the 'wild-cat' mobility caused by the knock-on effect of numerical restrictions in a given country.

What may happen when the decision is taken to maintain 'open' admission in such circumstances may be demonstrated with regard to Italy and the influx of in particular Greek students. In 1979/80, only one in five applicants were reported to have secured entrance to Greek higher education institutions following the introduction of competitive entrance examinations,[40] and this has served to quicken the already strong flow of Greek students to other countries. One quarter of all Greek students are currently enrolled abroad. Italy is the main receiver, and a glance at the latest figures for the highly sought-after field of Medical Sciences shows that 'open' admission is having an almost hypnotic effect on the inward flow of foreign students not only from Greece but also elsewhere. No fewer than 37·5% of Italy's foreign students are currently enrolled in medicine (1976/77), 57% of them Europeans, and medicine takes the largest proportion of students from all the main continents of origin (28·2% of the Africans, 31·8% of the Europeans, 47·8% of those from America, and 55% of the Asians).

'*Numerus clausus* mobility' is a highly significant phenomenon, in that it points up the fact that where students perceive a clear advantage in studying abroad, they will do so and that in this respect at least, the German, Dutch or Greek student seeking admission to medical studies in Austria, Italy, Belgium or Switzerland because of the impossibility of such admission at home, is motivated very much by the same considerations as the student from a developing country seeking admission to a subject area at a European university which is not provided in his country of origin: to treat intra-industrialised country mobility as being a fundamentally different phenomenon from that between developing and industrialised countries, may therefore require some basic re-thinking in the years to come. Some further remarks will be made on this in our conceptual comments contained in Part III below.

Distribution of foreign students by field and level of study, and sex
As regards the distribution of foreign students by *field of study*, analysis is hampered by the lack of internationally collected data after 1970. This is particularly unfortunate in that many of the numerical and other restrictions on admission were only introduced around or after that date, which makes it impossible to assess accurately and comprehensively their effect on the distribution of foreign students among the various subject areas. The dearth of statistics by both country/continent of origin *and* field of study is particularly frustrating in this respect.

National statistics are more readily available, but lack comparability, even of the subject nomenclature. To set the background for more in-depth research, the salient points to emerge from our analysis of Unesco data by field of study up to 1970 may therefore be useful for reference purposes.

Dividing foreign students into five main fields of study, 1970 figures showed a fairly even spread: 25% each in the humanities and technology, 20% in social sciences and 15% each in the natural sciences and medical sciences. A comparison with the distribution of the total student population on the same basis revealed a much higher percentage of the total student body in the humanities and social sciences and a correspondingly lower one than in the case of foreign students when it came to technology and the medical sciences. Over half the foreign students were then opting for the 'hard' sciences (natural sciences, technology, and medical sciences), as opposed to only 35% of the total student population. The percentage was even as high as 80% in Spain, the German Democratic Republic and Italy, 60% in Portugal, the Federal Republic of Germany, Turkey, Greece, Czechoslovakia and the USSR. The proportion of foreign students

studying 'soft' science subjects (humanities and social sciences) pre-
dominated in Finland, Denmark, Norway, Luxemburg, Switzerland and Japan, while the distribution was more or less balanced
in the remaining countries.

The second phenomenon to emerge is that of the exceptionally
high demand among foreign students for places in medicine. Twice
as large a percentage of the world's foreign students study medicine
as of the total student population as a whole, and almost all
countries under review showed a higher percentage of the foreign
than of the home students in medicine. Between 1964 and 1970, the
total number of foreign students studying medicine almost doubled
to around 60,000, over half of these being enrolled in France, Spain,
the USA and Italy. But that the rise in the numbers and percentage
of foreign students in the field of medical sciences has deprived host
country students of places, is not borne out by the statistics
available, for the percentage of host country students in this field
also grew between 1964 and 1970, albeit more slowly.

Although no precise data are available on the rejection rate in
medical sciences, there is a good deal of evidence to suggest that
students react in two ways to the introduction of severer admission
restrictions. One reaction is that of opting for another, usually in
some way related, field of study, either to 'park' there for a while
awaiting admission to medicine, or as a permanent choice. This may
be inferred from the fact that in countries where the proportion of the
total student body studying medicine has been falling, this has been
accompanied by an attendant rise in the proportions studying in
natural sciences and technology.

Of the twenty-four host countries under review, more than 75%
of all foreign students studying technology were enrolled in just three
of them in 1970, namely the USA, UK and the Federal Republic
of Germany, and the same three host countries plus France
accounted in the same year for over 80% of the foreign students
in natural sciences in the countries under review.

In the 'soft sciences', growth rates in the social sciences were tending to be appreciably higher than in the humanities, one contributing
factor probably being the increasing emergence and attraction of
courses in business management in many of the main host countries.

Later figures suggest that the broad outline indicated by the above
figures appears to be fairly stable, significant shifts from one subject
to another only taking place where specifically restrictive measures
are introduced (e.g. in medicine in Austria, France, Switzerland and
so on). The country studies to be published by the Institute in the
coming months will provide more precision on this topic, as also

on foreign student distribution by type of institution – another type-categorisation fraught with pitfalls.

More radical changes have, as we saw in Part I with regard to 'Policies', been making themselves felt concerning the distribution of foreign student numbers by their *level of study*. Most host governments have been laying greater emphasis on opportunities for further degree level study, and this is already making itself felt statistically. Thus in France, foreign students account for only 12·8% of all university enrolments (1979), but 18·2% of those at 'third cycle' level, and the proportion of the foreign student body enrolled in the latter has risen from 20·8% in 1973 to 24·3% in 1979. Switzerland, too, which also has a current (1979) ratio of 80:20 between its foreign students at first:further degree level, had been noticing an upswing in the latter. But nowhere has the trend been as marked as in the UK. From an already high percentage of 25·6% of the total student population at further degree level in 1970/71, the foreign student proportion rose to 37·0% by 1977/78, compared with a rise from 3·9 to 7·4% at first degree level.

Finally, it is worth noting that in the past two decades, the distribution of foreign students by *sex* has been undergoing steady and considerable change, as in the case of the student population as a whole. Between 1964 and 1976, the proportion of female students relative to the total student population rose by an average of 10% in the countries under review in this present report, standing at between 40 and 50% in most of these countries in the latter year. Only Turkey with 25% women students and Japan, the Netherlands and Switzerland with roughly one-third constitute exceptions to this pattern. But although the growth-rates of the female student population have been on average higher, there are signs, as Cerych and Colton have recently pointed out,[41] that in countries where the proportion of female students was already high, a certain stagnation of their growth-rates is beginning to set in.

The foreign student population, too, shows a marked and continuous rise in the proportion of women enrolled, though it still tends to be well below that of their male counterparts and lower than that for the home student population. Thus in the USA* and Austria (1977/78), it stands at only 29%, in France at around 30% (compared with 50% for French students), in Belgium at 23·9% (compared with 37% for Belgians), in the UK (1975/76) at only 21·2% (compared with 35·2% for the home student population). Only in Switzerland does the foreign student population show a higher percentage of

*Provisional figures from IIE for 1979/80.

females (36·3%) than is recorded for the home student population (30·2% in 1979/80); and indeed it has been consistently higher there for the past decade and a half, the female proportions in 1965 being 24·6% for foreigners and 18·1% for home students.

Part III General Conclusions and Areas for Future Research

The present report on trends and developments in the foreign student population in selected industrialised countries represents but one element in what one would hope might become a systematic analysis of student mobility in worldwide terms. For this is a highly complex phenomenon, influenced as it is by interacting factors related to the educational and social policy, economic and political development of both the 'sender' and 'receiver' countries, together with a multitude of less easily definable but in motivational terms nonetheless important considerations. We have therefore felt it appropriate to conclude our study with some brief remarks on avenues which might profitably be explored in future research, together with some conceptual comments on how we feel such research might be approached.

First, and to reiterate what was said at the outset, there is a pressing need for more adequate statistical data. At international level, the only available comparative source, Unesco, lacks many of the most important categories for analysing student flows, notably field of study, sex, new enrolments, rejection ratio at entrance and at other levels, distribution by phase of study (first or higher degree), success rates and social background. Some of these, it is true, are taken into consideration when collecting statistics at national level, but comparison across a large number of countries is at present well nigh impossible. Equally lacking are empirically founded calculations of the actual cost of providing higher education for foreign students, and the work being carried out under the current Overseas Students Trust project may well provide some much-needed guidance in this respect. Some of these categories are, of course, available when it comes to studying the student population as a whole or that of the host country concerned, and what is really needed is a means whereby developments in the foreign student population may be studied in genuine comparison with this. The annual *Open Doors* report, produced by the Institute of International Education in New York on foreign students in the USA and now efficiently computerised to facilitate unique opportunities for cross-correlation of categories, is an example of what can be done when manpower, resources and imagination are brought to bear on the task, and the signs are that the currently increasing interest in foreign student affairs may be encouraging other countries to follow suit.

Secondly, foreign student flows and policies must be viewed in the context of worldwide secondary, further and higher education development as a whole. For it is clear that drastic changes in higher education policy, together with other extrinsic factors such as changes in the labour market, are bound to affect host countries' attitudes to the reception of foreign students – and who would deny that such changes have characterised many of the statistically most important receiver countries in recent years? Similar changes in the situation of the sender countries are equally important, particularly that of the developing nations, which form the largest source of foreign students: many countries in Asia, Africa and South America have witnessed an unprecedented expansion of pre-tertiary education in recent years, and this is likely to give rise to a continuing, if not indeed quickening increase in the number of foreign students seeking admission to higher education in the more highly industrialised countries in the years to come. Foreign students' policies therefore seem likely to play an ever increasing part in the context of governmental development aid policies in future, and the beginnings of this trend are already in evidence, as well as a clear tendency towards greater differentiation. This trend will probably be heightened further by the increasing demand for places from students from OPEC countries, and in particular, countries with traditionally open access policies seem likely to be constrained to compromise on such policies.

A third area for further research is decidedly that of motivation and reasons for mobility, touched upon at various instances in this present report, and it may be regarded as crucial if policy-makers are to be provided with a more comprehensive basis on which to take their decisions. Our analysis of student flows has led us to forward the hypothesis that such flows may be usefully explained by reference to the 'cost-benefit' model, applying these concepts to the individual student's decision on whether to study abroad or not, and using them in a broader than the strictly economic sense. Quite apart from the higher financial cost (travel, subsistence in a foreign country) involved, other costs are inevitably incurred by a student wishing to study in another country: overcoming the language barrier and adapting to a different culture are just two of many. A student will, consciously or not, weigh up these costs against the possible benefits which may accrue (improvement in qualifications, enhancement of career opportunities, enrichment of personal cultural experience, etc.), and view them in the light of the resources at his disposal (availability of funds, knowledge of the foreign language, existing links with the country concerned, and so on). Unless he is convinced that the benefits outweigh the costs, he is unlikely to take the step of going abroad of his own volition.

On the basis of the analysis outlined above, three types of international mobility may be broadly distinguished according to their participants' motivation:

(1) Students go abroad because the opportunities of study which they seek are either non-existent, of inferior quality or subject to severe admission restrictions in their home country;
(2) They do so because a period of study abroad is either an intrinsic and obligatory part of their courses, or at least represents a demonstrable enrichment of them (language study etc.);
(3) Opportunity for study abroad is not of superior quality or range, but is less costly in financial terms (many US students cross the border into Canada).

And, as indicated in Part II of the study, in considering the phenomenon of what we have called '*numerus clausus* mobility', we feel that this approach may serve to call into question the veracity of the widely held view that mobility from developing to industrialised countries is of an essentially different nature from that, say, within Europe or between Europe and the USA.

As regards mobility between industrialised countries, our analysis suggests that the mere removal of administrative obstacles, important though this is, is unlikely to provide the key to increasing flows. In addition, measures would need to be taken to stimulate these actively by enhancing the benefits and reducing the costs to the student, in brief, by rendering study abroad more advantageous. Apart from the improved provision of financial support, one potentially effective means of achieving this is the development of structures for full integration of study periods abroad into a student's prescribed course, thereby overcoming a number of administrative problems and – as initial experience shows – improving the professional prospects of the students concerned. In addition, the creation of inexpensive and well integrated language courses for students of all faculties will be indispensable, if such mobility between countries with different languages is to be increased.

Naturally, the analysis, predictions and recommendations outlined above are somewhat rudimentary, and much more detailed research – both into the reasons behind student flows and into the factors determining government action – will be necessary on an international basis if a comprehensive view is to be obtained.

Happily, there are currently signs that the isolationism, which has so characterised decision-making in this in many respects crucial sector of policy-making, is being increasingly called into question. Thus in 1981 there will be major conferences organised by both inter-governmental (Council of Europe) and academic (European Rectors Conference: CRE) bodies on the whole question of foreign student flows and policies. We hope that the present report will contribute in some small way to providing them with food for thought.

Notes

1. For total enrolment of students, see G. Carceles, 'Development of Education in the world: a summary statistical review', *International Review of Education*, 1979, Vol. 2/3, pp. 147–76, especially p. 151.
2. 'Brain drain or reintegration after study abroad', in *Development and co-operation*, Vol. 1, 1977, p. 20.
3. See, for example, O. Klineberg, 'International Exchanges in Education, Science and Culture', *Social Science Information*, Vol. 4, 1966, pp. 91–143; O. Klineberg, and J. Ben-Brika, *Etudiants du tiers monde en Europe*. Paris, Mouton, 1972; O. Klineberg and W. F. Hull, *At a Foreign University. An International Study of Adaptation and Coping*, New York, Praeger, 1979; I. Eide, *Students as Links between Cultures*, Oslo, 1970; A. Sen, *Problems of Overseas Students and Nurses*, London, 1970; W. F. Hull, *Foreign Students in the United States of America. Coping Behaviour within the Educational Environment*, New York, Praeger, 1978; P. Aich, 'The Problems of Coloured Students in Germany', *Social Science Information*, Vol. 1, 1962, pp. 37–49; M. C. Viguier, *La vie sociale des étudiants étrangers à Toulouse*. Thèse du 3. cycle, Maison de Science de l'Homme, 1966.
4. R. G. Myers: *Education and Immigration*, Chicago and New York, 1972, p. 5.
5. For the Member States of the European Community, conditions of admission for students from other Member States are exhaustively enumerated in the annex to the Consultative Document XII/1151/77 – final (Brussels, 1978) entitled *Admission to Institutions of Higher Education of Students from other Member States* circulated by the Commission in 1978. This document, based on a report prepared for the Commission by L. Cerych and A. Smith of the Institute of Education of the European Cultural Foundation, has ultimately given rise to agreement between Member States on this topic (Ministerial meeting of 27 June 1980). Unless otherwise stated, the overview of policy measures contained in the present chapter draws both on this document, on research carried out by the same authors in the context of the 1978 Unesco/CEPES project on 'Access to Tertiary Education in Europe', and on the responses to the questionnaire distributed in connection with the present study.

6. L. Cerych, *Access and Structure of Post-Secondary Education* (= Occasional Paper no. 1) Paris, Institute of Education of the European Cultural Foundation, 1976.
7. *Le Matin*, 25 March 1980.
8. Österreichischer Auslandsstudentendienst (Zentrale Geschäftsstelle), *Gesperrte Studienrichtungen bzw. Aufnahmebeschränkungen bei bestimmten Studienrichtungen für ausländische Studienbewerber an den österreichischen Universitäten für das Studienjahr 1979/80.*
9. In particular, measures have been introduced to prevent as far as possible the selling of immigration papers (cf. article entitled 'Selling Immigration Papers', *The Chronicle of Higher Education*, 31 March 1980, p. 11.
10. Cf. M. Woodhall, *Review of Student Support Schemes in Selected OECD Countries*, Paris, OECD, 1978, p. 9f.
11. *Chronicle of Higher Education*, 7 April 1980, p. 17.
12. A. Phillips, *British Aid for Overseas Students*, London, World University Service, 1980.
13. For example, an article in *Higher Education and National Affairs*, Vol. 29, no. 19, 30 May 1980, p. 3, reported the state of Louisiana to be contemplating the exclusion of Iranian students from its institutions of higher education.
14. In the case of nationals of EC Member States, in accordance with Resolution 1612/68, the Belgian residence requirement related to students' parents or guardians is waived, though the students themselves must be resident there.
15. Cf. regulations of 5 January 1976 promulgated in the *Moniteur Belge*, Chapter III, Article 85ff. of the Budget for 1976.
16. Cf. also the system in the USA described in *NAFSA Newsletter* Vol. 31, no. 2, January 1980, p. 91.
17. Cf. A. Smith, 'From "Europhoria" to Pragmatism: towards a new start for higher education co-operation in Europe?' *European Journal of Education*, Vol. 15 (1980), no. 1, pp. 77–95.
18. B. Burn, (ed.) *Higher Education Reform: Implications for Foreign Students*, New York, Institute of International Education, 1978, p. 10.
19. L. Cerych, and S. L. Colton, 'Summarising Recent Student Flows', *European Journal of Education* Vol. 15 (1980), no. 1, pp. 15–35.
20. Cf. *Education Statistics*, Brussels, *Eurostat*, Annual Reports.
21. Paris, Unesco 1971, 1976.
22. Bucharest: Unesco/CEPES 1978.
23. On the problems of the comparability and validity of international statistics, cf. Sarah Colton's article entitled 'Chaotic Uniformity in European Higher Education Statistics', *European Journal of Education*, Vol. 14 (1979), no. 4, pp. 379–87.
24. *Statistics on Students Abroad 1969–1973*, p. 11.
25. *Statistical Yearbook 1975*, p. 345.
26. More information about changes in the definition of 'foreign student' in Britain can be found in Overseas Students Trust: *Overseas Students in Britain – some facts and Figures*, Annex I; A. Phillips, *British Aid*

for Overseas Students, pp. 12–15. The Race Relations Act of 1976 and changes in official interpretation of 'ordinary residence' are tending to raise the number of students classified as 'overseas', some of whom have previously been defined as 'home' students.

27. Overseas Students Trust, *Overseas Students and Government Policy*, London, 1979, pp. 4–8.
28. Cf. R. B. Armada, 'Foreign Students in Spain', in: B. Burn (ed.), *Higher Education Reform: Implications for Foreign Students*, New York, Institute of International Education, 1978, p. 155.
29. J. P. Jarousse, *Foreign Students in France* Paris Institute of Education, European Cultural Foundation, 1980 (mimeograph).
30. *Informationsdienst Austausch* 30 July 1980.
31. A. Phillips, *British Aid for Foreign Students*, pp. 16, 28–32.
32. Cf. also 'The dilemma facing the refugee and overseas student', *The Times Higher Education Supplement*, 14 March 1980, p. 13.
33. M. Peters, P. Zeugin: Zur ökonomischen und sozialen Lage der Studenten an der Universität Zürich, Zürich, U Zürich, 1975.
34. Cf. Commission des Communautés Européennes, *Les enfants des travailleurs migrants*, Collection Études. Série education no. 1, Bruxelles 1977, pp. 8–10 and 40.
35. H. Schulte, 'Reflections on the problem of student mobility in Europe', address to the CRE on 8 April 1976 (manuscript), p. 1 (French version in: *CRE-Information* 34 (2nd quarter 1976), pp. 11–37.
36. Cf. A. Smith, 'From "Europhoria" to Pragmatism: towards a new start for higher education co-operation in Europe?', *European Journal of Education*, Vol. 15 (1980), 100.1, pp. 77–95. The author discusses a considerable number of recent trends, policies and programmes related to higher education co-operation in Europe, many of which have a direct bearing on student mobility. Some four years previously, the Institute had already produced the 'Masclet Report' on 'Intra-European Mobility of Undergraduate Students'.
37. A table on student mobility throughout the 'European Region' of UNESCO, i.e. including North America, is published in the *Statistical Study on Higher Education* in Europe produced by Unesco/CEPES, pp. 61ff.
38. Cf. J. C. Masclet, *The Intra-European Mobility of Undergraduate Students*, Paris, Institute of Education of the European Cultural Foundation, 1975.
39. Cf. A. Smith, *Joint Programmes of Study. An Instrument of European Co-operation in Higher Education*, Brussels, Commission of the European Communities 1979 (Studies. Education Series, no. 7).
40. Cf. article in *The Times*, 11 December 1979.
41. L. Cerych and S. L. Colton, 'Summarising Recent Student Flows', *European Journal of Education*, Vol. 15 (1980), no. 1, pp. 15–35.

8. Conclusion: the Way Ahead

This concluding chapter by the Editor, Peter Williams, draws not only on the material in the book itself, but also on participants' contributions and the record of discussions at the Wiston House Colloquium convened by the Overseas Students Trust in October 1980.

The wide-ranging contributions to this book underline the multi-dimensional nature of the overseas student problem. It is a broader question than the narrow issue of whether or not overseas students have been contributing to Britain the equivalent of the full cost of their education. Beyond the important financial aspects there are considerations of trade, political and cultural influence, assistance to overseas development. There are also aspects which it has been possible to touch on only lightly in this volume – the academic importance of overseas students in British colleges and universities, and the relationship of overseas student policies with immigration. It is also clear that our provision for overseas students is of concern not simply to ourselves and the sending countries. British policies and practice in this field have an effect on other English-speaking 'receiving' countries in particular, and it is desirable to harmonise our approach with that of other friendly countries sharing common interests.

The papers assembled here combine to convey a central message that Britain needs urgently to develop a coherent policy on overseas students. This is a conclusion that others have also reached, most notably the two House of Commons Committees which examined the subject in some detail in 1980. The Education, Science and Arts Committee of the House of Commons concluded:

> The policy of previous governments over overseas student fees has been characterised by drift and infirmity of purpose. In contrast the decision of the present government to move to 'full-cost' fees within a matter of months is equally at fault ...
> Some of us support the Government's concept of 'full-cost' fees;

others would prefer to return to the earlier practice of non-discrimination between home and overseas students, fixing the fee at a percentage of 'full-cost'. All, however, agree that a definitive statement of policy, in the form of a White Paper, after consultation, is now essential.[1]

The Overseas Development Sub-Committee of the Foreign Affairs Committee expressed similar views:

> Enquiries have revealed both the need for and lack of a properly integrated, coherent policy on overseas student affairs....
> We formed the impression that, largely as a result of our inquiry, Departments which had hitherto been acting unilaterally had begun to perceive the need for co-ordination. We hope and expect that out of this experience there will arise a better degree of co-ordination in Whitehall and the development and communication to all parties concerned of a coherent and internally consistent set of policies on overseas students.[2]

The basis for any coherent policy on overseas students should be long-term rather than short-term. Certainly the short-term problems for individual students, for particular overseas countries, for award-giving agencies, for educational institutions have all been severe and have been aggravated by the suddenness with which changes were announced and by the lack of prior consultation. The full rigour of new arrangements may be reduced by short-term palliatives to help adjustment by the various parties over the transitional period. Whilst such measures are undoubtedly necessary to protect the once-in-a-lifetime opportunities of study in Britain for some foreign individuals, and to ensure the immediate survival of certain key institutions and courses in British higher education, it must be stressed that such actions do not collectively constitute a coherent policy. Thus far the Government has acted to reduce the cost to public funds of overseas students in Britain but has done little to identify, protect and promote long-term British interests. The reception of overseas students in Britain has been regarded not as an opportunity, nor as an investment in Britain's future, but rather as a tiresome and costly legacy from the past. Britain's image abroad has thus already suffered harm: but the cumulative damage to our long-term interests will only be felt over a longer period.

However, it is yet possible that this damage can largely be averted by timely thought and action, and this book constitutes in a sense a plea for constructive thought to be devoted to working out such a coherent approach for the longer term. When the very immediate short-term economic difficulties have been surmounted and controlled growth of public expenditure can again be contemplated it should be possible to embark with confidence on a new set of arrangements for the reception and support of overseas students in Britain.

Such policies should most usefully be discussed and developed separately from questions concerning the best way to fund British higher and further education. Financial support for overseas students has to be justified, if at all, on grounds other than that it is a means of channelling public resources to educational institutions. These two issues were fortuitously brought together in 1979 as a result of the method selected by Government to introduce full-cost fees for overseas students. They were one of the chosen means of imposing public expenditure cuts on the higher education sector. A good part of the opposition to the overseas student policy came from vice-chancellors and principals who could not see how their institutions were to remain solvent when faced with a withdrawal of part of their grants. They argued that they lacked the power to reduce their expenditure in the short term to the same extent as the grant reductions, principally because of the academic tenure system, and Blaug (pp. 52–55) lends some support to their stance. The question whether the intended savings can actually be realised in the short and medium terms remains basically unresolved. Because this is not, however, essentially an issue of policy with regard to overseas students, it will not be further addressed here.

Of course whilst noting that the two issues are distinct, any chosen method of financing overseas students must be consistent with, and accommodated to, the overall system for financing higher education in general. The terms of admission for overseas students must be fixed in such a way that they do not distort British education priorities and the planning of provision for UK students. As discussed below in relation to full-cost fees, there is certainly a possibility that this could happen. The best means of financing higher and further education in Britain generally is under intensive discussion at the present time, having been the subject of review by the House of Commons Education, Science and Arts Committee. In some quarters considerable interest is being shown in having a system that would involve nominal full-cost fees for all students and a system of grants and loans to enable students to meet these. This would probably involve the ending of discrimination in charges (fee levels) according to nationality, but with continuing differential access for home and overseas students to financial support from British public funds. British and European Community students (including those from, say, Réunion) would then be charged exactly the same fee as students from Commonwealth countries.

Any new policy that may be devised will have to differ quite radically from the regime that existed prior to 1979. Both major political parties were agreed that the previous arrangements had to be modified, being unsatisfactory in a number of major respects. In the first place they involved a heavy public subsidy from British funds which seemed to be rising rapidly not through Britain's own volition, but in reflex response to an underlying overseas demand for high quality tertiary education in the medium of English at costs which were relatively low given British fees policy and the level of the exchange rate. The sum involved in the subsidy – well over £100m by Treasury reckoning and nearer £200m by Blaug's subsequent calculation (p. 85) – was substantial, and even if the absolute numbers and proportions of overseas students were sustainable at their existing levels, the trend (a tripling of the number in publicly financed tertiary education and a doubling of the proportion) was indeed alarming and insupportable over a prolonged period. Moreover the subsidies were not being directed to serve the aims of British policy at all closely. A large part was going to support students on fairly low level courses (including GCE and SCE courses) with no obvious relevance to overseas developmental needs or to the further-ance of British trade. The country composition of the overseas student body was such that more places were taken by private students from Iran or Malaysia than by all our European Com-munity partners combined, and students from the probable economic giants of the twenty-first century – China, Brazil, Mexico and India for example – were few. Third, a rather unsatisfactory pattern of distribution by institution and course had emerged. Even leaving aside the special cases where courses in oriental languages and culture, or in tropical medicine, were specifically oriented to overseas concerns and so naturally attracted high proportions of students from abroad – there were concentrations of overseas students in institutions, subjects, departments and courses which seemed to reflect a maldistribution from the point of view of British interests. On the one hand there were sectors of British higher education where the admixture of overseas students was so diluted as to be unnotice-able. At the other extreme there were instances where the proportions were so high that one could only conclude that publicly subsidised courses were being laid on exclusively for an overseas clientele and in furtherance of institutional expansionist policies. In isolated cases British students may have even suffered positive disadvantage from being grouped with a preponderance of foreigners.

Undoubtedly it was the first of these considerations – the escalation of costs through the growth of numbers – that weighed most heavily with successive governments and two main regulatory instruments were considered. These were price (manipulation of fee levels) and quota. The price mechanism was used to contain the cost to British public funds from 1967 onwards, but although increases in some years were quite steep (Table 2.5) the resultant fees never constituted a high proportion of overall costs at the levels and in the subject areas (mainly science and technology) of most interest to overseas students. Certainly, as Phillips has shown (Figure 2.1 p. 32), the fee rises in the latter half of the 1970s affected the distribution of overseas students by countries of origin; but the overall number of students continued to rise. It was only in 1979 that really massive price rises were announced, with the intention that from 1980 fees should cover full costs.

This is the market approach to regulating the overseas demand for places in British tertiary education, and there are clearly many advantages in this approach. It avoids for the public exchequer any open-ended subsidy: indeed unless one decides to organise special scholarship or fee remission schemes it obviates the need for any public expenditure on foreign students at all, thus removing the main argument for imposing restrictions on numbers. As many as can pay will then be welcome. For individuals in a position to pay, it may thus offer greater possibilities of actually finding a place, for it is likely that any qualified student whose fee payment yields some 'profit' to an educational institution would be admitted. The public education system should become more efficient in its use of resources, being more alert to the requirements of the student market and more conscious of the need to reduce costs. It apparently offers institutions a real incentive to mount an 'export drive' in the field of educational services. If Britain has a greater comparative advantage in 'selling' university postgraduate courses – for reasons of quality, cost-effectiveness in terms of course length and drop-out rates, language, etc. – than in selling machinery, should she not deliberately set out to develop her export potential in this area of activity? And administratively it is cheap in so far as no controls are needed over the volume or composition of the inward student flow.

At the same time the drawbacks to full-cost fees are obvious. The case for subsidies to students in general (home, as well as overseas) is that if all students were asked to pay the full cost of their education, they would – from society's point of view – underinvest in it: and that one would then lose certain general benefits to society at large from investment in education that are 'external' to (inappropriable by) the individual being educated. The benefits to Britain outlined in Chapter 1, and spelled out more fully in Chapters 3 to 5, are all of this external kind, and it follows from the above argument that if *some* benefits from educating overseas students in the UK do indeed accrue to Britain on a sufficiently large scale, then an entirely respectable case may exist for modifying a full-cost fees policy through systems of fee remission or scholarships. One of the most powerful criticisms made of the initial arrangements under the full-cost fees policy was that it failed to apply the financial support instrument of awards schemes to help key categories of overseas student (Wallace, p. 131).

A second problem with full-cost fees centres around the precise reckoning of 'full-cost' and who is to make the reckoning. This issue cannot be discussed exhaustively here, but would have to be tackled sooner rather than later for overseas students and possibly also in the British student context if full charges and loans were to be introduced. The minimum 'full-cost fees' actually charged are bound to be calculated in a very rough and ready manner. If average costs are used, then in some cases these are probably above, and in other cases below, the true marginal costs of courses. Both average and marginal costs will vary by institution, by subject, by level of study, by course, and by level of enrolment. How much freedom should be exercised by educational institutions in calculating and prescribing their own fee levels for each separate course? Should minima be prescribed by government or should each institution be free to determine how to cover its own costs? Are institutions able to agree uniform fee levels for similar courses or must each decide individually?

These questions are potentially important in relation to attempts to maintain uniform standards of quality in British higher education. If those institutions with particularly high 'drawing power' were to raise overseas fees so as to increase their income, there would be the probably unwelcome prospect of concentrating the wealthiest group of overseas students in the best institutions in the UK. It might also 'pay' such institutions to maximise their income by allocating an increasing share of their sought-after places to overseas students, to the exclusion of British applicants. At the other end of the scale, institutions in financial difficulty might be tempted to respond either by lowering their fees or lowering their standards of admission for overseas students. The question that arises is whether the degree of 'disorder' in the system inherent in a competitive market system could be contained at an acceptable level, or whether it would spell the end of a unified higher education system in Britain.

The main alternative approach to fees as a regulatory instrument is quotas (quantitative restriction, or *'numerus clausus'* as it is known in some continental countries). Quotas are a very direct means of restricting total numbers and the first tentative steps to applying them were taken by the Labour government in 1976. Although the quota system operated only slowly and was thought even by Government itself to have been ineffective, it now seems (p. 37) that quotas may have had more impact on overall numbers of admissions in the years 1977–79 than had previously been thought. Since however the period of quota operation was also a time when tuition fees were rising and inflation was high, it is not certain what separate effect the quotas themselves had on admission levels, and what was a result of these other factors.

A major disadvantage of quotas is that they tend to require a rather large bureaucractic machinery to 'police' and operate them if, as must be assumed under the British system, students are admitted at institutional level and not farmed out to institutions by some central placement agency. This immediately raises distributional issues and gives rise to difficult questions about the basis for quota allocations. How are these to be determined? If allocation is on the basis of historic entitlement, the danger is that an obsolete set of arrangements may be perpetuated, and the possibility of dynamic change reduced. But if quota shares are allocated through competitive bidding by educational institutions, the requirements in time and administrative machinery seem overwhelming. Those who are familiar with import licensing systems for goods in international trade will be only too aware of the problems and even abuses to which such systems can give rise.

Both fees and quotas, then, have their advantages and disadvantages as means of control of overall numbers. They would also need substantial modification if they were to be used in a selective and discriminatory way to promote certain specific British interests by supporting particular groups of students. They have not thus far been used in Britain to secure desired distributional effects: rather they have been thought of as imposing numerical ceilings to regulate total numbers.

It is possible to conceive of both fees and quotas being used to affect distribution. In the case of fees this would involve a differential fee system with lower fees, implying some subsidy, for specified favoured groups (or a penalty level of fee for *dis*favoured groups, while favoured groups paid the normal full cost fee). Favoured groups might be chosen on the basis of individual country of origin, country category (e.g. all developing countries), personal characteristics of the student, subject studied, etc. Apart from deciding priorities, problems involved with this categorisation would be the reporting system needed to verify and pay the resource claims of institutions admitting students at concessionary fee levels and the mechanisms for establishing the credentials of individual students entitled to concessionary treatment. In the same way quotas could be operated to control the actual composition of the overseas student body, using a similar set of categories for the purpose as has been mentioned above in connection with fees. It would only make sense to use quotas if their purpose was to ration out a limited quantum of places, presumably in a system that did not charge full fees (the Conservative government that came into power in 1979 maintained that quantitative restrictions were no longer necessary if full-cost fees were charged). The disadvantages of using quotas on such a disaggregated basis (a quota for indigent students, a quota for refugees, a quota for Benin, a quota for Singapore, etc.), is that the administrative burden would be exceedingly great particularly if institutional autonomy in selection were preserved.

One area where quotas might be deemed appropriate is in establishing some guidelines on the proportions of overseas students that might best be admitted to British institutions and courses, in order to get the benefits of a more equal distribution. In the majority of courses a minimum target proportion of say 5% overseas students and a maximum of say 33% might ensure the benefits of international mixing while guarding against excessive concentration. However it must be admitted that the very notion of 'excessive' concentration raises severe conceptual difficulties if a market approach with fully cost-covering courses is being followed; for the implication of such a system is that Britain might deliberately create and sell to foreigners extra capacity in its education system. And whatever the orientation of the system might be, one can see that exceptions from recommended proportions would have to be made for cost-covering courses specially geared to overseas countries' needs, where higher proportions of up to 100% might be the expected norm.

An alternative approach to the distribution problem – i.e. to the problem of influencing the composition of the overseas student body, in order to ensure that British interests and obligations find due recognition – is to operate an award system of bursaries and scholarships. This actually has several advantages over differential fees or specific quotas. In the first place it is possible with an award scheme to incorporate payments other than tuition fees. Costs of travel and maintenance may also be included, and by meeting total costs in some instances the field of potential candidates will be widened. For without awards, even if tuition were free, the annual costs of board and accommodation in Britain – at not less than £3000 in 1980 – effectively prevent all but the well-to-do from taking advantage of places. Secondly an award scheme can 'target' support in a much more effective and directed way than the differential fee scheme or quota. Instead of regulation from above by the use of ceilings on numbers, the award scheme works up from the bottom so to speak by ensuring a specified number of places of a particular kind for particular purposes or particular groups of students. Third, used in conjunction with a system of full-cost fees the award scheme may be much less costly than an exemptions system, as it is possible to limit the numbers supported. With an exemption system – as applied in 1980/81 to European Community students or to refugees, both of which categories qualified for home fees – there is virtually no control over the number who may qualify under any prescribed category.

In the course of the recent discussions sponsored by the Overseas Students Trust a broad consensus view seems to have emerged that the way ahead in British provision for overseas students lies largely in the expansion of support schemes targeted to various priority groups coinciding with identified British interests and obligations. For this to take effect it would be necessary to build on already existing schemes in the form of technical co-operation awards on the vote of the Overseas Development Administration, Common-wealth Scholarships, British Council Scholarships and Bursaries, government contributions to the Confederation of British Industry Overseas Scholarship Scheme, support for academic exchange pro-grammes and the like.

One might envisage a very greatly expanded provision under these schemes, taking account of the much greater needs arising with the introduction of full-cost fees. Whilst the exact number of awards would depend on the government's perception of its interests and obligations at any particular time and on the state of the economy, it should be borne in mind that even 15,000–20,000 fully paid awards (including travel and subsistence) could be funded for a sum no greater than the estimated former net 'subsidy' (put by Blaug at £180m) and if the same amount were used to finance partial awards the coverage could be much more extensive still.

It is tempting to think that a system of this kind could establish a clear order of priorities for the future allocation of British public funds among different purposes and different categories of student. Certainly it would be desirable to attempt to define broad priorities at the outset and to institute a comprehensive review from time to time. On the other hand some caution about the possibilities of producing an agreed list of priorities is probably appropriate, bearing in mind, first, Wallace's point about the extent to which obligations and expectations have been inherited and, second, that many of the expected benefits are unquantifiable and cannot be reduced, for example through economic cost-benefit analysis, to a single scale of values. Different sets of decision-makers in different departments of government and in organisations outside government may have very different sets of value preferences.

It is not possible here to do more than hint at some of the principles which might inform the selection of priorities by the UK authorities in 'targeting' support funds to particular groups of overseas students

- Emphasis should be placed in all award schemes on the academic quality of the recipient: this is essential both as a rationing device and to maintain the standing of awards, and also ensure that standards of work including research are enhanced in our institutions.

- Generally awards for more advanced courses are to be preferred to those for lower level work, and for specialised training as opposed to general training.

- More emphasis could be given to studies which link up with British trade and investment overseas: this should be construed broadly to include more than just exports of machinery and engineering courses, and should take account of invisible exports of financial, insurance and other services and of business-oriented studies such as accountancy, management and economics.

- The temptation to equate individual indigence with country GNP should be avoided since it has been established by Blaug and others (Appendix A) that some of the poorest students come from the richest countries and vice versa. Whilst every effort should be made to ensure that students are not prevented by poverty from taking up awards, the limitation on scholarship schemes as a means of redressing poverty have, as Hunter points out, to be recognised and we must accept that foreign students will generally come from the more privileged groups in their countries.

- Country of origin is clearly one of the most important criteria for allocation of awards. Britain will want to have a balanced spread in the overseas student body between students from the First, Second and Third Worlds. In terms of country allocations of awards the authorities will wish to take account of the following factors among others:

- overseas countries' needs and development priorities;
- the extent of private access to the UK education system for its nationals;
- British commercial ties and prospects;
- strategic importance and the competition for influence;
- inherited patterns of educational interdependence between the overseas country and the UK, and of UK obligations to certain groups of countries; and
- reciprocal access for British students to other countries, particularly in cases where knowledge of foreign languages, technology and science, social and economic systems is in Britain's own national interest.

Although overseas students have increasingly become a matter for state concern, copious provision should be made within British arrangements for awards to provide for individual applicants from abroad. Clearly many awards, as at present, will be made on a nominated basis under technical assistance and other arrangements. But room should be found within our officially-funded awards schemes to support the individual applicant as well as the state nominee. This accords with our tradition of hospitality to the refugee scholar and the politically dissident student: it also reflects our preference for individual application and our insistence on institutional autonomy in selection and admission. Many people would regret the introduction of any kind of arrangement which put the power of selection and granting of student support entirely in the hands of officialdom in London and abroad. There should be room for the occasional maverick, freethinker or political dissident whom no official committee would nominate. In amplification of this, it is for consideration whether some form of limited earmarked fund could be available for institutions to use at their own discretion to assist overseas students, even if most public subsidy was operated through centrally administered selective programmes. To guard against undue preponderance of bureaucratic nominees therefore, there should be:

(a) competitive awards open on an international basis to overseas student applicants;

(b) country competitive awards to ensure an adequate spread of nationalities, as for example under the Commonwealth Scholarship Scheme;

(c) scholarship funds allocated through institutions themselves.

Close study is needed of the experience under these and other schemes, and also of the practices in other receiving countries in Europe and North America, to find the most suitable arrangements which combine (i) an element of competition and the winning of awards on merit; (ii) due attention, in fixing fields of study for awards, to the developmental needs and priorities of overseas countries; (iii) some role for British officials and overseas nationals in the basically independent bodies making nominations for awards; and (iv) actual selection and admission to particular courses by UK educational institutions. Undoubtedly a great deal of suitable experience already exists, which requires analysing and sifting, on whether and in what circumstances the most satisfactory arrangement is for selection for awards to be made from among students who have already obtained a place, or whether on the other hand the granting of the award should precede admission to a course. Procedures must be kept simple and speedy, whatever the sequence, if good applicants are not to be lost. And in that connection, the time may well be ripe for UK academic institutions to consider instituting joint arrangements, possibly with the help of the British Council, for handling applications overseas and for operating clearing house arrangements for rejected overseas applications in the UK at levels other than university undergraduates.

It has become apparent in the discussion that Britain's interest in overseas students is a multidimensional one involving education, foreign policy and aid, trade, finance and – though this has not been discussed here – migration. In the area of policy-making, recent experience suggests that while all those departments and other official bodies (e.g. the British Council) which have an interest in the matter should be able to contribute their perspective to policy formulation, a 'lead department' is needed to co-ordinate the process. The analysis of interests and obligations also suggests that overseas student policy is predominantly an aspect of international relations, and is not ultimately a question of financial support for the education system. If this is agreed it would seem to follow that while the Department of Education and Science (DES) has to be consulted at every stage on the capacity of the system in relation to overseas demand, and on the financial arrangements for admitting overseas students, the lead department in the co-ordination of policy should be the Foreign and Commonwealth Office (FCO). Amongst the advantages of this arrangement are that better arrangements for liaison and consultation with overseas governments might result.

Public funding of financial support schemes for overseas students, whether through scholarship or fee subsidies, might be provided according to the locus of interest. The system that has operated hitherto has been fatally flawed in the sense that funds were not expected to come from where the major interest and obligations lay. Faced with a Treasury-imposed choice between saving money on overseas students and cutting services to its British clientele, the choice that the DES made was inevitable.

There are, however, multiple loci of interest in attracting overseas students to Britain. It is fundamentally important that some of the budget for this purpose should continue to come from the DES so as to reflect its responsibility for making the education system internationally minded and outward-looking, for encouraging foreign scholars to work among us and make their substantial contribution to our research and development programmes. The Department of Trade should also be a source of funding for overseas students if the view is taken that such study and training brings commercial advantage to Britain. Substantial parts of the funding would properly fall to the budget of the ODA wing of the FCO; while those elements that stem from a desire for cultural contact, educational interchange and exchange, the meeting of our international obligations and the pursuit of political interests would fall on the FCO proper. Such a division of responsibility for funding would differ from that suggested by a number of Parliamentary Committees which recommended that all concessions from the full-cost fees policy should be financed from aid funds. Surely that would be to take too narrow a view of Britain's relations with the rest of the world and of her place within it? Is it not in Britain's interest to fund some Americans, Australians and Kuwaitis, as well as Angolans, Antiguans and Kenyans? Has not the Brandt Report reminded us of the need to move from a relationship of aid, dependence and inequality to a new style of relationship based on co-operation, interdependence and equality?

Whether such a division of financial responsibility would necessarily generate the needed articulation of Britain's interests in receiving overseas students cannot be answered in clear-cut terms. There are few vested interests to make the case to FCO/ODA for overseas students in terms of foreign policy and international assistance, whereas the DES has always been exposed to the pressures of the main interest group in Britain – the educational institutions themselves. External relations is an area without a constituency, unless one regards bodies such as the Royal Institute of International Affairs, the Overseas Development Institute, the Institute for Strategic Studies and the like as the constituency voice. In overseas student matters it has been left to the Overseas Students Trust and others to ventilate the issues and to present the case for a wider forum where needs and priorities could be articulated. When each department of state weighs budgetary allocations for overseas student support against other claims on its budget, the absence of sustained interest and representations from outside the government machinery may prove a serious weakness. Whilst education, foreign aid and trade have large operational programmes within which to cater for the financial requirements of overseas student support, in the case of the FCO proper (i.e. excluding the ODA wing) such funding would form a much larger proportion of the operational budget and compete rather directly with, say, diplomatic posts and personnel. The fate of the British Council's budget in recent times points to the potential dangers of having financial responsibility for overseas students concentrated exclusively in the FCO: a parallel that is all the more inauspicious in so far as an enhanced role for the Council both in Britain and overseas is essential if Britain is deliberately to embark on the commercial sale of educational services to other countries.

Whatever administrative and financial arrangements are ultimately adopted there would be advantage in establishing a small unit with responsibility for keeping policy on overseas students under review, for collecting and collating information from appropriate institutions in Britain and abroad, and acting as secretariat to any inter-departmental co-ordinating bodies that might be set up. Such a unit which might be based in the FCO or perhaps at the British Council would have as one of its tasks the close monitoring of the number and composition of supported and non-supported overseas students, so indispensable to any effective policy. The formulation of policy has been seriously hampered in the past by the lateness and inadequacy of the available statistics on overseas students. Whatever decisions may be made about the future location of responsibility for statistical data – and it is difficult to conceive of a really effective system unless the DES plays a leading role – it needs higher priority among official tasks than hitherto.

Whilst much of the foregoing discussion has necessarily been focused on domestic arrangements within Britain, our role should constantly be viewed in the broader international perspective. Overseas students in Britain are part of a much wider international exchange in which many other countries participate both as receivers and senders of students. Britons are themselves 'overseas students' in many Commonwealth and foreign countries, and this is a flow that needs to be encouraged both for the benefit of our own youth and our own scholarship, and in the wider national political and economic interest. The health of our own society depends on our learning the languages, customs and cultures of others and on gaining insights into their social, political and economic institutions. A much greater effort than in the past needs to be directed to sustaining award schemes for Britons studying overseas and for British participation in academic exchange schemes.

Simultaneously – as Wallace, Oxenham and Smith all stress – Britain should maintain contact with other countries and international organisations engaged in international student exchange. As is clear from Chapter 7, Britain is not the country receiving most students either absolutely or proportionately. If overseas students are regarded in any sense as a 'burden' and responsibility of industrialised countries, then others are carrying a heavier load than we. It is important for many reasons that Britain consults closely with her partners in the Western Alliance both because of shared interest in meeting the Soviet ideological challenge, but also because of the effect that one country's policies may have on another (the so-called 'knock-on' effect) and also because a close knowledge of each other's policies, practice and experience may help each country to formulate better national policies. Similarly consultation with the main sending countries – particularly in Britain's case the developing countries of the Commonwealth – will help to maintain good relations in a sensitive area and can ensure that our policies take into account vital interests in the area of manpower supply and educational development in the Third World. No country in the modern world is an island unto itself, and Britain's failure in 1979/80 to behave in a good neighbourly way by consulting with her overseas friends caused a great deal of unnecessary damage to her overseas relations.

Beyond these bilateral contacts Britain should be pressing for international student mobility to have a place on the agenda of the international organisations to which she belongs – the Commonwealth Prime Ministers' meetings, the European Community and the Council of Europe, the Organisation for Economic Co-operation and Development, Unesco and the United Nations. For the current international recession and a creeping restrictionism in policies towards foreign students pose a serious threat to the emerging concept of world community. Just as a General Agreement on Tariffs and Trade (GATT) was found necessary to contain the threat of unilaterally imposed restrictions on the growth of world trade, so the potential diminution in international student mobility should be regarded equally seriously. The international organisations should be pressed to allocate responsibilities and establish units to concern themselves with monitoring developments in this area and to develop practical instruments of international co-operation. Today's students will inherit tomorrow's world: let us help them to know their inheritance.

Notes
1. Education, Science and Arts Committee (House of Commons). *The funding and organisation of courses in higher education: interim report on overseas student fees* (HC 552–1), London, HMSO, 1980, paras 59 and 61.
2. Foreign Affairs Committee (House of Commons), *Overseas Students Fees: Aid and Development Implications*, (Third Report, Session 1979/80) London, HMSO, 1980, paras 35 and 36.

Appendix A
A Survey of Overseas Students in British Higher Education 1980
by Mark Blaug and Maureen Woodhall*

Description of the Survey

Our survey was based on a representative sample of students paying overseas student fees in advanced-level courses in universities and polytechnics in England and Wales.

We selected students in two stages. At the first stage, we selected fourteen institutions using a sampling procedure designed to ensure that there was a representative distribution of students across institutions, and that the overall selection probabilities were equal for all overseas students in advanced higher and further education in universities and polytechnics in England and Wales. The sample of fourteen institutions included at least one institution in each of the following categories:

(1) Oxbridge
(2) London University (counting the university colleges, institutes and non-medical schools separately)
(3) Old red brick universities (counting the colleges and schools of the University of Wales separately)
(4) New universities (having received their Charter since 1960)
(5) Polytechnics in Greater London
(6) Polytechnics outside Greater London

At the second stage, within each institution the students themselves

---

* As a basis for the study commissioned by the Overseas Students Trust which appears as Chapter 3 Mark Blaug directed a survey of overseas students in British universities and polytechnics. In this work he was assisted by John Mace, Sue Owen and Maureen Woodhall. The survey was executed on behalf of the research team by Social and Community Planning Research. The findings of the survey are summarised here by Maureen Woodhall. A full version of the report, which includes the survey instruments, is available from the Overseas Students Trust.

were selected by the individual institutions concerned. Each institution was asked to make a random selection of approximately 200 overseas students. All undergraduate and postgraduate overseas students were included in the sampling frame and 'overseas' was defined in terms of the fees paid by the student. In order to preserve confidentiality, the institutions contacted the sampled students by letter, asking them to take part in the survey, and in addition to the introductory letter, first and second reminder letters were sent to all those students who did not reply.

Some 62% (or 1697) of the 2735 students initially contacted, replied that they were willing to be interviewed; 15% said that they were unwilling to take part. Of the remaining 23% from whom nothing was heard, 3% were identified either as having left the course, or as ineligible for some other reason; whilst for the remaining 20% it was impossible to tell whether they refused to co-operate or were never located. Although in calculating the response, we have treated hearing nothing from the student as a refusal, it seems likely that a number of students from whom we heard nothing were either ineligible, or never received a letter because they had moved. The response rates given below have therefore been calculated on the most pessimistic basis. The effective response rate would probably prove to be somewhat higher if more information could be obtained about those students from whom nothing was heard.

At the interviewing stage another sixty-two students were found not to be known at their stated address, or to have moved away to an unknown address, leaving a productive sample of 1635 with whom successful interviews were achieved for 91% or 1484 students. Eliminating all those students who were, in the language of market researchers, 'out of scope', the total possible sample was 2607 and hence our response rate was 57%. Wherever we collected information on sample characteristics which are known for the total population of overseas students from published data, there is a high degree of congruence between our findings and those for all overseas students in the United Kingdom. We thus have considerable confidence in the unbiased character of our sample despite what is admittedly a low response rate.

The survey was carried out by Social and Community Planning Research, using face-to-face interviews, based on a lengthy questionnaire which was designed to provide information on:

(1) the level and length of course of students, together with details of subjects studied and the proportion of overseas students on the course;

(2)   age, marital status, nationality and normal place of residence;
(3)   family background, including parental occupation and level of education;
(4)   previous education, including level of previous qualifications, and where they were obtained;
(5)   reasons for choosing to study in Britain, sources of information or advice about study in Britain, choice of institution and course;
(6)   future educational and career plans;
(7)   levels of income and expenditure;
(8)   sources of income;
(9)   opinions about the announced increase in overseas student fees; and
(10) willingness to study in Britain at various alternative levels of fees.

The full questionnaire, which contained forty-five questions in all, together with a detailed account of the sampling procedure can be obtained from the authors or the Overseas Students Trust on request.

The results of the survey are summarised below, in terms of the percentage of the sample (N = 1484) responding to the various questions. All percentages are rounded to the nearest whole digit (except less than 0·5% which is represented in tables by $\emptyset$%). Hence the various responses to a particular question do not always add up exactly to 100%. The summary cannot hope to do full justice to the enormous amount of information collected by the survey. Such detailed information on overseas students had never previously existed in Britain.

What follows is first, an attempt to answer the question 'What are the characteristics of the typical overseas student in Britain?' and second, a sample of the rich harvest that cross-tabulations – particularly of the key variables of levels of course; countries of nationality grouped by continents; countries of nationality grouped by poor/rich, and Commonwealth/non-Commonwealth – can yield.

The Characteristics of the typical Overseas Student: a Summary

On the basis of national statistics it is possible to conclude that the typical overseas student in Britain is a postgraduate student in engineering and technology or else an undergraduate student in either engineering and technology or pure science. We can now go further than this, and say, on the basis of the replies to our survey, that the typical overseas student is (i) male (75% of all respondents) aged 30 or below (82%); (ii) studying for a first degree or a postgraduate degree in engineering and technology, science, or administrative and business studies, and (iii) likely to be studying a course in which more than half of all the students are overseas students (54% of MPhil and PhD students, and 66% of master's degree students said that overseas students outnumbered home students on their courses).

Similarly the survey showed that the typical overseas student is likely to be unmarried (72%); but if married he or she will probably be accompanied by wife or husband (72%) and possibly children (44%). The student tends to come from Asia (36%), Africa (16%), or the Middle East (16%), to be the son of a self-employed business-man, craftsman or farmer (40%) or a civil servant or other govern-ment employee (32%), and to have a father who has completed higher education (32%) or, at least, secondary education (26%). In other words, the average overseas student is not the child of poor or ill-educated parents. It is interesting to note, however, that an overseas student taking an MPhil or PhD is five times more likely to have a father who has completed higher education himself than an overseas student taking a higher national diploma (the proportions are 36 and 7%), but the differences in social background between those taking a first degree and postgraduate overseas students taking a master's degree are very slight. The typical overseas student is also likely (a 42% chance) to have obtained some previous qualification in Britain, either one or more 'A' levels (21% of all respondents) or a bachelor's or master's degree (12%).

Nearly half of all respondents had a scholarship or grant of some sort (46%), and the overseas student studying for an MPhil or PhD is particularly likely to have a scholarship (63%), usually from a foreign government (33%) or from British funds (22%). The mean annual income of the overseas students from all sources was £3233, and the mean fee paid by overseas students was £1137. It is clear that the availability of scholarship funds is crucial to the majority of overseas students. Of those who had a scholarship, 36% of all students – and 63% of those taking an MPhil or PhD – said they would not have come to Britain without a scholarship.

Whilst the foregoing brief summary gives a rough picture of the 'average' or typical overseas student, it must be emphasised that the student survey also revealed large differences and variations among overseas students, particularly regarding income and expenditure levels.

Fields of study and concentration

A central question about overseas students is how they are distributed over fields of study. Given the thousands of courses in universities and polytechnics, the Universities Statistical Record long ago adopted a standard set of ten subject groupings, and a somewhat similar scheme has been in use in polytechnics and further education colleges. We therefore analysed our sample of students in terms of these subject groupings.

Most of the students in our sample, whether undergraduates or postgraduates, were concentrated in engineering and technology, science, and social, administrative and business studies. This is also true of overseas students nationally: 34% of all overseas students in British universities in 1977 were studying in the subject group engineering and technology (the figure for our sample is also 34%); 20% were studying science (our figure is 25%); and 20% were studying social, administrative and business studies (which is also our figure). In polytechnics throughout Britain, 41% were studying engineering and technology (which is also our figure); 14% were studying science (as against 13% in our sample); and 27% were studying social, administrative and business studies (compared to our 29%). Clearly, our sample is by no means unrepresentative of all overseas students.

The fact that overseas students tend to be concentrated in science and engineering courses has important implications for the cost of educating overseas students in Britain, as discussed in Chapter 3. Additionally, questions of marginal versus average costs of overseas students are very much influenced by the extent to which overseas students are concentrated in individual courses. Some have suggested that overseas students are always a minority in higher education courses and in the effort to collect more information on this question, we asked our interviewees to estimate the proportion of students on their course that were from overseas. Research students found this a 'nonsense' question and even some other students studying split subjects or courses in different departments found this a difficult question to answer. Nevertheless, we received clear replies from a majority of the sample, showing that almost half of them (N = 1484) were in courses in which overseas students outnumbered home students, and almost a quarter were in courses where home students, and not overseas students, were marginal. The proportion of overseas students in different courses is shown, by level of course, in Table A.1.

Student background

The 1484 students in the sample held passports from 100 different countries but only 93% were born in their country of nationality and only 91% were resident in their country of nationality immediately before coming to study in Britain. They were distributed in terms

Table A.1   Proportions of overseas students on course by course levels (%)

Proportions on course	Base	MPhil/ PhD	Masters	Diploma	First degree	Higher national diploma	Teacher training	Professional qualification	Others
Base	1484	333	229	74	737	14	8	9	80
$<\frac{1}{4}$	493	18	14	19	47	29	88	67	31
$>\frac{1}{4}, <\frac{1}{2}$	292	15	18	9	24	7	—	11	19
$>\frac{1}{2}, <\frac{3}{4}$	290	23	18	16	19	29	13	11	19
$>\frac{3}{4}$	347	31	48	55	8	29	—	11	31
It varies	6	—	—	—	1	—	—	—	—
Irrelevant	17	5	—	—	—	—	—	—	—
Don't know	38	8	1	—	1	7	—	—	—

Notes: — = 0%

Base row and column are absolute numbers and all other figures in the table are percentages of column totals. Percentages of column totals can be translated into percentages of row totals by dividing the row base into the column base and multiplying the percentage entry by the resulting divisor.

Source: Student survey.

of the major nineteen nationalities as shown in Table A.2. We include for easy comparison, the corresponding percentages in 1977 of all overseas students in advanced higher education in universities and polytechnics. Once again, we can see how amazingly representative is our sample of overseas students in public sector institutions throughout Britain.

We were tempted to ask a great many questions about parental background, but in the final analysis we confined ourselves to some modest queries about parents' occupation and education. The results are shown in Tables A.3 and A.4.

Table A.2   Overseas students by countries of origin

Countries of origin	Sample survey respondents (%)	All overseas students 1977/78 in same categories
Malaysia	18	16
Nigeria	7	5
Iran	5	7
Greece	5	5
USA	5	5
Hong Kong	4	4
Iraq	3	3
Zimbabwe	3	2
Singapore	2	2
Sri Lanka	2	1
India	2	2
Turkey	2	1
Cyprus	2	2
Mauritius	1	$\emptyset$
Western Germany	1	1
Ireland	1	1
Japan	$\emptyset$	$\emptyset$
France	$\emptyset$	$\emptyset$
Switzerland	$\emptyset$	$\emptyset$
Others	36	40

Notes: $\emptyset$ = less than 0·5%
Sources: Student Survey and British Council, *Statistics of Overseas Students in Britain 1977/78*, London, 1979, Table A.

Table A.3   Parents' occupations

	Father's occupation (%)	Mother's occupation (%)
Self-employed businessman or woman	28	7
Self-employed craftsman or farmer	12	3
Self-employed professional	7	1
Civil servant	13	3
Government employee other than civil service (including army, teaching, nationalised industries)	19	8
Employee in private sector	18	6
Housewife not in employment	—	71
Other	1	$\emptyset$

Note: $\emptyset$ = less than 0·5%
Source: Student Survey.

Table A.4   Parents' education

	Father's highest level of education (%)	Mother's highest level of education (%)
None	7	16
Primary	23	30
Secondary	26	29
Vocational training	11	8
Higher	32	15
Don't Know	2	2

Source: Student Survey.

We asked students whether they had obtained any previous qualifications by study undertaken in Britain, having in mind the widespread conviction that the overseas students doing non-advanced work in further education colleges today are the higher education overseas students of tomorrow. Indeed, it transpired that 42% had done so and that as many as one out of five had taken one or more 'A' levels in Britain. Before starting their present course, 61% of the sample were in full-time education, 34% were in full-time employment, and the remaining 5% were in national service, part-time work or study, were unemployed, or were on holiday. We asked them what they intended to do after completing their present course and discovered that 30% of them intended to remain in Britain for study or work.

If we compare different groups of students in terms of their previous educational qualifications, their reasons for studying in Britain and their intentions after completing their study some interesting differences emerge. Naturally enough, postgraduate over-seas students are better qualified, in terms of levels of education previously completed, than those studying for a first degree or higher national diploma. Over 40% of those studying for an MPhil or PhD have previously obtained a degree or postgraduate diploma in Britain, but the proportion who had taken 'A' levels was only 5%. Among undergraduates, on the other hand, more than a third have pre-viously taken 'A' levels in Britain, and half of all overseas students taking higher national diplomas had taken 'A' levels in Britain. This confirms the impression that lower levels of education in Britain are used by overseas students to equip themselves for further study in this country.

There are some interesting variations in the educational back-grounds of overseas students from different countries. Latin American and Australian students appear to have the highest level of qualifications, in terms of levels of education completed abroad, before study in Britain. Over 60% of Latin American students have completed higher or postgraduate education before coming to Britain, and all the students from Australasia had completed higher education or postgraduate education. On the other hand, less than a quarter of the Asian students had completed higher or postgraduate education before coming here.

A comparison between Commonwealth and non-Commonwealth countries, at the same level of development, suggests that students from non-Commonwealth countries are more likely to have completed higher education, or even postgraduate education, before coming to Britain than students from Commonwealth countries. For example, 94% of students from very poor non-Commonwealth countries had previously completed higher or postgraduate education, compared with 56% from Commonwealth countries, and amongst countries with per capita GNP below $750 (classified as poor), the proportions were 66% from non-Commonwealth countries, and only 18% from Commonwealth countries. This may reflect a pattern of dependency on British higher education which has been fostered by historical or colonial links between Britain and Commonwealth countries in the past.

Certain differences between countries are also apparent when students are compared in terms of future career intentions. For

Table A.5   *Main reasons for decision to study in Britain by poor/rich countries*

Reasons	Base	Very poor Common-wealth	Very poor Non-Common-wealth	Poor Common-wealth	Poor Non-Common-wealth	Middle East OPEC	Middle East Non-OPEC	Rich
Base	1484	36	34	513	149	273	75	404
Course not available in own country	330	42%	50%	22%	19%	26%	17%	18%
Course not available at suitable time in own country	31	6%	—	2%	1%	4%	1%	1%
Course not available in other overseas country	6	—	—	0%	—	1%	—	0%
Better course	254	22%	21%	14%	24%	20%	20%	15%
Shorter course	24	—	—	1%	2%	1%	4%	2%
Cheaper course	15	—	3%	—	1%	1%	1%	2%
Selection procedure less complicated	21	—	—	3%	—	1%	3%	1%
Speak English better than other languages	41	3%	—	1%	3%	5%	3%	3%
Wish to improve English	26	—	—	0%	5%	1%	3%	3%

Friends or relatives in Britain	37	—	3%	2%	3%	4%	3%	2%
Believed qualification better for jobs or study	334	22%	15%	29%	16%	14%	23%	23%
Application not accepted in own country	101	—	—	12%	1%	7%	3%	5%
Application not accepted in another country	8	—	—	1%	—	∅%	—	∅%
Attraction to Britain	63	3%	—	2%	4%	4%	7%	8%
Attraction to abroad	46	—	—	1%	2%	4%	3%	6%
Political reasons	33	—	—	2%	9%	1%	7%	∅%
Competition stiffer at home	22	—	—	3%	—	2%	—	1%
Minority discrimination at home	14	—	—	2%	—	—	1%	1%
Scholarship or sponsorship	43	—	—	4%	4%	1%	3%	3%
Exchange agreement	5	—	—	—	—	1%	—	1%
Not answered	13	3%	3%	∅%	2%	1%	—	1%

Notes: — = 0%; ∅ = less than 0·5%. The columns in this table do not add up to 100% as the answers to the question are not mutually exclusive.

Source: Student Survey.

example, the proportion of overseas students who wanted to continue to study in Britain, or work in Britain, at the end of their course was between 30 and 35% among students from Africa, Asia and the Middle East, but only 10% of Latin Americans and 15% of North Americans wanted to remain in Britain. Nearly half of all Latin American students wanted to return to their previous job in their own country. On the other hand, among North Americans, the most popular option was to continue study in their own country (41%) and among Asian students it was to return to a new job in their own country (37%). Half of all higher national diploma students wanted to continue to study in Britain, but only 6% of MPhil or PhD students.

Reasons for study in Britain   (see table)
We tried to discover how and why students had come to study in Britain rather than elsewhere, distinguishing between the decision to study in Britain and the decision to study a particular course at a particular British institution (Table A.5). In the case of postgraduate students, 30 to 32% said that such a course was not available in their own country, whereas only 16% of undergraduates said this; they were more likely to cite, as reasons for coming to Britain, the superiority of British qualifications (25%) or courses (16%). More than half of all overseas students had made a careful comparison between courses in Britain and elsewhere. 89% of MPhil or PhD students who had made such a comparison had considered courses in North America, and amongst undergraduates it was 70%. The next most 'popular' area was Western Europe, but few students said they had considered Eastern Europe or Latin America. (See Table A.6.)

Students received advice from a variety of sources, although almost a half of all overseas students said that the idea to study in Britain was their own, rather than based on specific advice. Undergraduates were more likely to have been advised by parents, relatives or friends than anyone else (37%), whereas MPhil or PhD students and teacher training students were likely to have been advised by teachers (27%). When choosing individual courses, or institutions, students had consulted teachers, parents, relatives or friends, but few had consulted British Council officials, with the exception of those taking a postgraduate diploma (12%) or master's degree (6%).

Sources of income
35% of the sample earned something while studying in Britain, either from their own efforts or from the efforts of their spouse, the source being distributed as follows: teaching – 4%; research assistance –

Table A.6 Other continents considered by course levels

Continents considered	Base	MPhil/ PhD	Masters	Diploma	First degree	Higher national diploma	Teacher training	Professional qualification	Others
Base	795	192	115	34	406	5	2	4	37
Western Europe	180	22%	17%	21%	23%	60%	—	50%	38%
Eastern Europe	12	2%	3%	—	1%	—	—	—	—
North America	612	89%	87%	76%	70%	80%	50%	50%	65%
Latin America	3	1%	1%	—	—	—	—	—	—
Middle East	24	2%	4%	—	3%	—	—	—	3%
Asia	44	1%	3%	3%	9%	—	—	—	5%
Africa	24	1%	3%	—	4%	20%	—	25%	3%
Australia/New Zealand	162	9%	13%	18%	28%	20%	50%	25%	16%
Not Answered	6	1%	—	3%	1%	—	—	—	3%

Notes: see Table A.1. The columns in this table do not add up to 100% as the answers to the question are not mutually exclusive.
Source: Student Survey.

2%; publications – 0%; and non-academic work – 30%. These were not trivial earnings: 20% earned up to £500; 6% earned £501–1000; 3% earned £1001–2000; and 4% earned £2001 or more. As many as 46% of our sample received a scholarship or grant to study in Britain, of which about one-third came from British funds and about two-thirds from overseas funds (see Tables A.7–A.10). 9% said that they would still have come to study in Britain if they had not received the scholarship or grant but 36% said that they would definitely not have come to Britain without financial support.

It is evident that self-financed students relied principally on their parents, relatives and friends. When we add this to the fact that the parents of all students are generally highly educated and predominantly self-employed business people and government officials, we do not get an impression that overseas students are typically poor. At the same time, it is striking to witness the diverse sources of their finance and, even more striking, the diverse amounts which individual overseas students receive under various headings.

The level of income of overseas students is related to whether or not they receive scholarships or grants. The mean income of students with no scholarship was only £2988, compared with mean incomes of over £3500 for those with a scholarship or grant. Students from certain countries appear to be much more likely to have a scholarship than certain other groups of students. Over 90% of the students from very poor non-Commonwealth countries (Afghanistan, Ethiopia, Nepal, Somalia, Sudan, Western Samoa, Yemen Peoples Democratic Republic) had scholarships, whereas only 40% of students from the Middle East (non-OPEC) countries (Bahrain, Egypt, Israel, Jordan, Lebanon, Syria) had scholarships. On the other hand, there is no obvious relation between the level of economic development of countries and the number of students receiving scholarships. The proportion of students from poor Commonwealth countries (including India, Kenya, Malaysia, Mauritius, Sri Lanka and Zimbabwe) who have no scholarships (58%) is almost as high as the proportion from the most developed countries (including Europe and the USA), who had no scholarship (64%). There is a much closer relation between the level of course and the proportion of scholarship holders. More than 75% of all MPhil and PhD students hold scholarships, but only 26% of undergraduates. The MPhil and PhD students were most likely to receive a scholarship from a foreign government (33%), a scholarship from British funds (22%) or a private scholarship (12%).

Students who had a scholarship were asked whether or not they would have come to study in Britain without a scholarship,

Table A.7   Income sources in Britain by course levels

Income source	Base	MPhil/ PhD	Masters	Diploma	First degree	Higher national diploma	Teacher training	Professional qualification	Other	Mean (£)	Standard deviation (£)
Base	1484	333	229	74	737	14	8	9	80		
Public scholarship/grant	201	22%	19%	22%	7%	21%	25%	4%	9%	2333	1188
Private scholarship/grant	10	2%	—	1%	0%	—	—	—	3%	2404	1205
Industrial scholarship	24	5%	1%	—	1%	—	—	—	—	2736	1278
Bank loan	3	—	0%	3%	—	—	—	—	—	317	202
Loan from parents, relatives etc.	15	1%	0%	·	2%	—	—	—	—	839	751
Gift from parents, relatives etc.	27	1%	—	1%	3%	7%	—	—	1%	1156	826
Private savings	30	2%	4%	3%	1%	—	—	22%	1%	1436	1264
Spouse's income	53	6%	5%	5%	2%	7%	—	—	3%	2758	2011
Own job	70	5%	4%	4%	5%	14%	—	—	4%	1489	1811
University hardship fund	21	2%	—	—	2%	—	—	—	1%	345	485
Others	4	1%	1%	—	—	—	—	—	—	2600	1615

Notes: see Table A.1. The columns in this table do not add up to 100% as not all students had income sources in Britain. ∅ = less than 0·5%
Source: Student Survey.

Table A.8   Income sources in Britain by poor/rich countries

Income source	Base	Very poor Common-wealth	Very poor Non-Common-wealth	Poor Common-wealth	Poor Non-Common-wealth	Middle East OPEC	Middle East Non-OPEC	Rich
Base	1484	36	34	513	149	273	75	404
Public scholarship/grant	201	33%	15%	18%	19%	5%	11%	11%
Private scholarship/grant	10	—	—	1%	1%	0%	—	1%
Industrial scholarship	24	3%	—	1%	3%	1%	4%	2%
Bank loan	3	—	—	—	—	1%	—	0%
Loan from parents, relatives etc.	15	3%	—	2%	—	1%	—	1%
Gift from parents relatives etc.	27	6%	—	3%	2%	0%	1%	2%
Private savings	30	6%	—	1%	2%	2%	3%	4%
Spouse's income	53	3%	3%	4%	2%	4%	1%	3%
Own job	70	3%	3%	6%	1%	3%	4%	5%
University hardship fund	21	—	—	1%	2%	1%	1%	2%
Other	4	—	—	0%	1%	—	—	0%

Note: see Tables A.1 and A.7.   0% = less than 5%
Source: Student Survey.

Table A.9 Income sources outside Britain by course levels

Income source	Base	MPhil/ PhD	Masters	Diploma	First degree	Higher national diploma	Teacher training	Professional qualification	Others	Mean (£)	Standard deviation (£)
Base	1484	333	229	74	737	14	8	9	80		
Public scholarship/grant	312	33%	22%	27%	15%	36%	38%	33%	16%	2762	1535
Private scholarship/ grant in own country	97	10%	10%	4%	4%	—	—	11%	5%	2534	1683
Scholarship/grant abroad not Britain	37	5%	4%	4%	1%	—	—	—	1%	2665	1109
Industrial sponsorship	11	1%	2%	—	1%	—	—	—	1%	2946	1167
Government loan	43	2%	2%	4%	3%	—	—	11%	4%	2098	1057
Bank loan	15	0%	0%	1%	1%	—	—	—	1%	1571	829
Loan from employer	11	—	3%	—	1%	7%	—	—	—	2062	959
Salary from employer	93	14%	11%	8%	1%	—	—	11%	8%	2978	2040
Loan from relatives etc.	139	7%	7%	7%	12%	—	13%	11%	5%	2027	1067
Gift from relatives etc.	648	21%	25%	23%	61%	36%	25%	56%	54%	2343	1287
Private saving	138	8%	18%	11%	7%	—	—	—	9%	2151	1810
Spouse's income	22	3%	3%	4%	0%	—	—	—	—	2827	2251
Own job	11	1%	—	—	1%	—	—	—	—	1555	1417
Unearned income	5	0%	1%	—	0%	—	—	—	—	2660	3006
'Other' loan	6	0%	0%	—	1%	—	—	—	—	945	986

Note: see Table A.1. 0% = less than 0·5%. The columns in this table do not add up to 100% as not all students had income sources outside Britain, and some had more than one source of income.

Source: Student Survey.

Table A.10 Income sources outside Britain by poor/rich countries

Income source	Base	Very poor Commonwealth	Very poor Non-Commonwealth	Poor Commonwealth	Poor Non-Commonwealth	Middle East OPEC	Middle East Non-OPEC	Rich
Base	1484	36	34	513	149	273	75	404
Public scholarship/grant	312	17%	56%	16%	26%	37%	20%	13%
Private scholarship/grant in own country	97	8%	9%	4%	6%	5%	5%	11%
Scholarship/grant abroad not Britain	37	14%	9%	3%	3%	1%	—	2%
Industrial sponsorship	11	—	3%	∅%	1%	1%	1%	∅%
Government loan	43	—	—	1%	3%	1%	—	8%
Bank loan	15	—	—	1%	1%	—	—	2%
Loan from employer	11	—	—	1%	1%	—	1%	1%
Salary from employer	93	3%	21%	3%	18%	7%	4%	5%
Loan from parents, relatives etc.	139	3%	3%	9%	4%	7%	14%	13%
Gift from parents, relatives etc.	648	14%	—	47%	36%	43%	49%	48%
Private saving	138	3%	3%	3%	6%	5%	8%	24%
Spouse's income	22	—	3%	1%	3%	1%	1%	2%
Own job	11	—	—	∅%	—	∅%	—	2%
Unearned income	5	—	—	—	1%	∅%	1%	∅%
'Other' loan	6	—	—	∅%	1%	—	1%	1%

Notes: See Tables A.1 and A.9. ∅ = less than 0·5%.
Source: Student Survey.

and only 9% said that they would. However, the proportion of those taking higher national diplomas (29%) or teacher training (25%) who would have studied in Britain even without a scholarship was surprisingly high, and very much higher than the proportion of scholarship-holders taking a first degree, who said that they would have studied here without a scholarship (5%). On the other hand, 73% of those taking a first degree did not have a scholarship; a very high proportion of these undergraduates (61%) were financed by gifts from parents or other relatives.

The level of income of students is determined not only by whether or not they have a scholarship, but on whether or not they earn any money in the UK. Less than half (35%) of the respondents did earn money in Britain, but the proportion of higher national diploma students with a job in this country was much higher (64%) than the proportion of students taking a master's degree (20%). The amounts earned by overseas students in this country varied considerably, with 20% earning under £500 in a year, but 4% earning more than £2000.

Apart from scholarships and earnings from a job in Britain, there are many different sources of income for overseas students. A common source is gifts from parents or other relatives. Over 60% of all undergraduates are financed in this way, and about a quarter of those taking a master's degree or a PhD. A few postgraduates are financed by means of loans from relatives or government loans, but very few have bank loans or loans from employers. On the other hand, 14% of those taking an MPhil or PhD financed their studies by salaries from an employer abroad, and 9% financed themselves through the earnings of their spouse.

Different patterns of financing emerge if we compare students from different groups of countries. For example, about half of all students from rich countries (e.g. USA and Western Europe), from Middle East countries and from poor Commonwealth countries finance themselves through gifts from parents or other relatives. But no students from very poor non-Commonwealth countries finance themselves in this way, and the majority are financed by scholarships or by their employers abroad.

Levels of income of overseas students

Although the average (mean) income of all overseas students was £3233, some 15% of all respondents had incomes of under £2000 and 5% had incomes of over £7000 a year. The majority of those in the lowest income bracket (under £1000) were undergraduates (61%) and the majority of those with incomes above £9000 were doing master's degrees. But it is interesting that the proportion of those in the lowest income bracket who were doing an MPhil or PhD (13%) was the same as the proportion of undergraduates with annual incomes in excess of £9000. This underlines the great disparities that exist between different overseas students.

The wide dispersion of income in our sample was matched by an equal if not greater dispersion of expenditure: the standard deviation of total expenditure is 86% of the average expenditure, meaning that there were as many students who spent as little as four to five hundred pounds over a six-month period as students spending five to six thousand pounds. Clearly, there are poor and rich overseas students, and it is extremely dangerous to advance strong generalisations about the absolute level of income and expenditure of overseas students.

There appears to be some tendency, however, for poorer students to come from poorer countries. Thus, among the major sending countries only students from Malaysia, Mauritius and Singapore had mean incomes as low as £2500 and only students from India, Iraq, Nigeria, Greece, Iran, Japan and the USA had incomes above the overall mean of £3233. On *average* overseas students whether publicly or privately supported, seem to be better off than home students. Home students in 1979 received means-tested maintenance grants which at their maximum (London-based students living away from home) were worth £1485. In addition, they are likely to have vacation earnings and to be in receipt of social security benefits. If we update a sample survey of full-time home students on first-degree courses in Britain in the academic year 1974, it appears that home students in 1979 had an *average* income, exclusive of fees, of £1502.* Overseas students in 1979 paid a fee as high as £1230 if they were postgraduates, and thus needed £2732 (£1502 + £1230) to be at least as well off as the average home student. In fact, postgraduate overseas students in our sample had an average income of £3905–£4293, depending on whether they were MPhil/PhD or master's students. Of course, overseas students are also somewhat older than home students, and one doubts that as many as 20% of home students

---

*The survey showed that their average annual income in 1974 was £729, made up to £376 in Maintenance award, £161 in actual parental contributions, £167 in net vacation earnings, £11 in social security benefits, £5 in term-time jobs and £9 in gifts from relatives and friends (Office of Population Censuses and Surveys, Social Security Division, *Undergraduate Income and Expenditure*, by P. Busch and S. Dight, London, HMSO, 1979, pp. vii–viii, 11). If we update the figure of £729, using the implicit GNP deflator, we obtain £1502 as our best estimate of the annual income of home students in the academic year 1979/80.

have relatives who are financially dependent on them, which the survey showed was the case for overseas students. Moreover, the large variance in the income of overseas students and the fact that only 10% of home students receive the maximum grants inhibits any confident statements about the income differences between overseas and home students.

We have already noted that students from Malaysia, Mauritius and Singapore had mean incomes below £2500, while students from Iraq, Japan and Nigeria had mean incomes above £3500. However, even if we compare students from the same country, there are marked differences. For example, students from Iran had a mean income of £3481, or slightly above the overall average, yet more than a quarter of students in the lowest income category (under £1000) were from Iran. On the other hand, Greek students had a mean income very close to the overall average, yet 17% of all students with incomes between £8000 and £9000 were Greek. Therefore it can be very misleading to generalise about overseas students, particularly regarding income levels.

It is particularly dangerous to generalise about 'rich' and 'poor' students. During recent debates on overseas student fees, a number of commentators have suggested differential fees which vary according to the income level of the sending country. The implication seems to be that students from 'rich' countries can afford to pay higher fees than students from 'poor' countries. Yet if we compare the incomes of individual overseas students and the income levels of their countries, we find that 22% of the poorest students (those with incomes below £1000 a year) come from rich countries such as USA or Western Europe, whereas 27% of students in the highest income category (£9000 or more) come from countries classified as poor, with per capita GNP below $750 (see Table A.11). Similarly, we found that whereas 75% of the poorest students came from Asia or the Middle East, and only 4% from Europe, more than a third of the richest students also come from Asia and the Middle East, and the proportion from Europe is once again only 4%.

The differences in levels of income of different overseas students are matched by differences in expenditure patterns. As would be expected, postgraduate students have a higher mean level of expenditure (£1756 in a six-month period) than undergraduates (£1051), but the standard deviations are again high, which indicates very considerable disparities between those with the highest and lowest levels of expenditure, particularly among those studying for a first degree.

The level of student income is closely related to the question of

Table A.11   Poor/rich countries by income of students

Country/ Income-level	Base	Up to £1000	£1001-2000	£2001-3000	£3001-4000	£4001-5000	£5001-6000	£6001-7000	£7001-8000	£8001-9000	£9001+	RF	DK	NA	Mean (£)	Standard deviation (£)
Base	1484	23	205	526	352	139	74	39	34	12	26	3	13	38	3233	1778
Very poor																
Commonwealth	36	4%	2%	3%	2%	4%	—	—	3%	—	—	—	8%	—	2824	1188
Non-Commonwealth	34	4%	0%	3%	2%	6%	1%	3%	—	—	—	—	—	—	3299	1080
Poor																
Commonwealth	513	26%	53%	43%	29%	17%	20%	18%	15%	8%	8%	33%	15%	42%	2692	1313
Non-Commonwealth	149	—	8%	7%	11%	15%	9%	26%	18%	17%	19%	33%	23%	5%	3858	2189
Middle East																
OPEC	273	35%	12%	14%	22%	25%	28%	36%	21%	17%	19%	33%	—	11%	3545	1819
Non-OPEC	75	9%	2%	2%	9%	7%	8%	3%	9%	—	15%	—	—	3%	3871	2039
Rich	404	22%	22%	27%	27%	26%	32%	15%	35%	58%	38%	—	54%	39%	3387	1947

Notes: RF = refused to answer; DK = don't know; NA = not answered.
0% = less than 0·5%. — = 0%

Source: Student Survey.

Table A.12   Willingness to study in Britain if fees higher, by course levels

Student decision/ fee level	Base	MPhil/ PhD	Taught Masters	Diploma	First degree	Higher national diploma	Teacher training	Professional qualification	Others
Base	1484	333	229	74	737	14	8	9	80
Not Student's Decision	458	46%	34%	42%	22%	50%	63%	44%	25%
Not if £200 Higher	462	25%	24%	23%	38%	36%	25%	11%	29%
Not if £500 Higher	271	14%	21%	16%	20%	7%	—	33%	18%
Not if £1000 Higher	185	8%	12%	9%	15%	—	13%	—	16%
Not if £2000 Higher	39	2%	4%	3%	2%	—	—	11%	4%
Yes if £2000 Higher	39	3%	4%	7%	1%	7%	—	—	4%
Not Answered	30	0%	0%	—	0%	—	—	—	3%

Notes: see Table A.1.   0% = less than 0·5%
Source: Student Survey.

whether or not students have dependent relatives. Over 80% of all students with incomes below £3000 a year have no dependants, whereas over 60% of students in the top income bracket had a dependent spouse or children. Students from Latin America and Africa were more likely to have dependants than students from other areas. In fact, over half of all Latin American students had either a spouse or children financially dependent upon them, whereas over 88% of students from Europe or North America had no dependants.

Response to fee increases
Finally, it is interesting to consider what variations were revealed in the willingness of students to study in Britain if fee levels had been higher (see Table A.12).* In the case of postgraduate students, a high proportion (46% of MPhil and PhD students) said that the decision whether or not to study in Britain if fees were higher was not their decision. No doubt this reflects the high proportion of post-graduate overseas students who have a scholarship or grant, and it emphasises that the policy of foreign governments and grant-giving agencies may well be crucial in determining how many overseas students will pay the increased fees. A quarter of both MPhil/PhD and master's degree students said that they would not come if fees were £200 higher; if fees were £1000 higher only 5% of MPhil/PhD students would still be willing to come to Britain, and 8% of master's degree students, whereas if fees were £2000 higher, only 3 or 4% would be willing to come. Of course, this question about willingness to pay higher fees may not be a good guide to actual behaviour. Nevertheless, the responses to this question showed that students' declared willingness to pay higher fees was strongly influenced by the size of the fee increase and by their course. If fees were £200 higher, then 38% of undergraduates said they would still be willing to study in Britain, 41% of master's degree students, but only 27% of MPhil/PhD students; if fees were £2000 higher, then only 1% of undergraduates said they would be willing to come, compared with 7% of diploma and higher national diploma students. It is not surprising that students' response to this question was also related to their income level. Those in the highest income bracket (£9000 a year or more) were most likely to express willingness to study at higher levels of fees, which is only to be expected. However, what is less easy to explain is that the students who expressed willingness to come to study in Britain even if fees were £2000 higher had a lower mean income level (£4095) than those who said they

*The survey was conducted before 'full-cost' fees were implemented, so the students questioned were paying the fees applicable in 1979/80 (see Table 2.5).

would *not* come if fees were £2000 higher (£4511). The numbers in these categories were very small, so that not too much significance can be attached to such results. However, perhaps they serve as a reminder that students' attitudes to fee increases may not always be predictable!

We concluded the interviews with an open ended question, to give students a chance to express their opinion on the increase in overseas student fees, and this showed a wide range of opinion. Far more negative comments were received than positive ones. For example 'It will involve a lot of hardship for the students, who will have to economise on even the bare necessities of life'; 'It's unfair'; 'All students should be treated the same'; 'It's short-sighted'. A quarter of all the students believed that the new level of fees was too high, and 20% believed that students would go to other countries, where fees were lower. Nevertheless, 9% of the students said that they could understand the government's need to reduce subsidies to overseas students; 'Despite the increases, fees are still reasonable'; 'You don't feel like a parasite if you pay'; 'In Africa it would cost three times as much to do the same thing and take a longer time too'. A handful of students said that they would be willing to pay even more. In other words, overseas students vary in their opinions, just as they do in their characteristics. Our survey helped to reveal this striking diversity.

Appendix B
Statistics*

Tables Supplementary to Chapter 2

Tables Supplementary to Chapter 7

---

*The country names are those given in the Unesco *Statistical Yearbook* 1978/79.

Table B.1   Overseas students in Britain 1950/51 and 1958/59 – 1978/79

Years	A. Publicly financed institutions								B. All other institutions[b,c]	Grand total
	Higher education						Non-advanced further education	Total publicly financed higher and further education		
	(i) Universities			(ii) Other advanced higher and further education						
	Under-graduate	Post-graduate	Total	Colleges of education	Poly-technics, further education colleges	Total				
1950/51	n.a.	n.a.	8242				4258			12500
1958/59	n.a.	n.a.	10672	a		10441		21113	20987a	42100
1959/60	n.a.	n.a.	11001	2053		11944		24998	22522	47520
1960/61	n.a.	n.a.	12199	2450		12862		27511	27576	55087
1961/62	n.a.	n.a.	13293	2960		14143		30396	29769	60165
1962/63	n.a.	n.a.	13919	1582	4500b	20001b	11083	31084	33235	64319
1963/64	n.a.	n.a.	14014	1028	6000b	21042b	10425	31467	32702	64169
1964/65	7535	7446	14981	704	6964	22643	9766	32409	36065	68474
1965/66	8204	8052	16256	596	5801	22653	10021	32674	38713	71387

1966/67	8343	9135	17478	532	6529	24539	11180	35719	37674	73393
1967/68	6947	8919	15866	499	5676	22041	9050	31091	38740	69831
1968/69	6956	9019	15975	500	5054	21529	8744	30273	39546	69819
1969/70	7141	9799	16940	504	5140	22584	9315	31899	42858	74757
1970/71	7471	10867	18338	514	5529	24381	10183	34564	34719	69283
1971/72	7735	11975	19710	543	6724	26977	12387	39364	39982	79346
1972/73	8825	13585	22410	563	7259	30232	14978	45210	37624	82834
1973/74	10177	15141	25318	577	9178	35073	18091	53164	42045	95209
1974/75	11874	16390	28264	667	11907	40838	21910	62748	37861	100609
1975/76	14244	17587	31831	736	16465	49032	26764	75796	38268	114064
1976/77	16021	18433	34454	795	20678	55927	26847	82774	42168	124942
1977/78	17336	18552	35888	22675		58563	27544	86107	37652	123759
1978/79	18225	18915	37140	22485		59625	27154	86779	32780	119559

Notes: [a] In 1958/59 student teachers included in 'non-public and private sector' total.
[b] Approximate.
[c] Mainly private sector.

Source: British Council, *Statistics of Overseas Students in Britain*, Annual Reports.

Table B.2   Overseas students in Britain outside the publicly financed sector 1958/59–1978/79[a]

Year	Inns of court (approx) No. (%)	Nursing No. (%)	Other hospital (approx) No. (%)	Language assistants No. (%)	Industry (approx) No. (%)	Business and professional (approx) No. (%)	Government (approx) No. (%)	Private colleges etc. (approx) No. (%)	Total No.
1958/59	2000 (9·5)	6000 (28·6)			9987 (47·6)			3000 (14·3)	20987
1959/60	2775 (12·3)	5850 (26·0)			7747 (34·4)			6150 (27·3)	22522
1960/61	2748 (10·0)	8484 (30·8)			9921 (36·0)			6423 (23·3)	27576
1961/62	2674 (9·0)	9954 (33·4)			9711 (32·6)			7430 (25·0)	29759
1962/63	2333 (7·0)	13542 (40·7)			11826 (35·6)			5534 (16·7)	33235
1963/64	2056 (6·3)	12603 (38·5)			13078 (40·0)			4965 (15·2)	32702
1964/65	2360 (6·5)	14526 (40·3)			16526 (45·8)			2653 (7·4)	36065
1965/66	1482 (3·8)	15673 (40·5)	—	2135 (5·5)	5800 (15·0)		5882 (15·2)	7741 (20·0)	38713
1966/67	1816 (4·8)	16745 (44·4)	—	2404 (6·4)	4318 (11·5)		5582 (14·8)	6799 (18·0)	37674

Year									Total
1967/68	1697 (4·4)	17735 (45·8)	—	2858 (7·4)	4038 (10·4)	3818 (9·9) ——→		8594 (22·2)	38740
1968/69	1822 (4·6)	16356 (41·4)	—	3177 (8·0)	3691 (9·3)	3947 (10·0) ——→		10553 (26·7)	39546
1969/70	2003 (4·7)	17208 (40·2)	890 (2·0)	3172 (7·4)	3933 (9·2)	2569 (6·0)	1799 (4·2)	11284 (26·3)	42858
1970/71	1605 (4·6)	18546 (53·4)	333 (1·0)	3424 (9·9)	3298 (9·5)	1454 (4·2)	1296 (3·7)	4762 (13·7)	34719
1971/72	694 (1·7)	20120 (50·3)	522 (1·3)	3718 (9·3)	3140 (7·9)	1165 (2·9)	1704 (4·3)	8919 (22·3)	39982
1972/73	538 (1·4)	19839 (52·7)	385 (1·0)	4021 (10·7)	1656 (4·4)	1626 (4·3)	483 (1·3)	9076 (24·1)	37624
1973/74	528 (1·3)	19877 (47·3)	405 (1·0)	4502 (10·7)	1094 (2·6)	826 (2·0)	534 (1·3)	14279 (34·0)	42045
1974/75	592 (1·6)	16974 (44·8)	612 (1·6)	4521 (11·9)	688 (1·8)	453 (1·2)	176 (0·5)	13845 (36·6)	37861
1975/76	900 (2·4)	17444 (45·6)	558 (1·5)	4692 (12·3)	261 (0·7)	250 (0·7)	174 (0·5)	13989 (36·6)	38268
1976/77	424 (1·0)	14202 (33·7)	1330 (3·2)	3379 (8·0)	1093 (2·6)	1155 (2·7)	237 (0·6)	20348 (48·3)	42168
1977/78	383 (1·0)	9910 (26·3)	1324 (3·5)	3206 (8·5) ←——— (8·0) ←———		——→ 19826 (52·7)			37652
1978/79	278 (0·8)	7421 (22·6)	1352 (4·1)	3188 (9·7)	2446 (7·5) ←———	——→ 18095 (55·2)			32780

Note: [a]Figures in brackets are percentages of row totals.
Source: British Council *Statistics of Overseas Students in Britain*, various editions.

Table B.3   Overseas countries classified by number of students in Britain and in British publicly financed educational institutions in relation to the appropriately-aged population 1977/78

Country	National income Per head† ($)	Population 1977 (in thousands)		Number of students in UK 1977/78 (1978/79 in brackets)		Students in UK public sector education per 1000 population aged 20–24 in 1977/78
		All ages	20–24*	Total	Public sector	
Commonwealth countries						
Antigua	425	72	6	45 (28)	13	2·167
Australia	6278	14074	1178	1089 (1107)	834	0·708
Bahamas	n.a.	220	17	81 (93)	55	3·235
Bangladesh	106	82713	7514	557 (444)	499	0·066
Barbados	1486	254	24	350 (293)	145	6·042
Belize	639	149	10	27 (26)	19	1·900
Bermuda	n.a.	57	5	90 (85)	53	10·600
Botswana	515	710	46	91 (94)	83	1·804
British Virgin Islands	1789	12	1·33	6 (5)	4	3·008
Brunei	1178	190	18	648 (729)	598	33·222
Canada	6322	23280	2165	1464 (1383)	1137	0·525
Cayman Islands	n.a.	11	0·66	13 (20)	8	12·121
Cyprus	1084	640	60	1789 (1711)	1601	26·683
Dominica	349	80	8	80 (62)	41	5·125
Falkland Islands	n.a.	2	0·1	2 (7)	2	20·000
Fiji	1133	596	58	108 (79)	89	1·534
Gambia	228	553	52	135 (164)	102	1·962

Ghana	463	10475	833	1177 (1123)	813	0·976
Gibraltar	n.a.	30	2·8	174 (178)	154	55·000
Gilbert Islands	n.a.	70	6	21 (22)	17	2·833
Grenada	417	97	10	145 (94)	33	3·300
Guyana	596	827	76	498 (426)	308	4·053
Hong Kong	1599	4514	467	5030 (5557)	4585	9·818
India	136	625818	54947	1770 (1477)	1340	0·024
Jamaica	1265	2085	145	885 (764)	252	1·738
Kenya	213	14337	1150	1635 (1404)	1356	1·179
Lesotho	216	1250*	108	72 (91)	56	0·519
Malawi	124	5526	430	315 (523)	251	0·584
Malaysia	716	12600	1221	16001 (15470)	12856	10·529
Malta	1417	332	31	161 (226)	100	3·226
Mauritius	589	909	94	1718 (1347)	812	8·638
Montserrat	812	13	1	16 (9)	3	3·000
New Hebrides	n.a.	99	8	8 (13)	6	0·750
New Zealand	4026	3105	258	308 (310)	222	0·860
Nigeria	363	66628	5298	7011 (6595)	6251	1·180
Papua/New Guinea	448	2905	243	19 (30)	17	0·070
Zimbabwe/Rhodesia	474	6740	545	1850 (1872)	1446	2·653
St Helena	n.a.	6	0·3	13 (13)	7	23·333
St Kitts/Nevis	464	66	3	58 (33)	14	4·667
St Lucia	464	112	7·6	56 (39)	33	4·342
St Vincent	281	95*	7	48 (46)	19	2·714
Seychelles	618	62	4·5	110 (99)	78	17·333
Sierra Leone	201	3470	259	495 (447)	400	1·544
Singapore	2292	2308	265	1942 (2002)	1718	6·483
Solomon Islands	289	207	18	15 (20)	14	0·777

Table B.3 – cont.

Country	National income Per head† ($)	Population 1977 (in thousands)		Number of students in UK 1977/78 (1978/79 in brackets)		Students in UK public sector education per 1000 population aged 20–24 in 1977/78
		All ages	20–24*	Total	Public sector	
Sri Lanka	238	13971	1399	2836 (2376)	2353	1·682
Swaziland	420	507	40	61 (90)	40	1·000
Tanzania	159	16086	1208	740 (749)	657	0·544
Tonga	363	91	7·6	8 (7)	5	0·658
Trinidad/Tobago	1850	1050*	100	827 (655)	324	3·240
Turks/Caicos Islands	656	6	0·3	12 (9)		6·667
Uganda	250	12353	933	307 (329)	200	0·214
Zambia	421	5302	465	1029 (1002)	935	2·01
Foreign Countries						
Afghanistan	141	17447	1530	87 (73)	70	0·046
Albania	n.a.	2616	200	3 (1)	3	0·015
Algeria	803	17910	1300	1368 (1300)	1027	0·790
Andorra	n.a.	24	2	3 (1)	0	0·000
Angola	404	7000*	600	3 (6)	2	0·003
Argentina	1954	26056	2180	139 (153)	83	0·038
Austria	4377	7518	519	295 (247)	54	0·104
Bahrain	2935	267	20	442 (469)	317	15·850
Belgium	5887	9830	751	367 (396)	149	0·198
Benin	162	3286	249	11 (10)	2	0·008
Bhutan	66	1232	100	9 (1)	6	0·060

Bolivia	415	5950	527	21	(21)	14	0·027
Brazil	1095	112239	10681	762	(788)	434	0·041
Bulgaria	n.a.	8804	673	25	(26)	13	0·019
Burma	90	31512	2665	50	(70)	30	0·011
Burundi	69	3966	304	7	(6)	7	0·023
Cameroon	363	7914	630	155	(164)	130	0·206
Central African Empire	205	n.a.	n.a.	7	(5)	7	n.a.
Chad	165	4213	379	9	(14)	6	0·016
Chile	625	10656	985	392	(385)	356	0·361
China	n.a.	865677	76000	125	(144)	88	0·001
Colombia	508	25048	2260	305	(323)	165	0·073
Congo	521	1440	130	2	(5)	1	0·008
Costa Rica	910	2071	185	56	(56)	37	0·200
Cuba	n.a.	9596	775	11	(2)	2	0·003
Czechoslovakia	n.a.	15031	1307	31	(17)	16	0·012
Denmark/Faroes	6745	5129	377	260	(294)	110	0·292
Dominican Republic	696	4978	409	12	(5)	7	0·017
Ecuador	566	7556	673	64	(56)	30	0·045
Egypt	308	38741	2800	1040	(988)	791	0·283
El Salvador	427	4255	358	75	(46)	31	0·087
Ethiopia	91	28981	2700	120	(137)	88	0·033
Finland	5045	4737	416	447	(352)	90	0·216
France and deps.	5710	53079	4510	3320	(3557)	514	0·114
Gabon	n.a.	534	45	31	(13)	3	0·067
German DR	n.a.	16765	1318	66	(62)	11	0·008
German FR	6019	61396	4220	2519	(2587)	911	0·216
Greece	2204	9284	656	3946	(3657)	3325	5·069
Guatemala	517	6436	586	10	(9)	2	0·003
Haiti	184	4749	442	10	(8)	5	0·011

Table B.3 – cont.

Country	National Income Per head† ($)	Population 1977 (in thousands)		Number of students in UK 1977/78 (1978/79 in brackets)		Students in UK public sector education per 1000 population aged 20–24 in 1977/78
		All ages	20–24*	Total	Public sector	
Honduras	357	2800*	240	35 (29)	8	0·033
Hungary	n.a.	10648	939	39 (34)	20	0·021
Iceland	4783	222	20	177 (186)	142	7·100
Indonesia	200	143282	9721	961 (851)	668	0·069
Iran	1600	34274	2789	12294 (10691)	10079	3·614
Iraq	1159	11907	948	2363 (2653)	2163	2·282
Ireland	2417	3192	244	3173 (2812)	681	2·791
Israel	3232	3465	333	481 (461)	389	1·168
Italy	2800	56446	3891	1371 (1262)	315	0·081
Ivory Coast	732	5152	470	98 (116)	35	0·074
Japan	3856	113863	8701	1950 (1772)	512	0·059
Jordan	457	2500*	208	1698 (2087)	1482	7·125
Kampuchea	100*	8606	800	8 (5)	6	0·008
North Korea	n.a.	16651	1499	12 (4)	10	0·007
South Korea	519	36437	3281	87 (93)	56	0·017
Kuwait	11431	1129	101	777 (893)	602	5·960
Laos	100*	3464	300	12 (11)	9	0·030
Lebanon	700*	3056	231	633 (626)	471	2·039
Liberia	360	1684	131	49 (71)	26	0·198
Libya	4618	2500*	181	1069 (1414)	610	3·370
Liechtenstein	n.a.	25	2	11 (4)	0	0·000
Luxemburg	6780	356	27	69 (57)	55	2·037

Madagascar	230	8520	640	26	(20)	12	0·019
Maldives	98	140	10	7	(7)	6	0·600
Mali	96	5994	443	16	(20)	15	0·034
Mauritania	240	1500*	121	23	(11)	23	0·190
Mexico	1191	64594	5645	880	(949)	359	0·064
Mongolia	n.a.	1531	130	2	(3)	2	0·015
Morocco	440	18245	1589	124	(91)	42	0·026
Mozambique	275	9678	790	28	(17)	26	0·033
Namibia	n.a.	n.a.	n.a.	25	(25)	22	n.a.
Nepal	104	13136	1102	89	(65)	67	0·061
Netherlands	5491	13853	1148	525	(671)	298	0·260
N. Antilles	1275*	252	21	21	(14)	19	0·905
Nicaragua	678	2312	191	37	(24)	17	0·089
Niger	124	4859	370	31	(17)	31	0·084
Norway	5996	4042	306	1029	(907)	671	2·193
Oman	2139	817	70	168	(199)	83	1·186
Pakistan	175	75278	6226	1222	(1106)	1127	0·181
Panama	1037	1771	155	40	(29)	23	0·148
Paraguay	536	2805	261	8	(11)	5	0·019
Peru	518	16358	1447	119	(127)	78	0·054
Philippines	333	45028	4344	542	(365)	70	0·016
Poland	n.a.	34698	3500	148	(113)	71	0·020
Portugal/Macao	1482	9000*	750	425	(423)	339	0·415††
Qatar	8440	98	8	166	(148)	82	10·250
Romania	n.a.	21658	1844	8	(6)	6	0·003
Rwanda	131	4368	318	13	(4)	7	0·022
Saudi Arabia	4371	9522	900	942	(910)	493	0·548
Senegal	333	5000*	399	44	(52)	22	0·055

Table B.3 – cont.

Country	National income Per head† ($)	Population 1977 (in thousands)		Number of Students in UK 1977/78 (1978/79 in brackets)		Students in UK public sector education Per 1000 population aged 20–24 in 1977/78
		All ages	20–24*	Total	Public sector	
Somalia	151	3354	300	26 (52)	21	0·070
South Africa	1170	25000*	2126	869 (833)	693	0·326
Soviet Union	n.a.	258932	18600	36 (37)	31	0·002
Spain	2651	36672	2733	1199 (1277)	245	0·090
Sudan	274	16953	1500	907 (1015)	761	0·507
Surinam	1040	448	40	3 (4)	3	0·075
Sweden	7561	8255	563	559 (543)	102	0·181
Switzerland	7820	6327	467	3026 (2658)	400	0·857
Syria	676	7845	579	283 (312)	201	0·347
Taiwan	n.a.	n.a.	n.a.	127 (141)	120	n.a.
Thailand	323	44039	4073	1026 (889)	685	0·168
Togo	250	2348	155	5 (13)	2	0·013
Tunisia	728	6065	495	60 (114)	24	0·048
Turkey	854	42134	3708	2333 (2053)	1585	0·427
United Arab Emirates	n.a.	236	20	327 (340)	210	10·500
USA (incl. Puerto Rico, Samoa, Virgin Is.)	6294	220234	20200	4116 (4341)	3424	0·170
Upper Volta	85	6319	475	7 (9)	4	0·008
Uruguay	1231	2846	210	32 (17)	24	0·114
Venezuela	2128	12737	1239	1641 (1309)	1076	0·868
Vietnam	n.a.	47872	3590	69 (89)	37	0·010

Yemen Arab Republic	168	7078	492	92 (113)	62	0·126
Yeman PDR	122	1797	125	35 (39)	18	0·144
Yugoslavia	n.a.	21767	2013	235 (164)	64	0·032
Zaire	127	26313	1975	36 (30)	17	0·009

Notes: *Estimated from nearest available years
†Generally for 1975: intended only to give a rough indication of relative wealth. For comparison the UK figure in 1975 was 3664
††Portugal only

Sources: Table compiled by Sir Charles Carter.
National income per head and population: *Demographic yearbook for 1977* United Nations.
Number of students in UK: British Council *Statistics of Overseas students in Britain*, 1977/78 and 1978/79 editions.

Table B.4   Enrolment of foreign students compared with total student population by host country 1960–76

Host country	Year	Enrolment			Index 1960 = 100	
		Total student population (to nearest hundred)	Foreign student population	Foreign students as % of total student population	Student Population	Foreign student population
Austria	1960	38500	10374	26·9	100	100
	1965	49300	9438	19·1	128	91
	1970	59800	8573	14·3	155	83
	1974	84100	9716	11·6	218	94
	1975	96700	10320	10·7	250	100
	1976	104500	10696	10·2	271	103
Belgium[a,c]	1960	30700	2696	8·8	100	100
	1965	48800	6326	12·9	159	235
	1970	75100	8611	11·5	245	319
	1974	81000	9369	11·6	269	348
	1975	83400	9748	11·7	272	362
	1976	169700	15439	9·1	553	573
Canada[a,d]	1960	114300	7251	6·3	100	100
	1965	205900	11284	5·5	180	156
	1970	477300	22263	4·7	418	307
	1973	491500	54453	11·0	430	751
	1975	546800	48055	8·8	478	663
	1976	567500	52087	9·2	497	718

Czechoslovakia					
1960	92200	1849	2·0	100	100
1965	145000	3131	2·2	157	169
1970	131100	3619	2·7	142	196
1974	144300	3400	2·4	157	184
1975	155100	3370	2·2	168	182
1976	168700	2428	2·0	183	185
Denmark[e]					
1960	28300	373	1·3	100	100
1965	51800	716	1·4	184	192
1970	76200	1644	2·2	270	440
1974	105400	—	—	374	—
1975	110300	1958	1·8	391	525
1976	110600	3227	2·9	392	865
Finland					
1960	23600	126	0·5	100	100
1965	38800	133	0·3	164	106
1970	59800	250	0·4	253	198
1974	71500	461	0·6	303	366
1975	77200	529	0·7	327	420
1976	79700	573	0·7	338	455
France[f]					
1962	272500	22132	8·1	100	100
1965	413800	32454	7·9	152	147
1970	662200	34500	5·2	243	156
1974	772100	77382	10·0	283	350
1975	811300	93750	11·6	298	424
1976	821600	96409	11·7	302	436

Table B.4 – cont.

Host country	Year	Enrolment			Index 1960 = 100	
		Total student population (to nearest hundred)	Foreign student population	Foreign students as % of total student population	Student population	Foreign student population
Federal Republic of Germany	1960	291300	21701	7·5	100	100
	1965	373100	26225	7·0	128	121
	1970	503800	27769	5·5	173	128
	1974	786700	47096	6·0	270	217
	1975	1041200	53560	5·1	357	247
	1976	1054300	54080	5·1	362	249
German Democratic Republic[g]	1960	69100	—	—	100	—
	1965	220600	—	—	319	—
	1970	303100	3350	1·1	439	100
	1974	306800	4864	1·6	444	145
	1975	386000	5383	1·4	559	161
	1976	382200	5351	1·4	553	160
Greece	1960	29300	729	2·5	100	100
	1965	58000	1681	2·9	198	231
	1970	76200	5748	7·6	260	789
	1974	97800	9929	10·2	334	1362
	1975	111400	10049	9·0	380	1378
	1976	117200	9448	8·1	400	1296

	Year					
Ireland[b]	1960	12400	2146	17·6	100	100
	1965	21800	2930	—	176	137
	1970	28500	—	10·3	230	—
	1974	37900	1464	4·0	306	68
	1975	46200	1513	3·3	373	71
	1976	46500	1263	2·8	375	59
Italy	1960	191800	2572	1·4	100	100
	1965	408100	6130	1·5	213	238
	1970	687200	14357	2·1	358	558
	1974	930200	20803	2·2	485	808
	1975	976700	18921	1·9	509	736
	1976	1020700	28390	2·8	532	1104
Japan[a]	1960	630500	4182	0·7	100	100
	1965	1017100	8274	0·8	161	198
	1970	1503300	10471	0·7	238	250
	1974	1762000	13564	0·8	279	324
	1975	1840700	14485	0·8	292	346
	1976	1896900	14737	0·8	301	352
Luxemburg	1960	100	—	—	100	—
	1965	600	48	7·8	600	100
	1970	400	66	18·2	400	138
	1974	—	84	—	—	175
	1975	500	38	7·9	500	79
	1976	400	70	17·5	400	146

Table B.4 – cont.

Host country	Year	Enrolment			Index 1960 = 100	
		Total student population (to nearest hundred)	Foreign student population	Foreign students as % of total student population	Student population	Foreign student population
Netherlands[a]	1960	40700	1264	3·1	100	100
	1965	64400	1240	1·9	158	98
	1970	103400	1721	1·6	254	136
	1974	112200	n.a.	—	276	n.a.
	1975	120100	1943	1·6	295	154
	1976	129200	n.a.	—	317	n.a.
Norway[i]	1960	9300	185	2·0	100	100
	1965	27400	276	1·0	295	149
	1970	50100	420	0·8	539	227
	1974	64600	741	1·1	659	401
	1975	66600	931	1·4	716	503
	1976	73300	926	1·3	788	500
Portugal	1960	24200	112	0·4	100	100
	1965	34600	147	0·4	143	131
	1970	50100	902	1·8	207	805
	1974	64700	n.a.	—	267	n.a.
	1975	79700	672	0·8	329	600
	1976	95800	976	1·0	396	871

	Year				
Spain[j]	1960	87400	3381	3·9	100	100
	1965	131800	7656	5·8	151	226
	1970	224900	7878	3·5	257	233
	1974	453400	8417	1·9	519	249
	1975	540300	8909	1·6	618	264
	1976	581100	7814	1·3	665	231
Sweden[k]	1960	36900	n.a.	—	100	n.a.
	1965	77800	1366	1·8	211	370
	1970	141200	—	—	383	—
	1974	128900	2365	1·8	349	641
	1975	162600	2723	1·7	440	738
	1976	171200	n.a.	—	464	n.a.
Switzerland[al]	1960	21300	6987	32·8	100	100
	1965	32900	8649	26·3	155	124
	1970	42200	9469	22·4	198	136
	1974	50700	10031	19·8	238	144
	1975	52600	10113	19·2	250	145
	1976	54200	12204	22·5	255	175
Turkey[m]	1960	65300	2526	3·9	100	100
	1965	97300	3325	3·4	149	132
	1970	169800	6125	3·6	260	242
	1974	218900	6385	2·9	335	253
	1975	323000	5907	1·8	495	234
	1976	287500	6246	2·2	440	247

Table B.4–cont.

Host country	Year	Enrolment			Index 1960 = 100	
		Total student population (to nearest hundred)	Foreign student population	Foreign students as % of total student population	Student population	Foreign student population
United Kingdom[n]	1960	163100	12410	7·6	100	100
	1965	432700	22793	5·3	265	184
	1970	601300	24606	4·1	369	198
	1974	703700	40838	5·8	431	329
	1975	733000	49032	6·7	449	395
	1976	n.a.	55927	—	n.a.	450
USA[o]	1960	3582700	52107	1·5	100	100
	1965	5526300	82709	1·5	154	159
	1970	8498100	144708	1·7	237	278
	1974	10223700	154580	1·5	285	297
	1975	11184900	179344	1·6	312	344
	1976	11010100	203070	1·8	307	390
USSR[p]	1960	3260700	15000[b]	0·5	100	100
	1965	3860500	15600	0·4	118	104
	1970	4580600	27918	0·6	140	186
	1974	4751000	30563	—	146	204
	1975	4854000	n.a.	—	149	n.a.
	1976	4950000	n.a.	—	152	n.a.

Notes: [a] Data are for universities and equivalent institutions only.

[b] Estimated figure.

[c] *Belgium* Data are for universities and equivalent institutions only, except for 1976.

[d] *Canada* Data for 1973 and 1975 for foreign students include part-time students.

[e] *Denmark* Data for total student population for 1976 not comparable with previous years because of classification changes.

[f] *France* Data for total student population are for universities and equivalent institutions, while data for foreign students are for universities only. From 1973 data on foreign students differ from previous years as more complete information now available.

[g] *GDR* All years except 1960 include correspondence and evening courses. Data for foreign students do not include 'Fachschulen'. Data from 1975 not comparable with previous years because of classification changes.

[h] *Ireland* Data for 1960 for universities and equivalent institutions only. Data given for foreign students in 1965 are in fact for 1966.

[i] *Norway* Data given for foreign students in 1974 are in fact for 1973.

[j] *Spain* Data for total student population for 1975 and 1976 include 'Universidad de Educacion a Distancia' (UNED) which had 24,506 students in 1975 (including 6383 foreign students) and 25,571 students (including 5233 foreign students) in 1976. In 1975 only, the total student population also includes correspondence courses.

[k] *Sweden* Data for 1960 for universities and equivalent institutions only. Data given for foreign students in 1974 are in fact for 1973, first-year university students only. Data for foreign students for 1975 are for first-year university students only. From 1975, total student population data include some schools (26,000 students in 1975) previously classified with education at secondary level.

[l] *Switzerland* For 1976, the foreign student percentage counted with Swiss data is 18.6.

[m] *Turkey* Data for 1975 for total student population include non-formal education and correspondence courses (85,361 students).

[n] *United Kingdom* Data for foreign students for 1960 are for universities only. For 1965 onwards they also include full-time research or study at polytechnics and technical colleges (advanced courses only) and colleges of education. Source: Education Statistics for the UK.

[o] *USA* Source for foreign student data: *Open Doors*. Data from the 1977/78 *Open Doors* report are about 15% lower for the years 1962–73 than the Unesco figures.

[p] *USSR* Data given for foreign students in 1974 are in fact those for 1972.

Source: Unesco *Statistical Yearbook*, 1965, 1972, 1977, 1978/79 editions.

*Table B.5　Individual sending countries with more than 10,000
students abroad in 1976: data for 1970 and 1976*

Country	Students abroad 1970	1976	Annual average growth-rate 1970–76 (%)
1. Iran	13575	40422	19·9
2. USA	18789	31190	8·8
3. Greece	14147	31063	14·0
4. Hong Kong	13241	20854	7·9
5. Malaysia	9476	19811	13·0
6. United Kingdom	10927	19370	10·0
7. China	17022	18517	1·4
8. Nigeria	4423	18088	26·5
9. Vietnam, Soc. Rep. of	11585	16587	6·2
10. India	16486	15338	−1·2
11. Canada	15042	14342	−0·8
12. Italy	8332	13750	8·7
13. Korea, Republic of and Democratic People's Republic of	9662	13721	6·0
14. Jordan	19776	13010	−6·7
15. Germany, Federal Republic of	7072	12937	10·6
16. Lebanon	4077	11015	18·0
17. Japan	5507	10886	12·0
18. Morocco	2827	10776	25·0
19. Turkey	4908	10359	13·3
20. France	9205	10236	1·8
21. Cyprus	8199	10101	3·5

Source:　Unesco *Statistical Yearbook*, 1972, 1978/79 editions.

Table B.6 Foreign students by country of origin in selected host countries in 1976

	Host country								
Country of Origin	Austria	Belgium	Canada	France	Germany, Fed. Rep.	Italy	Switzerland	United Kingdom	USA
Algeria	17	178	106	6970	448	—	130	652	770
Austria		22	117	159	2573	50	357	39	220
Cameroon, United Republic of	2	39	64	2599	74	—	24	97	470
Canada	55	66		1011	309	96	105	994	11120
China	87	36	1150	678	404	20	37	67	12420
Cyprus	12	12	75	417	100	126	7	989	210
Czechoslovakia	37	4	129	83	919	30	407	9	49
France	81	1230	803	.	2357	294	1479	360	1780
Germany, Federal Republic of	2633	738	780	2092	.	490	2593	718	2040
Greece	938	417	568	3302	3869	165593	381	2511	1960
Hong Kong	8	—	7000	52	—	—	1	2078	10970
India	53	74	1684	333	1432	94	45	1356	9410
Indonesia	49	252	260	110	3543	—	44	338	1090
Iran	881	163	387	2469	4118	1291	225	3775	23310

Table B.6 – cont.

Country of origin	Austria	Belgium	Canada	France	Germany, Fed. Rep.	Italy	Switzerland	United Kingdom	USA
					Host country				
Iraq	49	8	70	349	221	60	8	1541	720
Israel	62	73	296	451	410	1618	90	247	2140
Italy	1857	1448	984	1339	1066	·	950	266	720
Japan	266	12	290	1082	1206	—	68	344	7160
Jordan	65	17	64	259	639	825	11	457	1480
Korea, Democratic Republic of	53	19	241	182	792	—	15	35	3630
Lebanon	6	400	317	5309	233	239	91	243	2220
Luxembourg	189	811	3	758	682	11	161	49	15
Malaysia	1	70	955	60	52	—	3	8057	2870
Morocco	2	448	49	9494	149	—	52	18	160
Netherlands	39	1276	429	333	1460	34	238	201	850
Nigeria	47	56	788	101	671	36	15	3690	11870
Syria	94	95	59	1326	629	393	23	142	430
Trinidad, Tobago	—	2	1535	16	7	—	2	247	1060
Tunisia	2	298	29	8677	296	41	66	28	37
Turkey	423	145	136	1117	4756	88	253	1250	1400
United Kingdom	113	202	10580	2004	1161	189	226	·	5580
United States of America	435	735	9897	3720	3250	1668	471	3151	·
Vietnam	14	329	431	2227	1112	143	256	12	8910
Yugoslavia	414	22	171	316	1151	191	173	78	310
Zaire	3	1258	18	800	56	87	70	18	210

Source: Unesco *Statistical Yearbook*, 1978/79

Host country	Foreign student enrolment	% distribution by continent of origin					
		Africa	North America	South America	Asia	Europe	Oceania
Austria	10696	2·9	4·8	1·5	21·0	68·0	0·3
Belgium	15435	25·3	6·7	3·3	11·5	46·1	0·1
Canada	52087	7·8	26·5	3·3	29·0	31·5	1·9
Czechoslovakia	3438	9·4	1·0	1·7	46·8	33·5	0·03
Denmark	3227	4·2	9·5	2·8	5·2	73·6	0·3
Finland	573	n.a.	n.a.	n.a.	n.a.	n.a.	n.a.
France	96409	46·6	6·2	5·0	19·8	17·7	0·2
Germany, Federal Republic	54080	7·4	7·4	3·5	39·0	39·3	0·3
Germany, Democratic Republic	5350	17·2	3·2	5·2	35·3	32·8	—
Greece	9448	5·8	3·5	0·2	84·4	4·1	0·6
Ireland	1263	27·2	23·0	0·2	17·7	30·7	0·8
Italy	28390	4·1	7·1	3·4	17·9	67·2	0·2
Japan	14737	0·3	6·4	1·3	88·5	2·7	0·5
Luxembourg	70	n.a.	n.a.	n.a.	n.a.	n.a.	n.a.
Netherlands	n.a.	n.a.	n.a.	n.a.	n.a.	n.a.	n.a.
Norway	926	n.a.	n.a.	n.a.	n.a.	n.a.	n.a.
Portugal	976	27·8	3·8	47·1	1·6	12·0	—
Spain	7814	3·3	23·6	21·8	16·7	9·3	0·01
Sweden	n.a.	n.a.	n.a.	n.a.	n.a.	n.a.	n.a.
Switzerland	12204	5·7	5·4	3·0	10·2	68·8	0·3
Turkey	6246	0·3	—	—	89·9	—	—
United Kingdom	55927	20·7	9·7	3·0	48·9	12·3	2·0
United States of America	203070	12·7	15·4	8·2	53·4	8·1	1·6
USSR	n.a.	n.a.	n.a.	n.a.	n.a.	n.a.	n.a.

Source: Unesco Statistical Yearbook, 1978/79

Table B.8   Foreign students received by individual European Community host country 1964–76

Host country	Total foreign student population	Foreign students from EC countries		
		Total	as % of all foreign students	as % of all European foreign students
Belgium[a]				
1963	4424	1373	31·0	70·4
1970	8611	2457	28·5	72·3
1975	9748	2916	29·9	71·7
1976	15435[b]	5555	35·9	78·0
Denmark				
1964[b]	716	n.a.	n.a.	n.a.
1970	1644	253	15·4	28·5
1975	1958	237	12·1	18·3
1976	3227	693	21·4	29·1
France[c]				
1964	35584	5044	14·1	61·6
1970	34877	3208	9·2	58·9
1975	93750	7173	7·7	45·4
1976	96409	7478	7·8	43·9
Germany, Federal Republic of				
1964	25594	2389	9·3	24·6
1970	27769	3659	13·1	33·8
1975	47298[b]	6750	14·2	36·5
1976	54080	7486	13·8	35·8

Country	Year				
Ireland	1964	2855	n.a.	n.a.	n.a.
	1970	2930	1941	66·2	95·5
	1975	1513	392	26·0	72·5
	1976	1263	268	21·2	69·3
Italy	1964	3800	171	4·5	12·4
	1970	14357	580	4·0	7·1
	1975	18921	657	3·5	5·5
	1976	28390	1148	4·0	6·0
Luxemburg	1964	48	n.a.	n.a.	n.a.
	1970	66	n.a.	n.a.	n.a.
	1975	38	n.a.	n.a.	n.a.
	1976	70	n.a.	n.a.	n.a.
Netherlands[a]	1964	1194	n.a.	n.a.	n.a.
	1970	1721	419	24·3	51·8
	1971	1943	496	25·5	61·3
	1976	n.a.	n.a.	n.a.	n.a.
United Kingdom[e]	1964	15084	631	4·2	28·8
	1970	24606	1020	4·2	28·1
	1975	49032	2247	4·6	34·3
	1976	55927	2378	4·2	34·4

Notes: [a] Universities and equivalent institutions only.
     [b] Except for 1976, data refer to universities and equivalent institutions only.
     [c] Universities only. France undertook an exhaustive survey on its foreign student population in 1973/74, and due to this improved collection of data the figures almost doubled. Comparability with previous years, for which the country of origin of nearly 1/3 of the foreign students is not known, cannot therefore be guaranteed. B. Burn, *Higher Education Reform: implications for foreign students*, New York 1978, p. 23, puts the 1970 figure in retrospect at 46409 for the entire higher education sector.
     [d] Full-time study or research at universities, polytechnics and technical colleges (advanced courses only) and colleges of education, from 1970 onwards.

Source: Unesco *Statistical Yearbook*, 1965, 1972, 1977, 1978/79 editions

Select Bibliography

Official reports and publications
Board of Trade, *Exports and the Industrial Training of People from Overseas: report of a working party*, HMSO, 1969.
British Council, *Statistics of Overseas Students in Britain*, London, British Council, published annually.
Central Office of Information, *Britain and Education in the Commonwealth*, HMSO, reference pamphlet 66, 1964.
Central Office of Information, *Britain and the Developing Countries: Education*, HMSO, reference pamphlet 79, 1967.
Central Policy Review Staff, *Review of Overseas Representation*, HMSO, 1977
Commonwealth Secretariat, *Eighth Commonwealth Education Conference Report*, London, Commonwealth Secretariat, 1980.
Department of Education and Science, *Government Observations on the First Report from the Education, Science and Arts Committee* (HC 552-1), HMSO, Cmnd. 8011, August 1980.
Foreign and Commonwealth Office, *Overseas Student Fees: Aid and Development Implications. Government Observations on the Report of the Sub-Committee on Overseas Development of the Select Committee on Foreign Affairs*, HMSO, Cmnd. 8010, August 1980.
Home Office, *Immigration Act 1971: A General Guide for Commonwealth Citizens*, Home Office, 1973.
House of Commons Education, Science and Arts Committee, *The Funding and Organisation of Courses in Higher Education: Interim Report on Overseas Student Fees*, HMSO, HC 552-1, April 1980.
House of Commons Foreign Affairs Committee, *Overseas Students' Fees: Aid and Development Implications*, HMSO, HC 553, 407-i to v, April 1980.
Immigration Act, 1971.
Ministry of Overseas Development, *What is British Aid?* ODM, 1976.
Race Relations Act, 1976.
Robbins Report, *Report of the Committee on Higher Education*, HMSO, Cmnd. 2154, October 1963.
Unesco Statistical Yearbook, Paris, Unesco, published annually.

Books, pamphlets and Handbooks

Bristow, R. and Thornton, J. E. C., *Overseas Students and Government Policy 1962–1979*, Overseas Students Trust 1979.

British Council of Churches, *Overseas Students and the Churches: report of a working party*, BCC, 1970.

Burns, D. G. (ed.), *Travelling Scholars: an enquiry into the adjustment and attitudes of overseas students holding Commonwealth Bursaries in England and Wales*, National Foundation for Educational Research, 1965.

Canadian Bureau for International Education, *Cross Canada Survey of Foreign Student Services*, 1977.

Centre for Studies and Research in Qualifications, *Study of the Relation between Employment, Trainihg and Qualifications: consequences of policies of labour, employment and vocational training*. Note prepared by the Commission of the European Communities, Paris, 1977.

Dunlop, F., *Europe's Guests, Students and Trainees: a survey on the welfare of foreign students and trainees in Europe*, Council for Cultural Co-operation of the Council of Europe, 1966.

Hunter, G., *Education for a Developing Nation: a study in East Africa*, George Allen & Unwin, 1963.

Inter-University Council, *British Universities and Polytechnics and Overseas Development: report of a working group chaired by Sir Michael Swann, FRS*, 1977.

Institute of Education of the European Cultural Foundation, *Intra-European Mobility of Undergraduate Students*, 1976.

Institute of International Education, *Open Doors*, New York, published annually.

Kendall, M., *Overseas Students in Britain: An annotated Bibliography*, Research Unit for Student Problems (University of London), in association with the United Kingdom Council for Overseas Student Affairs, 1968.

Kendall, M., *Overseas Students and their Families: a study at a London college*, Research Unit for Student Problems (University of London), 1968.

Kendall, M., and Williams, P., *Overseas Students in Britain: Some Facts and Figures*, Overseas Students Trust, 1979.

Laing, A., *International Campus: an Adviser to Overseas Students looks at his Job*, United Kingdom Council for Overseas Student Affairs, 1970.

Lancaster, P., *Education for Commonwealth Students in Britain*, Fabian Commonwealth Bureau, 1962.

Manderson, W. G., and Sclare, A. B., *Mental Health Problems in a Student Population*, Royal Infirmary, Glasgow.

Morris, B. S., *International Community?* National Union of Students and the Scottish Union of Students, 1967.

Overseas Development Institute, *Background Papers for Discussion on the Robbins Report and the Developing Countries*, ODI, 1963 and 1964.

Phillips, A., *British Aid for Overseas Students*, World University Service (UK), 1980.

Plunkett, D., *Students from Africa: report of a survey*, The Africa Centre & The Sword of the Spirit, 1960.

Political and Economic Planning, *New Commonwealth Students in Britain: with special reference to students from East Africa*, PEP, 1965.

Sen, A., *Problems of Overseas Students and Nurses*, National Foundation for Educational Research, 1970.

Singh, A. K., *Indian Students in Britain,* Asia Publishing House, New York, 1963.

The Grubb Institute, *Freedom to Study: Requirements of Overseas Students in the U.K.*, Overseas Students Trust, 1978.

United Kingdom Council for Overseas Student Affairs, Guidance Leaflets.

World Student Christian Federation, *Foreign Students: A New Ministry in a New World. An interpretative report of the World Student Christian Federation consultation, Ecumenical Institute, Bossey*, WSCF, 1963.

Main Parliamentary Debates on Overseas Students

House of Lords	*House of Commons*
14 February 1967	23 February 1967
21 January 1976	16 February 1976
17 March 1976	13 January 1978 (on universities)
22 March 1976	13 March 1978
9 June 1976	May 1979 (Debate on the Queen's speech)
11 November 1976	5 June 1980
9 May 1978	
20 July 1978	
17 January 1979	
5 July 1979	
12 December 1979	

Index